SHOT IN SOHO

SHOT IN SOHO

PHOTOGRAPHING LOVE AND LAWLESSNESS IN THE HEART OF LONDON

FOREWORD

'Shot in New York. Hung in Soho' was the compelling strapline on the poster accompanying Weegee's first UK exhibition at The Photographers' Gallery in 1980. The American photographer's striking image of a fallen figure lying dead on the pavement was of course 'shot' in Soho, New York, in the 1930s; fifty years later it was displayed at the gallery, then located on Great Newport Street on the southern edge of London's Soho. In the public imagination, the phrase encapsulated the reputations of both areas as places of unorthodox activity; in the 1960s the writer P. D. James had described London's Soho as 'the most sordid nursery of crime in Europe'.[1]

From marketplace to movie set, sex shop to coffee bar, crime scene to cabaret, Soho has always been a constantly evolving, multi-layered spectacle. Long a locus for the music, fashion, design, film and sex industries and a vibrant hub for LGBTQ+ communities, it has also been home to a variety of immigrant populations over the centuries, from French Huguenots to Italians, Maltese, Chinese, Hungarians, Jews and Bengalis.

For nearly five decades, The Photographers' Gallery has embraced Soho as its natural home, relocating in 2008 from its original site to a larger space in northern Soho, where it currently resides as a gateway to this internationally renowned area. Harnessing our position and role as the only public gallery within the neighbourhood, we have always sought to illuminate Soho's essence through an ongoing series of projects. These have ranged in scale and depth from community-based commissions such as *Over the Threshold*, developed in 2011 by artist duo French-Mottershead, who worked collaboratively with local residents to identify shared themes and responses to living in the area; to the *Soho Nights* exhibition in 2008, which showcased the work of five photographers, including Magnum member David Hurn's candid images of strippers backstage in 1965, and filmmaker Ken Russell's glorious 1950s photos showing people doing the hand-jive at the Cat's Whisker club.

As a reflection of Soho's notorious history, creative legacy and openness to difference and change, the gallery has consistently challenged conventional ways of seeing and defining this vibrant quarter, focusing instead on showing unorthodox perspectives. Personal highlights from among the new artworks we have commissioned in and around the area include Jordan Baseman's 2009 project *Dark is the Night* – a narrative, semi-documentary film centred around a transsexual prostitute reflecting on her life in Soho, which we screened in a concrete bunker in our unrenovated building in 2008; and Anders Petersen's

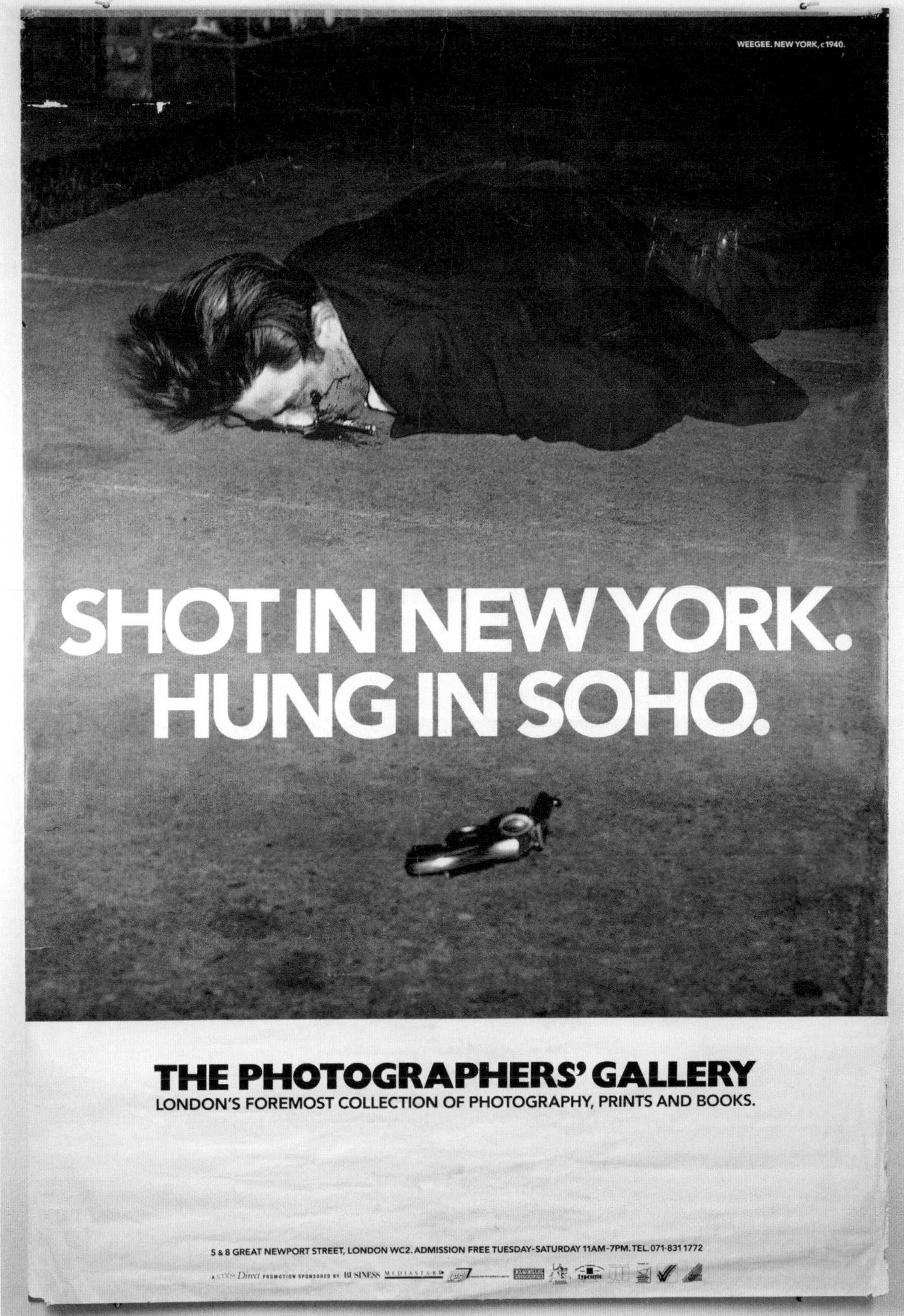

Poster for the exhibition *Weegee the Famous* at The Photographers' Gallery, 1980.

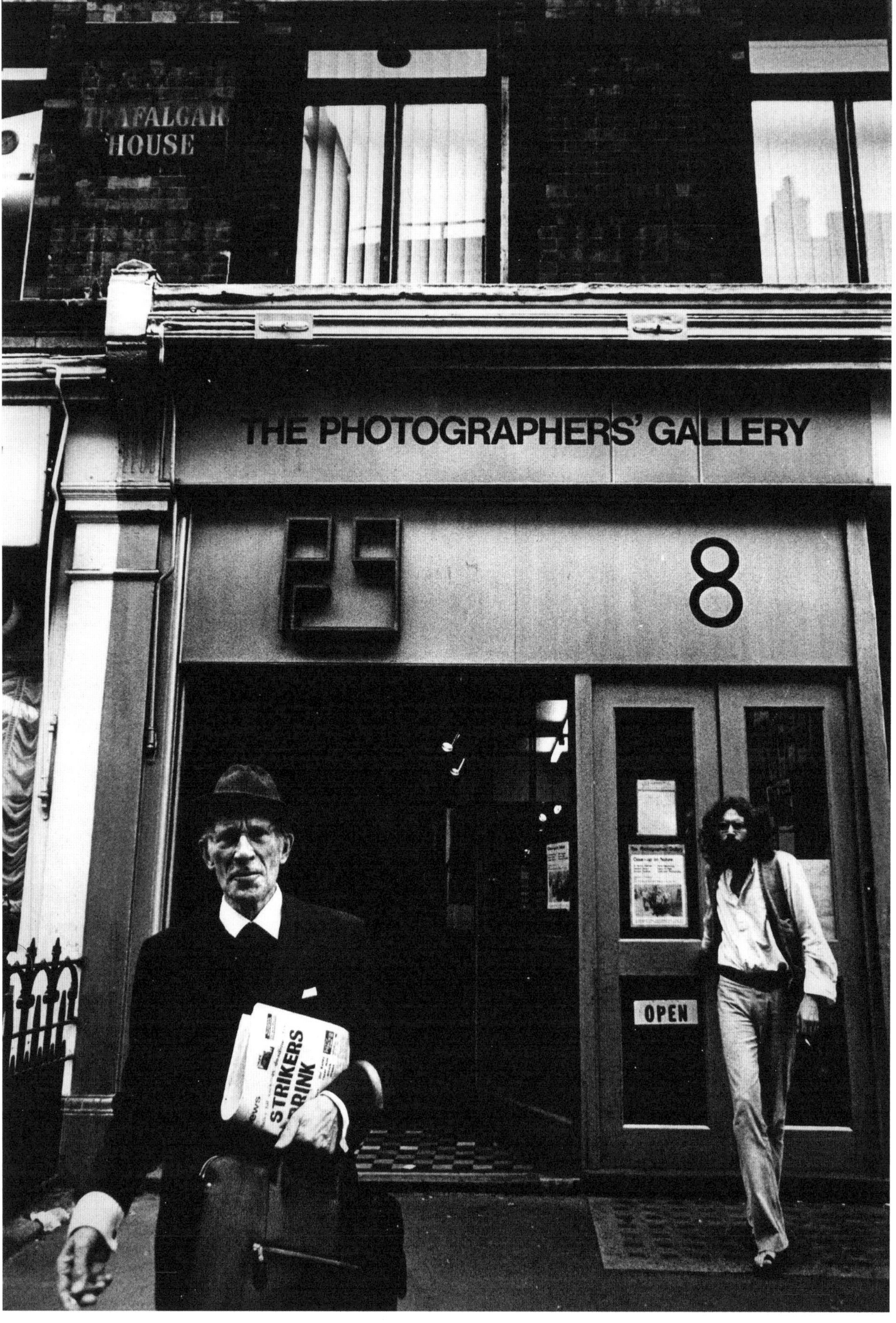

No. 8 Great Newport Street in 1973, photographed by Dorothy Bohm.

Soho (2011), a diaristic chronicle of the area also published as a book to coincide with our reopening in 2012.

This new exhibition, *Shot in Soho* (the title a neat throwback to that 1980 Weegee exhibition), allows us to evidence our commitment while further interrogating Soho's role and significance at a time when it is facing radical transformation. The imminent completion of Crossrail, the major railway line that will skirt Soho's northern border, threatens to make the area a prime target for development and further gentrification, and has already resulted in the disappearance of many independent businesses and key historical landmarks. More than at any other time in its history, it seems vital to ensure the spirit of this fabled quarter is preserved. *Shot in Soho* seeks to present the uniqueness of the place and the resilience that has characterised it over the centuries through the lenses of seven photographers.

In making their selection from the vast array of work produced in Soho over the past fifty years, our curators Julian Rodriguez and Karen McQuaid have focused on individuals who have engaged with 'monumental slabs of Soho history' – be that policing and crime; sex, love and contemporary relationships; fashion, music or melancholy. Through their gaze, we gain a fuller appreciation and understanding of the potential for photography to capture what so often remains invisible or hidden behind closed doors, but which inevitably has made Soho the place it is.

We would like to extend our thanks to the curators and to the participating photographers and their representatives, who have made the exhibition and this accompanying publication possible – Clancy Gebler Davies, Michael-John Jennings (on behalf of Kelvin Brodie), William Klein, Anders Petersen, Marcelle Price (on behalf of John Goldblatt), Mark Szaszy (on behalf of Corinne Day) and Daragh Soden – as well as to the residents, workers and devotees of Soho, who continue to contribute to its unique character. Soho may have transformed almost beyond recognition over the past decade, but it remains a hive of creative energy and innovation and a mecca for photographers and other artists.

Brett Rogers
Director, The Photographers' Gallery

SHOT IN SOHO: PHOTOGRAPHY AND RESISTANCE

BY JULIAN RODRIGUEZ

On the night of 29 January 1963, Tony Mella staggered from the dimly lit Bus Stop strip club he owned in Dean Street with three gunshot wounds, to bleed kerbside into one of his hostess's laps. Mella was a hard man, said to be responsible for keeping the Kray Twins out of Soho, but this night changed that. He had been shot by his minder, Alfred Melvin. After discharging his handgun three times into his boss, Melvin blew out his own brains with one careful shot under the chin. As Mella lay bleeding, photographers from the *Daily Herald* were quickly dispatched. The resulting bleak, direct-flash picture shows the police, their Triumph motorcycles parked up, having arrived expecting a routine gangland shooting only to be faced with a personal attack. The photograph looks strangely Weegee-esque, suggesting a New York crime scene rather than London Town. Clip joints like Bus Stop promised punters no-holds-barred stripteases and strong beer, but in reality both the beer and the performances were watered down. These were wallet-stripping rackets with no recourse to complaint. Soho, a square mile in the heart of the city, stained by police corruption, had become a law unto itself. A 1957 picture-led feature in *VUE* magazine described it as 'the world's wickedest mile' and 'like a cancerous sore',[2] while contemporary sociologist Dick Hebdige recognised the area's unfettering qualities: 'Soho became the perfect soil on which thriller fiction fantasies and subterranean intrigue could thrive.'[3]

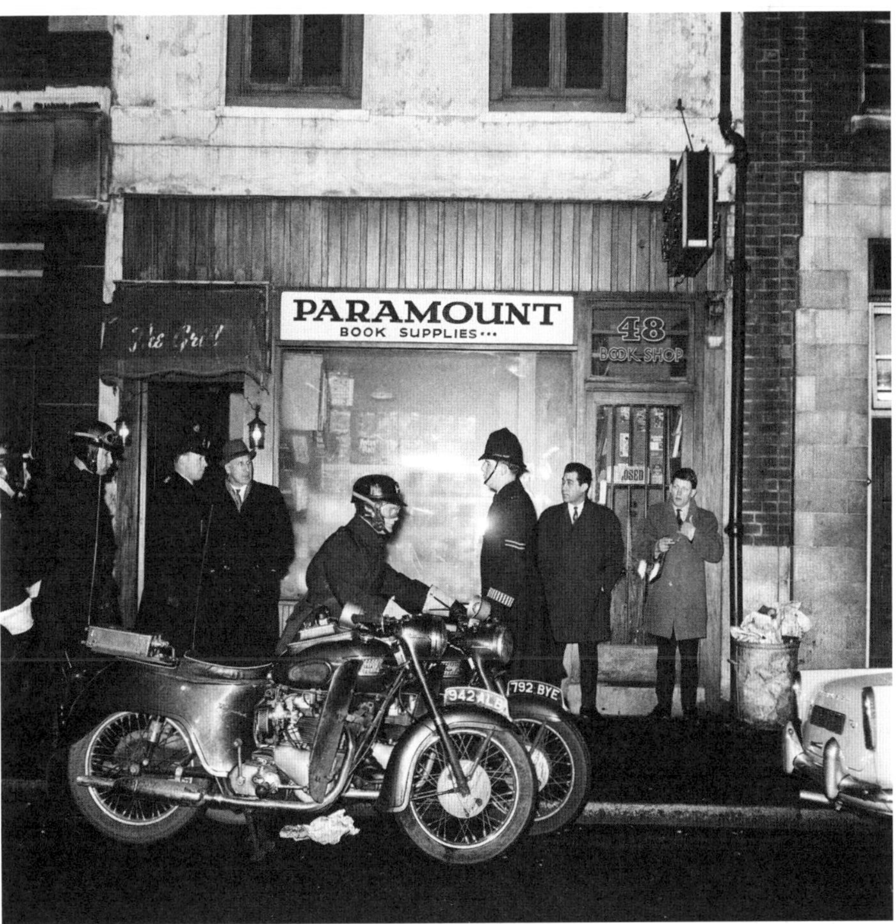

Police investigating the shooting at the Bus Stop strip club, Dean Street, January 1963.

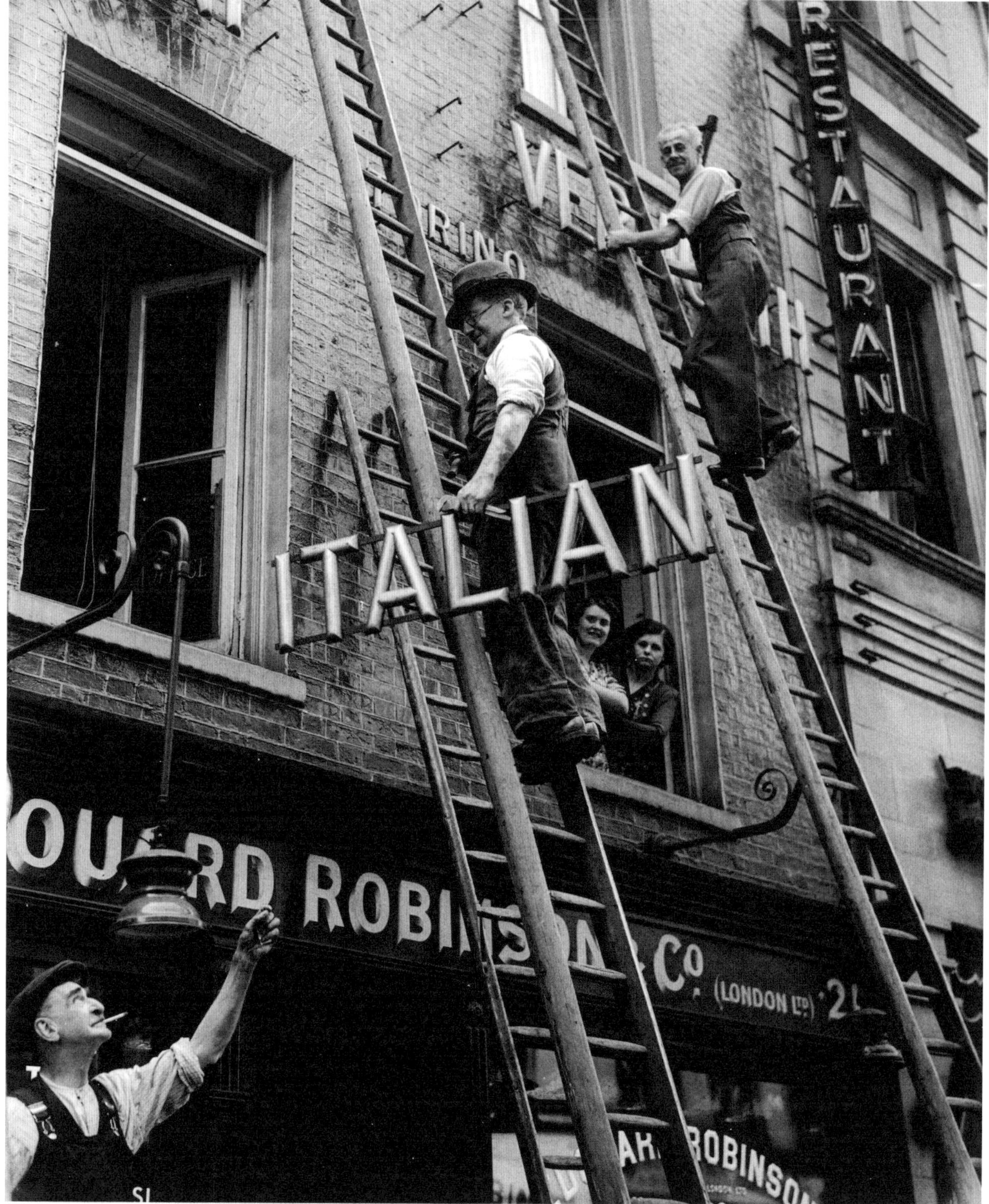

A shopkeeper removing the word 'Italian' from the sign above his Soho restaurant in May 1940 following anti-Italian riots across Britain during the Second World War.

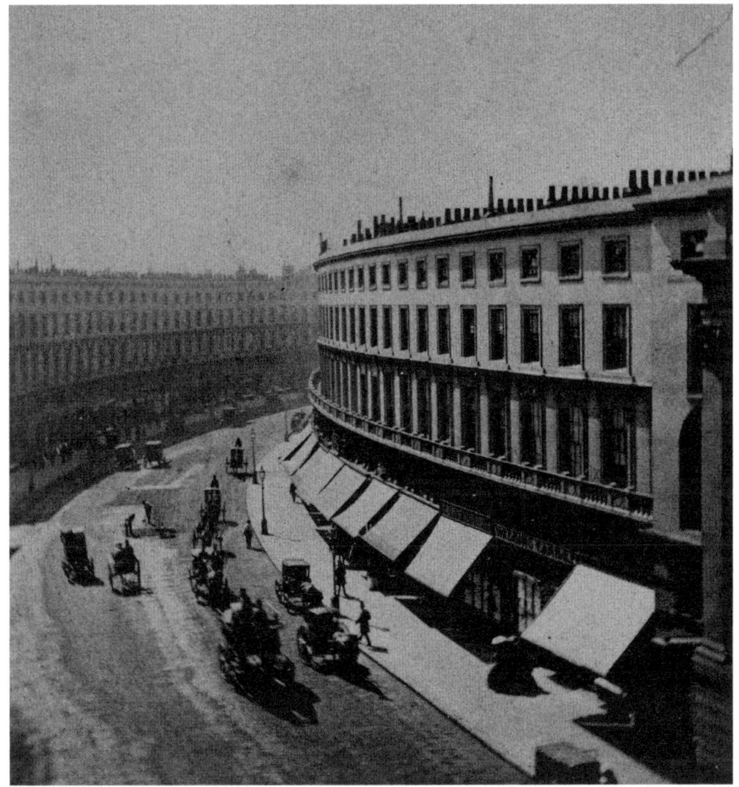

View of Regent Street, looking north, taken between 1865 and 1870.

Emerging from the greyness of 1950s post-war rationing, Soho lay behind the sweeping classical curve of John Nash's Regent Street, designed to create a kind of architectural modesty panel between posh Mayfair and a debauched hinterland. A Historic England archive photograph of Regent Street in the 1860s – sun awnings extended, horse-drawn traffic flowing – shows the curve fulfilling its function admirably. The cocaine-fuelled clubs of the 1920s like The 43 on Gerrard Street had been lively enough, but by the 1960s Soho was outperforming even its own reputation for sleaze, overrun with 'fixed' roulette wheels, one-armed bandits, adverts for 'French lessons', three-card trick teams and bent coppers. Sensibly, the UK's first all-night store, Boots the chemist, was conveniently positioned on Piccadilly Circus – visitors could pick up French letters before venturing into the area. All components of the market economy – speculation, concealment, exploitation – existed in Soho in microcosmic form. Soho's emergence as the international epicentre of youth fashion, pop, rock and punk was still to come.

Today's Soho – with its juice bars, galleries, retro stores, chain shops and thriving LGBTQ+ community, and now bracing for the footfall explosion that will result from Crossrail's new stations – seems a world away from that fateful 1963 night. Its porn shops have faded, now numbering just a dozen or so, with those that have survived seeming like quaint heritage features. Institutions like the Gay Hussar (haunt of Leftist politicians), Madame Jojo's, the Valbonne (a Jagger and Hendrix hangout with decadent heart-shaped pool, chronicled by Fleet Street's first female staffer, Doreen Spooner) and Hopkins, Purvis & Sons (purveyors of artists' pigments and dating back almost to when Canaletto attempted to sell his paintings from his Soho home)[4] – all these monumental slabs of Soho history are gone, and a total collapse of community is now feared. There are survivors, such as the immutable pocket-sized Bar Italia, Ronnie Scott's jazz venue (captured in Val Wilmer's moody 1969 image of drummer Andrew Cyrille), the Groucho Club (whose golden era in the 1990s drew David Bowie and George Michael) and I Camisa & Son delicatessen (est. 1929) on Old Compton Street, the mingling smell of Parmigiano and Milanese still inciting passers-by.

The area retains a high level of historical colour and entrenched political resistance. Soho was, after all, where Karl Marx thought through *Das Kapital*. It was also the birthplace of groundbreaking feminist magazine *Spare Rib* (driving issues of the day such as domestic violence), the home of *Private Eye* (perfecting speech-bubble satire) and the site of the invention that took the world by storm: television, with its first public transmission from the garret of what is now Bar Italia. In the 1960s and 1970s, offbeat characters like Soho stalwart Jeffrey Bernard – infatuated by the anarchy of the place and its watering holes – could be seen with Francis Bacon, Dylan Thomas and Marlene Dietrich. It is no surprise, then, that Soho has been crisscrossed by so many great photographers, including Margaret Bourke-White, Ernst Haas, Ida Kar, Kurt Hutton, Jill Freedman, Henry Dixon, Robert Doisneau, Henri Cartier-Bresson and even Beaumont Newhall, the father of what turned out to be quite a flawed history of photography. This truncated list is astonishing for just one square mile and allows Soho to be analysed from contrasting temporal perspectives.

Stephen Fry, who co-founded the Save Soho campaign in 2014, commented in a BBC radio interview: 'It's the most creative square mile on the surface of the planet ... such a magical place – there's nowhere else like it.'[5] From the beginning, Soho had been a Georgian experiment in racial liberalism, with the area being transformed from green hunting land into a commercial powerhouse mostly by French Huguenots, first-rate artisans and speculators despite their sober outlook. 'Invention' became part of Soho's DNA, mysteriously passed down through centuries. Soho became famous for piano makers, camera manufacturers, diamond cutters and, later, home to recording studios, advertising agencies and the film industry (Soho stories providing a scriptwriter's heaven).

Photographs such as those from Historic England make evident the loss of industry that has taken place. These include a 1905 image of Wardour Street's Mitchell Motor Works car park, which ferried theatregoers' cars over five storeys via a system of lifts and turntables, through to the majestic Salle Erard concert hall on Great Marlborough Street, a bronze medallion head of Mozart visible on the front elevation (the child composer having lived and performed in Soho in 1764–65). A print showing this long-gone building is preserved in the City of Westminster Archives, and the materiality of this photograph when held in the hand adds to the sense of loss. Just around the corner in Argyll Street, Edith Garrud trained suffragettes in jujitsu martial arts,[6] the photographs providing a fascinating glimpse into the women's preparedness for physical confrontation with the police.

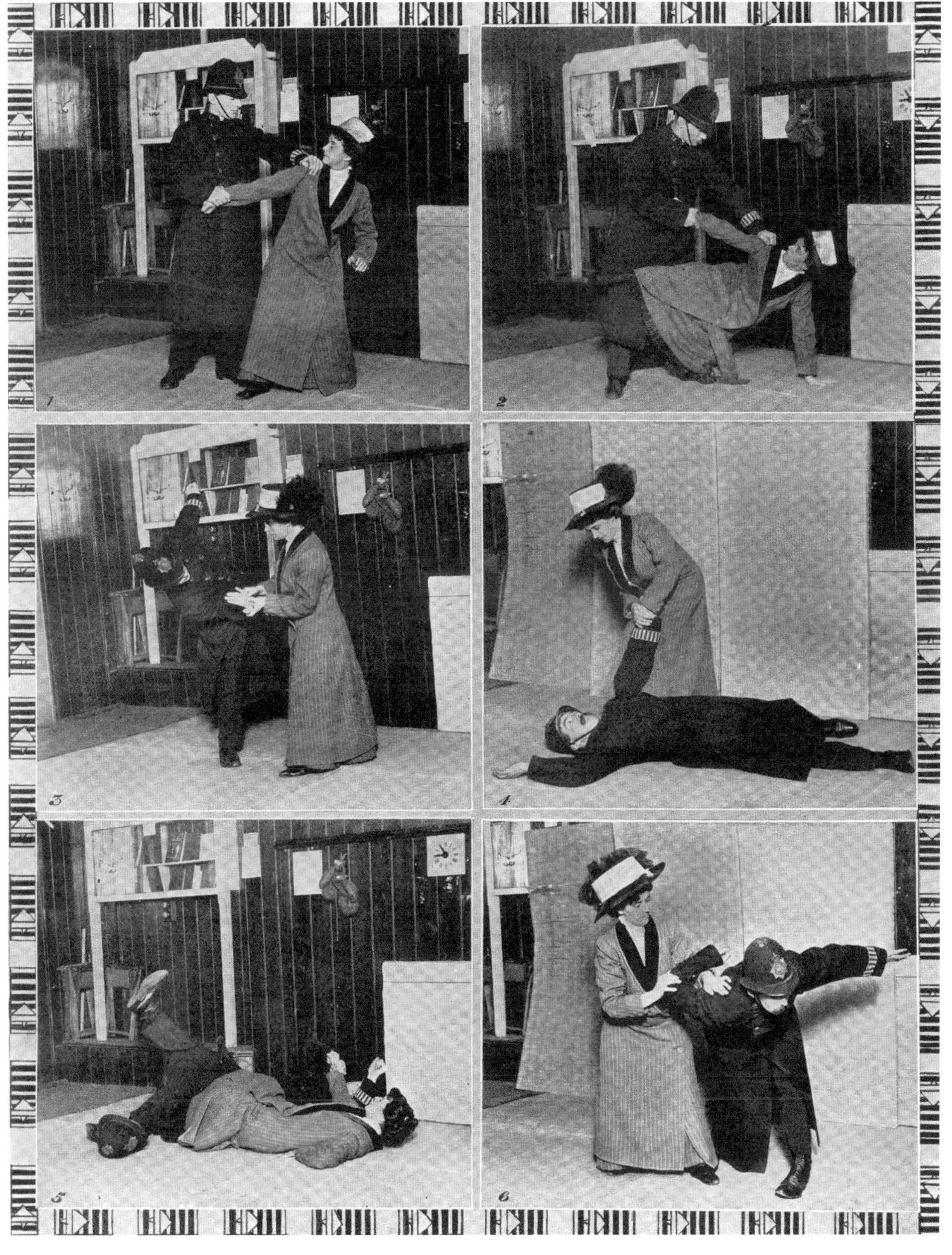

Edith Margaret Garrud training the bodyguard unit of the Women's Social and Political Union in jujitsu in 1910. Garrud's training room in the Palladium Academy on Argyll Street was also used as a suffragette bolt-hole following activist activities.

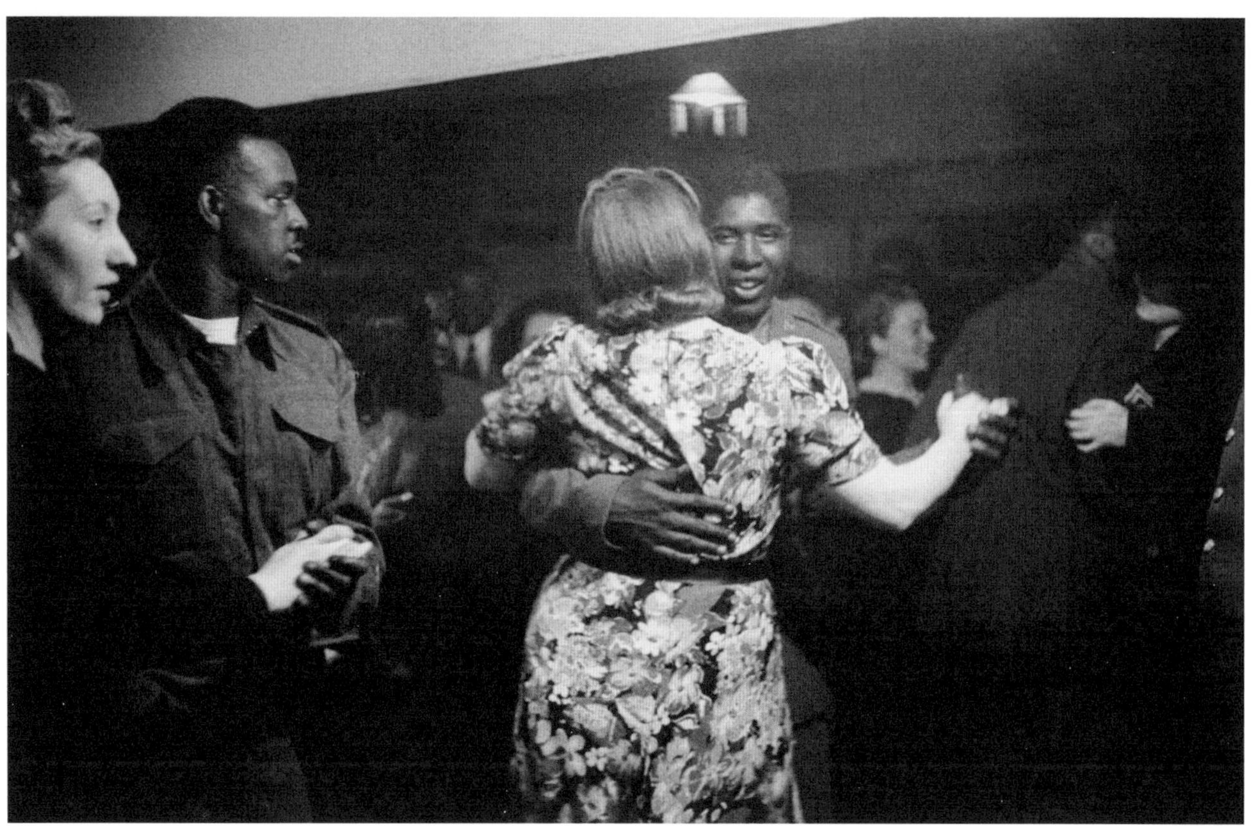

An American GI dancing with a woman at the Bouillabaisse Club, New Compton Street, 17 July 1943. The image was taken for a piece titled 'Inside London's Coloured Clubs' for the picture-led weekly magazine *Picture Post*.

The Second World War temporarily put a damper on Soho. Photographs of the Blitz – bomb damage on Ramillies Street (home to The Photographers' Gallery); St Anne's Church missing its nave; a spectacular crater on Charing Cross Road; gas mask training on Shaftesbury Avenue – show how destructive the air raids were. The Windmill Theatre, famous for French-inspired burlesque, prided itself on never closing its doors. Bill Brandt was there on assignment in 1942, to prove it to readers of *Lilliput* magazine. While not averse to staging a deceptive moment, Brandt produced brilliant wartime pictures of Soho that demonstrated the area's resistance. His caption for an image showing Windmill dancers peeping out at the servicemen in the audience reads, 'They are as nervous as troops going over the top'.[7] His 1942 picture of a waiter delivering a silver-service lunch amid bombed streets exemplifies Soho's resilience. A Hulton Archive image of the Windmill dancers in 1940, their outfits completed by gas masks and hard-hats, stands testament to the difficulties of the decade.

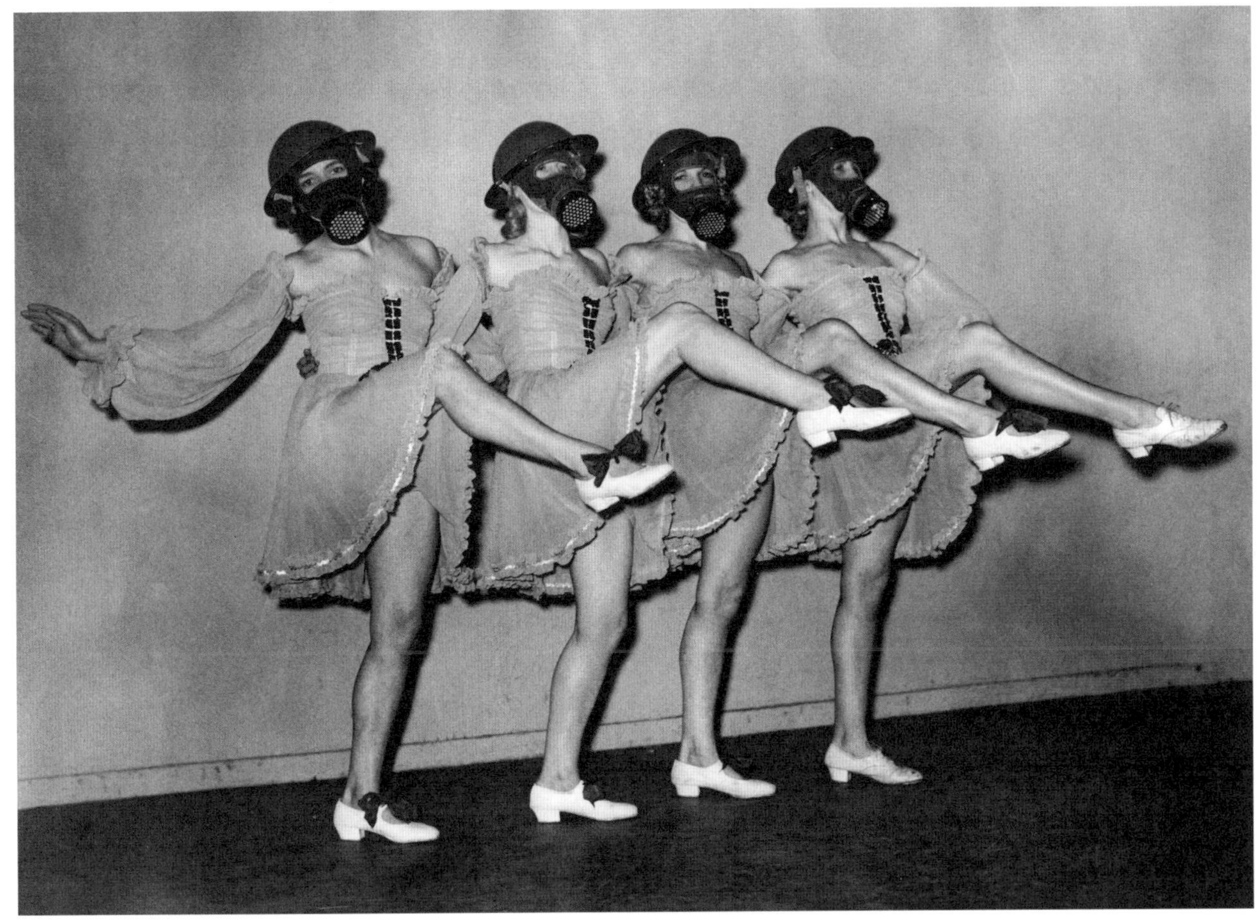

Dancers wearing gas masks and hard-hats with their costumes practise a routine at Soho's Windmill Theatre, Great Windmill Street, in January 1940.

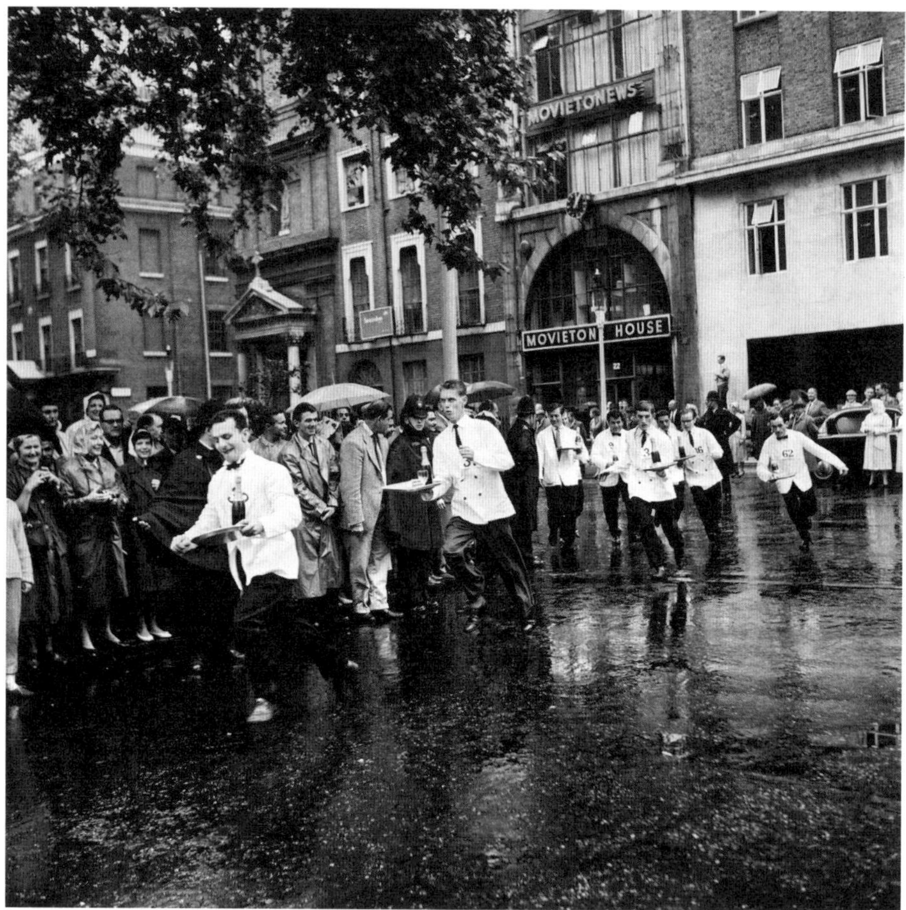

Waiters run in the waiters' race through Soho Square at the annual Soho Fair and Carnival, July 1960.

By the late 1940s recovery was signalled by new arrivals like Dean Street's Colony Room Club (opened by Muriel Belcher, with Francis Bacon as a founding member). A sign behind the bar that read 'Violence and Sensation' seemed to sum up Soho well. Forty years later, photographer Clancy Gebler Davies would be given full access to the club when working to pay off her extensive bar bill, leading to candid photography of the shenanigans of Brit artists including Tracey Emin, Damien Hirst and Gavin Turk.

Benefiting from the post-war boom, it was business as usual by the 1950s and the internationalisation of Soho was in full flow. Jazz and Jamaican vibes rose from basement clubs; photographs like Sergio Larraín's 1959 image of a Soho pub perhaps conceal the complexities of racial tensions. The annual Soho Fair with its traditional waiters' race was joyful – even 'art' photographer Jean Straker, who later brushed with the Obscene Publications Act, had a float in 1956. Writer Frank Jackson commented in 1959: 'It's unlikely that anywhere else can you buy, in addition to all the usual things, meat from a Pakistan butcher, killed Muslim style, or such Far East delicacies as Salt Fish Pickles, Gulab-Jamun and Rosogolla and Formosa Jasmine Tea.'[8] Willy Ronis's dreamy 1955 shot of the French House pub on Dean Street shows

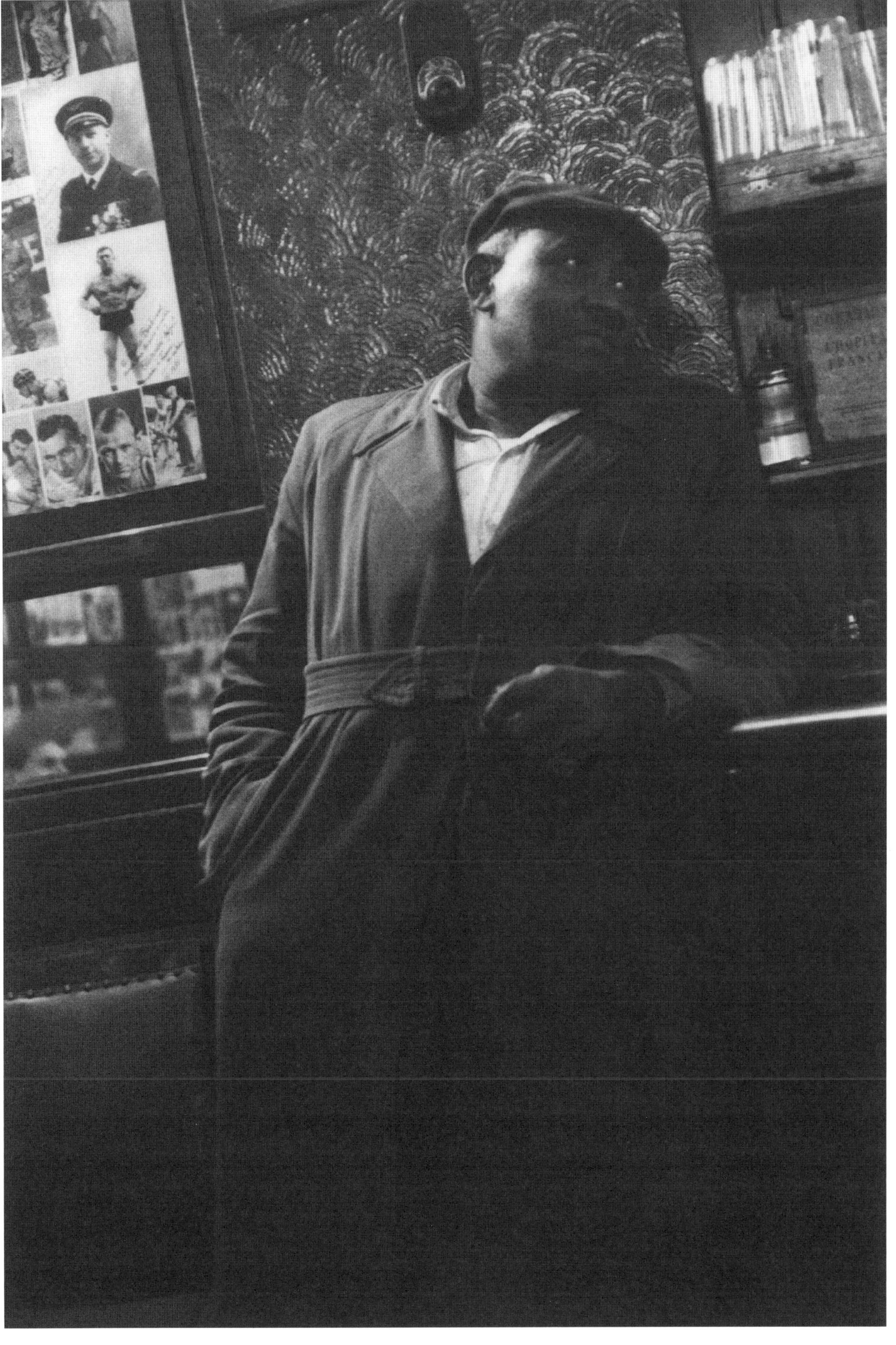

Sergio Larraín's 1959 photograph of a man in a Soho pub.

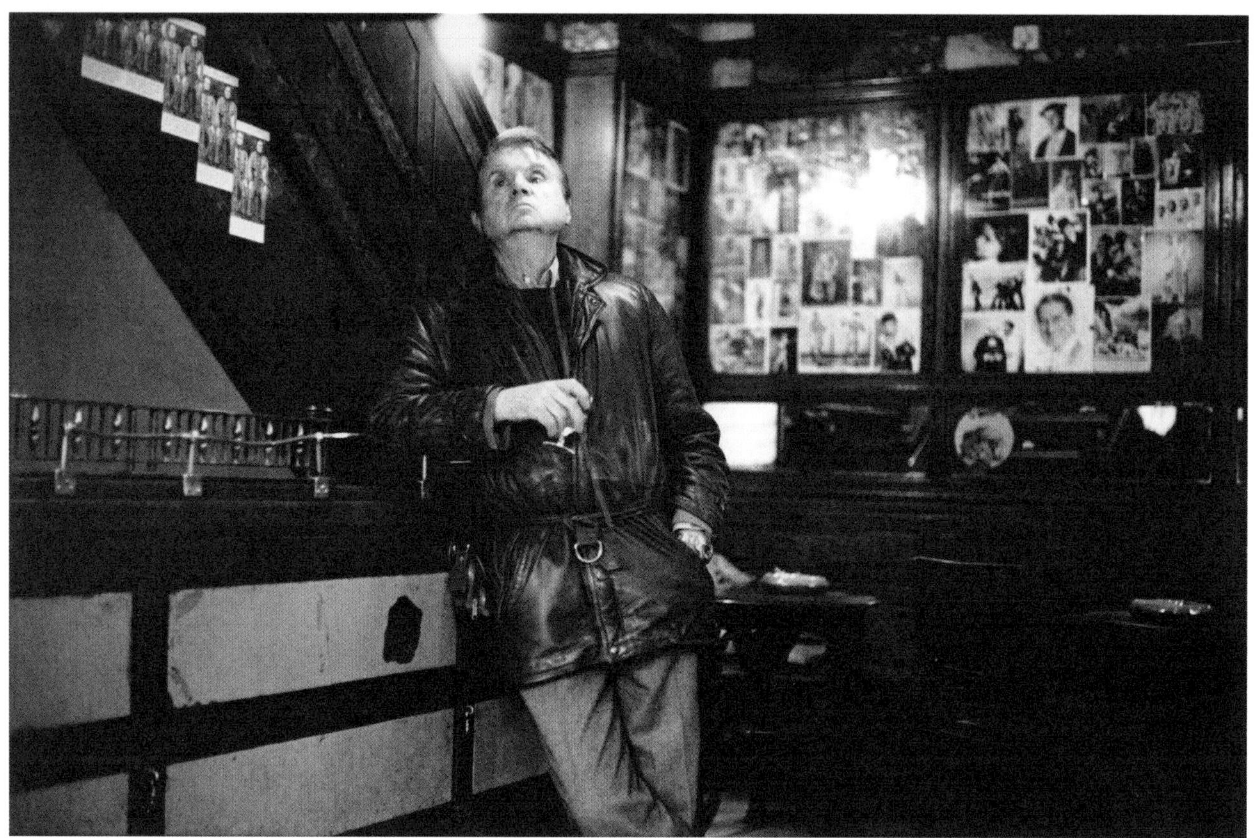

Francis Bacon at the French House in 1984, photographed by Neil Libbert, who would go on to photograph the 1999 bombing of Soho's Admiral Duncan pub.

a lazy sun-drenched afternoon, inviting contemplation of what creates tangible atmosphere in a photograph. And, following in the footsteps of the original Chinatown in London's Limehouse, Soho developed its own around Gerrard Street – new restaurants cashing in on returning servicemen's cultivated taste for East Asian food, fusing business growth with the needs of the local Chinese community.

By 1966, Soho's time in the international limelight had arrived. Carnaby Street became minted. The force of Mary Quant, Twiggy, Justin de Villeneuve and Leonard of Mayfair drove a new fashion-led counter-culture, culminating in punks and New Romantics. Carnaby Street, however, soon became a victim of its own success, a jingoistic tour-bus destination. Burt Glinn's 1969 photograph of a shopper in a flower-power minidress gazing into Carnaby's first women's boutique, Lady Jane, conjures its best times, along with a memorable shot of the trend-setting John Stephen, 'King of Carnaby Street', outside his shop.

Soho was also developing serious pop and rock credentials. Photographs from inside Trident Studios on St Anne's Court show their sought-after Bechstein grand piano, cradle of 1970s hits including 'Life on Mars', 'You're So Vain', 'Hey Jude', 'Without You', 'Walk on the Wild Side' and 'Bohemian Rhapsody', the piano much fancied for its brittle timbre. In 1969 Ray Stevenson captured Trident's laid-back vibe with a picture of David Bowie, John 'Hutch' Hutchinson and Hermione Farthingale (recording as Feathers) unwinding with guru Tony Visconti,

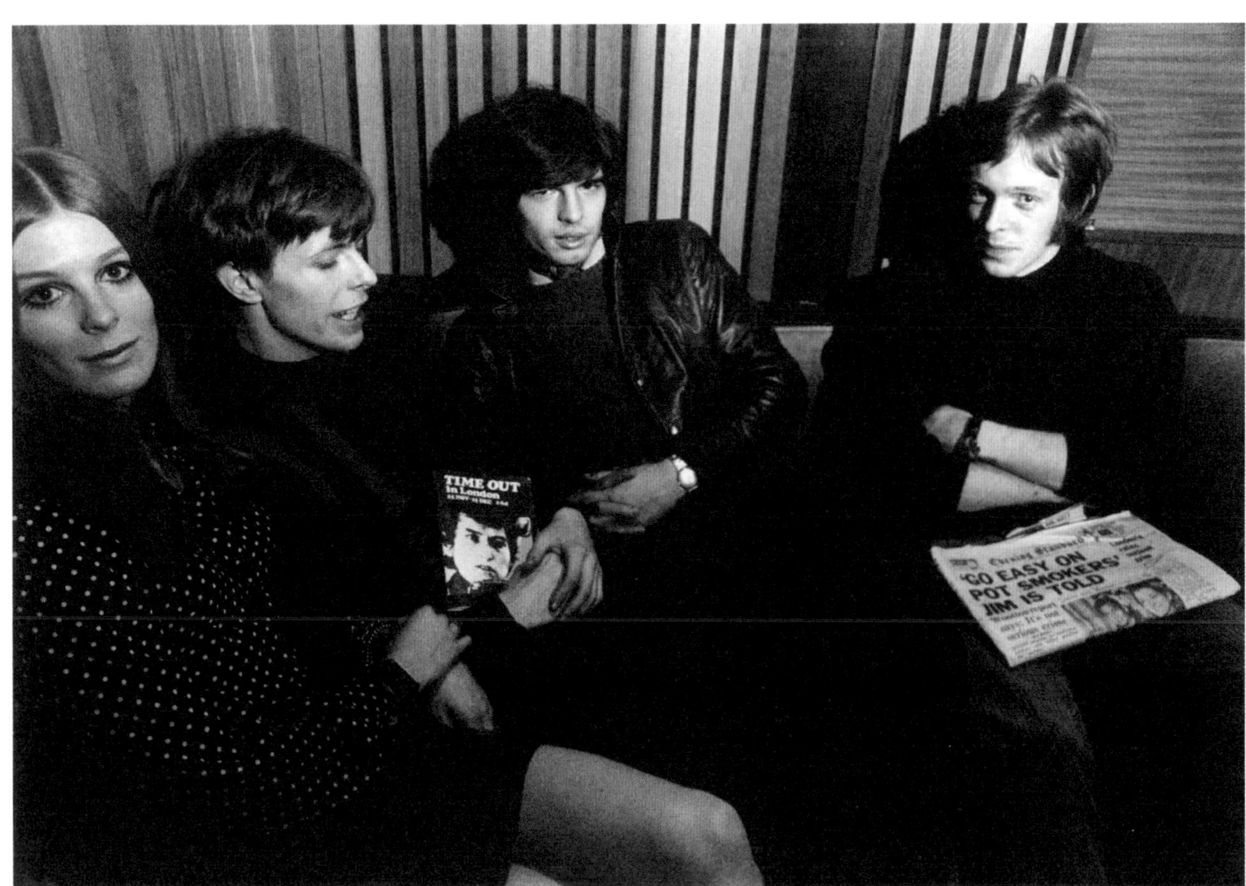

Hermione Farthingale, David Bowie, Tony Visconti and John Hutchinson at Trident Studios, 17 St Anne's Court, in 1969.

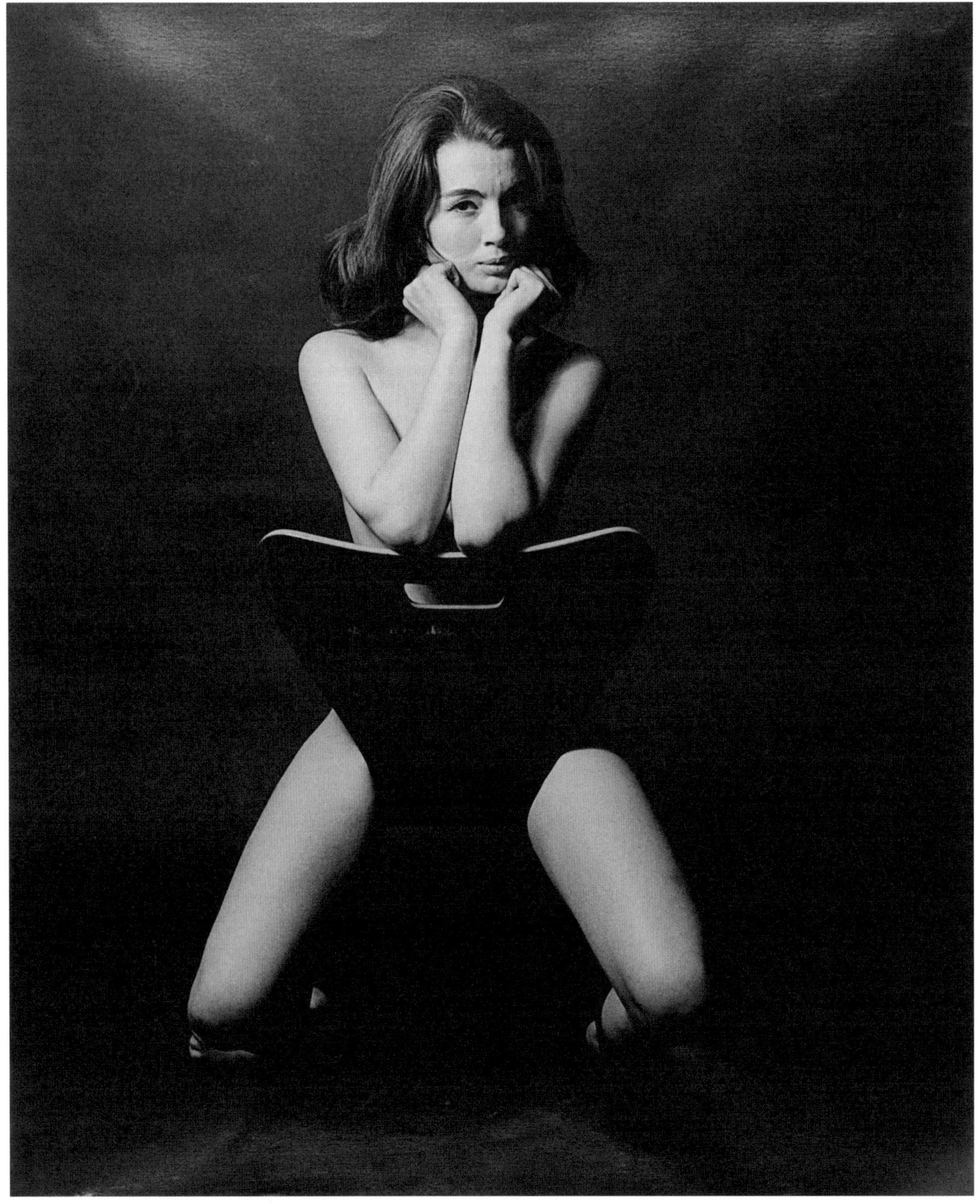

Lewis Morley's photograph of Christine Keeler astride a replica Arne Jacobsen chair was taken in 1963 in the photographer's studio, on the first floor of the satirical Soho nightclub The Establishment at 18 Greek Street.

an *Evening Standard* planted on Hutchinson's lap with the headline '"Go Easy on Pot Smokers" Jim is Told'. We are fortunate to have documents showing The Beatles (wearing kaftans), The Yardbirds, Joan Armatrading, Marianne Faithfull, Jimi Hendrix, Led Zeppelin, Sex Pistols and The Jam, as well as earlier artists like Tommy Steele and The Vipers Skiffle Group (all finding their feet at the 2i's Coffee Bar), Georgie Fame (an auspicious portrait at just sixteen by Roger Mayne), Sammy Davis Jr and Frank Sinatra, all of whom could be seen performing in Soho.

In the 1960s and 1970s, news photographers had to be hardened to operate at Soho's criminal edge. *Sunday Times* staffer Kelvin Brodie's physicality and hard-as-nails look made him a perfect fit. Describing his *Times* photographers, editor Harold Evans said: '[They] struck me rather like Battle of Britain pilots, lounging around with their cameras around their neck ready to take off on hazardous missions at a moment's notice.'[9] East Ender Brodie was in great company: Bryan Wharton, Sally Soames, Philip Jones Griffiths and Don McCullin had all put their lives on the line in global conflicts. Brodie was persistent, working up close to his subjects without impacting circumstances and making the most of low light despite the limitations of film. His Soho work from the late 1960s – as he worked alongside West End Central police, sweeping for drifters and extricating young teenagers from Soho's dirtier clubs – really gets under the skin. His work also went into the trailblazing *Sunday Times Magazine*, which was working to proprietor Roy Thomson's principle that 'there was money to be made in Britain with colour'.[10] Evans recalls, 'We weren't aware of it at the time but the magazine was itself a tiny chip in the mosaic of the swinging 1960s.'[11] Investigative and unflinching, the magazine's photo spreads and grids (shaped by art director Michael Rand) still look fresh today. Pictures, often shocking, jumped off the page straight onto Sunday breakfast plates. In addition to the staffers, international giants including Eve Arnold, Bruce Davidson, Eugene Richards, Brian Duffy, Lord Snowdon, David Bailey, Terence Donovan, Diane Arbus and William Klein were commissioned, all attracted by the magazine's reputation. Soho fortuitously got the irreverent Klein in 1980; it was a match made in heaven. Back in 1956 Klein had shaken up street photography forever with his book *New York*, a series of 'prototypes' for how photography could bend reality rather than reflect it. In Soho he managed to strip back the square mile to bare essentials – the last gunmakers, strip clubs, punks, the local Rotondos family, the Raymond Revuebar and, of course, Francis Bacon – the feature abetted by Denis Herbstein's clever words.

A few months prior to Klein's shoot, on a muggy August night, the mass murder of thirty-seven people occurred on Denmark Street, a disaffected customer having taken petrol and rag to the club El Hueco (also known as the Spanish Rooms and popular with Latin Americans),[12] in the same street that saw the first Rolling Stones album recorded and which was home to La Giaconda, a café frequented by The Kinks, Bowie and Elton John. So rapidly did the fire spread that distressed Soho firemen attending the scene said, 'People seem to have died on the spot ... with drinks still in their hands.'[13] It is perturbing that there is still so little awareness of this attack that took the lives of many immigrant workers.

There are many striking photographs that have given form to the ever-changing moods and iconic figures that define Soho, ranging from Christine Keeler astride *that* chair (hers was the perfect Soho story, involving model, government minister and Soviet attaché) to an awkward Johnny Rotten on Carnaby Street. Captured moments of lust, celebration and hedonism are quickly overturned by outbursts of violence and desperation, as is the case in what might be two of Soho's most affecting images: Neil Libbert's photograph of the racist and homophobic nail bombing of the Admiral Duncan pub in April 1999 – surely a direct attack on the inclusivity that is synonymous with the area – and the monochrome image of boxer-turned-celebrity Freddie Mills sitting lifeless in the backseat of his Citroën DS in Goslett Yard.[14] As a collection, Soho photographs offer a heady mix of scrutiny and nostalgia. They show the street as stage and go a long way to identifying Soho's neoteric disposition: a place in which instinct and interaction are at their most heightened.

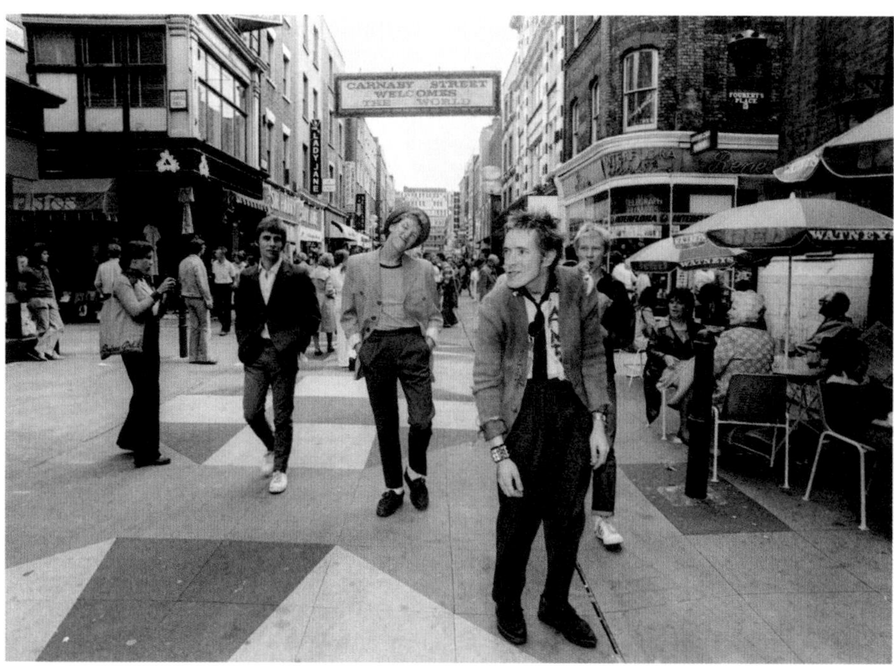

The Sex Pistols (Glen Matlock, Steve Jones, Johnny Rotten and Paul Cook) on Carnaby Street in 1976.

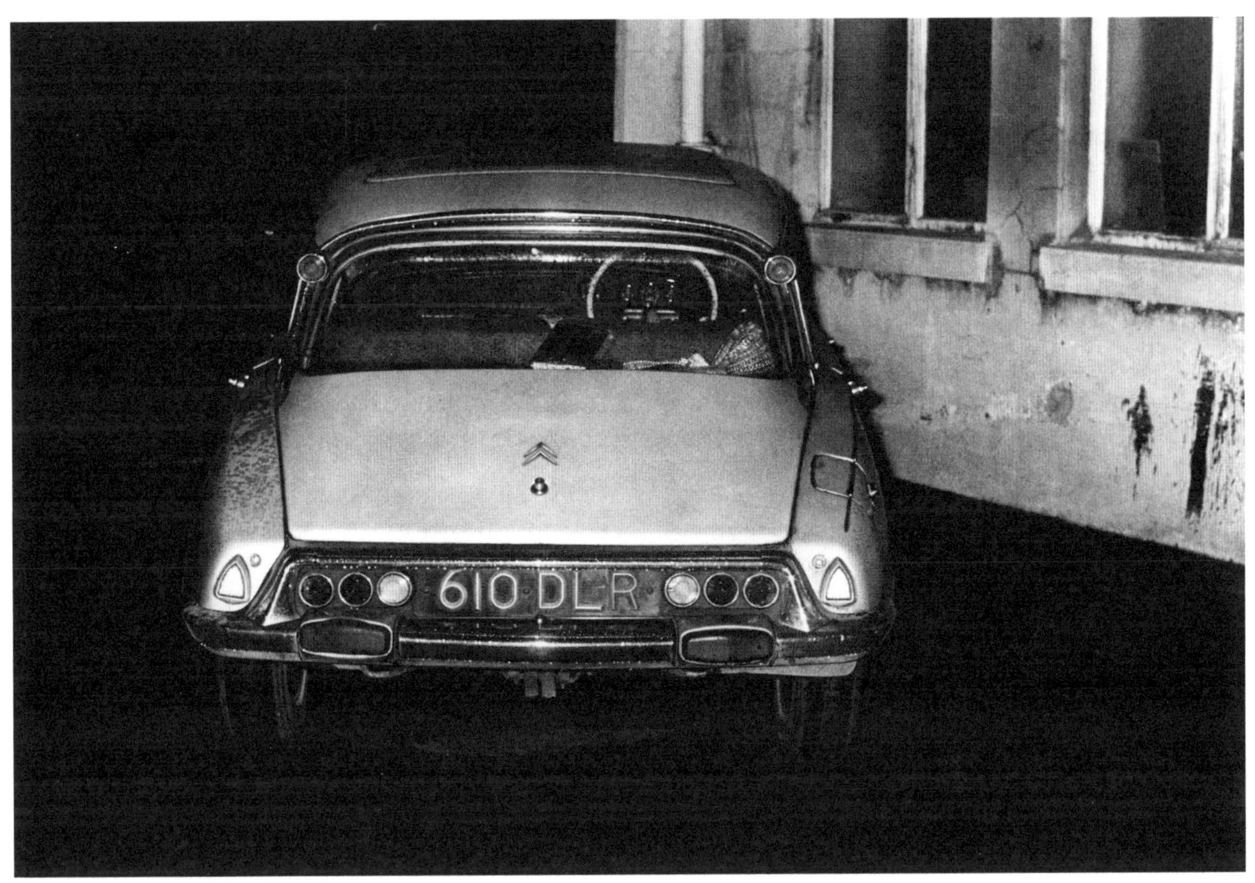

Champion boxer and TV celebrity Freddie Mills was found dead in his Citroën DS behind his nightclub in Goslett Yard in July 1965.

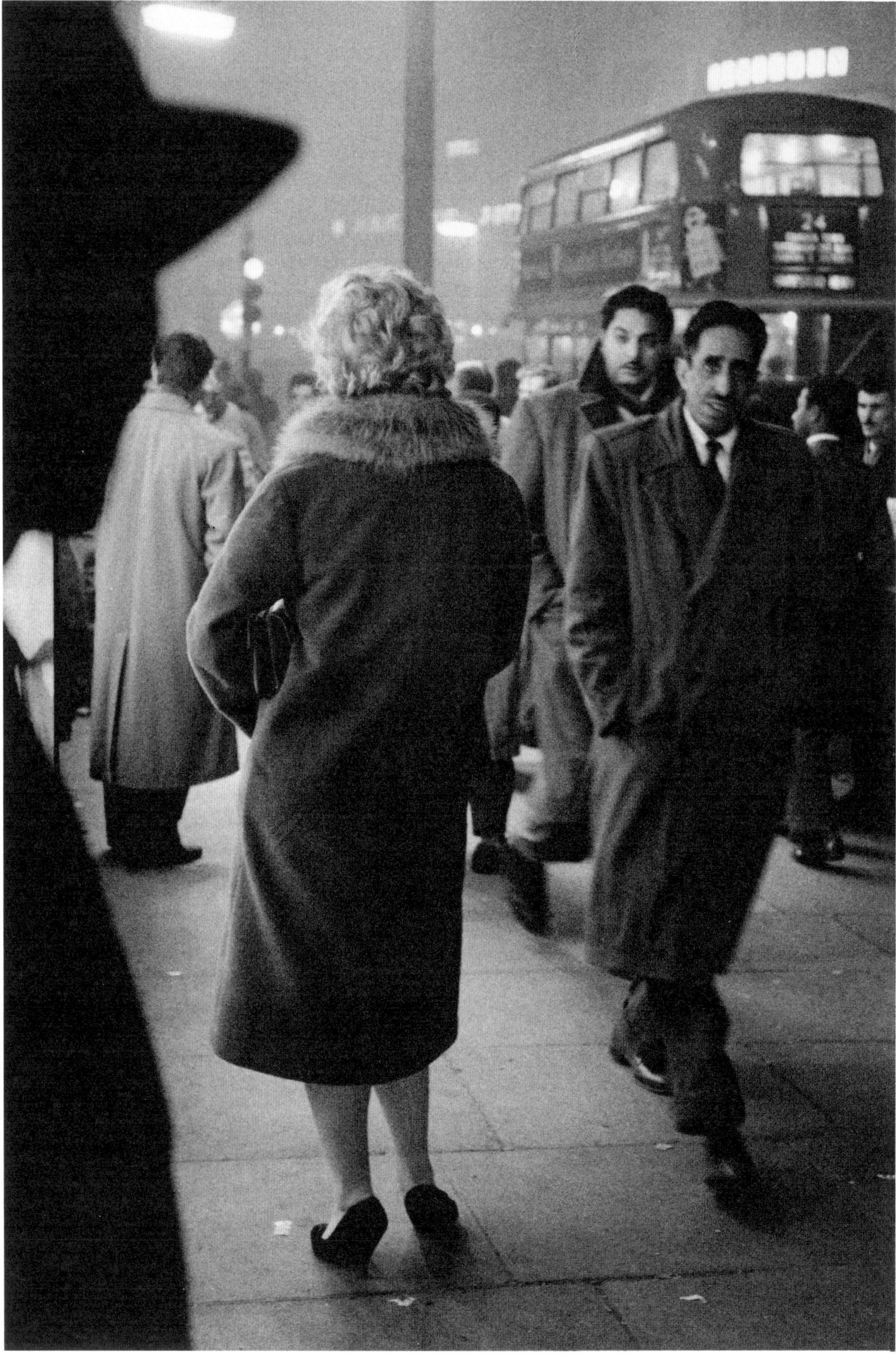
24

Sergio Larraín's 1959 image of a woman walking on the edge of Soho evokes the sense of intrigue and human connection that came to define the area.

NEON GLORY

BY PAUL FLYNN

One of the common conversations unique to Londoners concerns the stultifying effects of gentrification on Soho. In Soho's fragrant history, just close enough to touch, there was subversion, social defiance and sex. Now, there is only the incumbent monolith of Crossrail – a symbol of government bureaucracy, an administrative gravestone on how not to get things done and a totem of London's vulgar and theatrical tendency to spend, spend, spend. Soho, in the local parlance, is a shadowy and magnificent thing of the past; a place that used to be; a place that no longer exists.

However, the belief that this little mile of mischief has become its own ghost doesn't square with my own experiences of the area. Crossing the threshold from a bus stop on Oxford Street into Soho Square at the north end or by the Windmill Theatre at the south still feels like an esoteric, philosophic shift. It conjures a palpable sense of transference, from the you in the past to the you in the present. One's naughty valve cannot help but get loosened. Perhaps this is connected to the area's history, perhaps not. I tried to think of some of the lovelier things I've done in Soho over the past twelve months, some thirty-five years since first stumbling upon it as a Mancunian schoolboy on a day trip and inwardly genuflecting to its neon glory. The list, it turned out, was virtually endless.

1. Watching a voluble, hirsute and charismatic bear belt out a hilariously inappropriate Oasis song on karaoke night at the Kings Arms.

2. Stealing a napkin from Dean Street Townhouse.

3. Spotting a woman in a saucy uniform changing the Pop Art window display at Agent Provocateur.

4. Eating a coffee éclair from Maison Bertaux.

5. Short of a birthday present for a friend, purchasing a vial of amyl nitrite from one of the area's remaining sex shops – a useful and still entirely legal five pounds spent.

6. Clocking the new demographic of confused mums standing patiently in line, trying to understand what it feels like for their teenage sons to queue for elite, limited-edition streetwear at Supreme and Palace.

7. Dining in Quo Vadis.

8. Having lunch at Bone Daddies.

9. Drinking fifty black coffees while seated on the Bar Italia pavement.

10. Cackling in the audience as Lady Bunny grapples with the reverberating echoes of global drag culture as it hits the mainstream, downstairs at a basement residency.

11. Wowing at Sandra Bernhard bringing the fierce to Ronnie Scott's.

12. Buying re-edited disco twelve-inches you can't get anywhere else at Phonica, from a salesman stood behind turntables, sporting the customary and familiar surly, record-shop-boy frown.

13. Enjoying the familiar whiff of Breton cider across the threshold of the French House.

14. Watching previews of unseen films from an unreconstructed banquette at the D'Arblay Street screening rooms.

15. Sitting under the Ivy Brasserie canopies, casually spying the cottagers' comings and goings from the underworld of the Broadwick Street Victorian public conveniences.

16. Getting purse-lipped at the appalling Carnaby Street Christmas lights.

17. Becoming regular enough to be on first-name terms with one of the addled booze experts at Gerry's on Old Compton Street.

18. Watching confused suburban visitors with Harry Potter merchandise realise they've taken a wrong turn.

19. Observing, with a quaint smile, straight men taking photos of one another under the 'G-A-Y' signage to show their wives on Facebook.

20. Putting a pound in a box and lighting a candle at St Patrick's, Soho Square.

As the list began escalating, I started thinking of Soho not as a fantastical place where legends and myths are built – where artists, fashion designers and thinkers came to radicalise – it wasn't a fêted place of the past or a swinging, vertiginous roll call of hookers and their clientele. Instead, I started to think of Soho as a real, robust and weighty place that can handle change of any sort. If governmental conformity is the latest pressure on its soul, it will withstand that, too.

In confusing times, Soho remains a reliably tacit testament to the social temperature. We now know enough about addiction, compulsion and mental illness to recognise what once looked like jolly carousing as something darker. The radical shifts in the freedom around sexuality have removed the LGBTQ+ community from the netherworld and landed us in the mainstream for appraisal (not all good, but that's another matter entirely; we actually are here and queer now). Indeed, if you wanted to locate the busiest gay club in Soho in 2019, you might be well advised to walk up to the bustling sexual health services at the Dean Street clinic, with its specialism in chemsex aftercare. A sign of the times that we really ought to be talking about more than we do.

My first understanding of Soho arrived, fittingly, from the two-dimensional imagery of a record jacket. I was eleven years old when I first pored over the sleeve of Soft Cell's *Non-Stop Erotic Cabaret*. Peter Ashworth's photographs whisked this young mind off to an illicit place of sin and secrecy, of wit and wonder, of the night. Twenty-odd years later I went to interview Marc Almond, one half of the creators of this wonderful year-zero British synth-pop record, this epic ode to the grab-bag wonders of sleaze, in the lost playground of Soho's storied clip-joint history, Madame Jojo's. Mr Almond was recovering from a near-fatal motorcycle accident. Yet his tart humour remained unscathed. On my commenting what a perfectly appropriate teenage fantasy it was to be meeting him in a Soho nightclub, he simply rolled his eyes, as if his interviewer had not noticed the passing of time. 'It's not quite what it used to be,' he mused, 'But then, why should it? Sometimes I think I prefer it this way.'

For a London postcode to remain preserved in aspic feels fundamentally contradictory to the natural mutability of cities. They are not static, complete, finished entities. Some of the old scions of Soho's most celebrated days will disappear, like Central Saint Martins' crumbling fashion school outlet on Charing Cross Road. Some will stay, like the gaudy boozer just metres down the street. The passing of industry into history – however influential its epoch – cannot sustain the gradual passage of time that carves up cities in its wake, leaving just a scent of its wreckage underfoot: a sniff in the ether, a lost shoe on the footpath, a broken glass in the stairwell.

If we accept Soho as shifting sands, it's all the more remarkable to acknowledge the steadfast spirit of the area. Soho may not always look a certain way, but it will always feel it. For once you accept that your whole person can change in accordance with its surroundings, freedom and liberation from repression are but a whisker away. They might once have found outward expression in the area's sex industries, now dwindling, having been commodified and internalised online, a whole new ether the old Soho could not even have dreamed of. But an eagerness to allow the wind beneath your sails, to access the parts of yourself you might normally reserve for post-daylight hours, cannot be integral to the streets you're walking. What Soho really represented was that thing that is not policeable, by governments, by gentrification, by bureaucracy or by change. It is the excitement of thoughts, the candid flair of the imagination unhinged.

None of this should necessarily undercut the geographic and emotional significance of the one corner of London's showy, aggressive, palatial wealth reserved for fun. In many ways, these reasons all play into the fact that it is still perfectly permissible to walk into Soho feeling like a nobody, then metamorphose into a somebody on turning that first, magically transcendent corner. The application of the simple idea of accessing your best self is still a cornerstone of art, fashion and philosophy, wherever it lives.

So when Londoners talk about the death of Soho – when they romanticise its past with a collective lump in their throats – what they really mean is not that a physical space has lost its ardour, that the bulge in its trousers has lost all tumescence. What they mean is something to do with the mood music of leisure writ large, taking on a different, more tangential and quizzical tempo. For now, Soho is still the cranky, sharp-tongued, scarlet-lipped, ratchet big sister we will always love, no matter how many Tesco Metros are built in it.

KELVIN BRODIE

Kelvin ('Steve') Brodie (1932–1978) grew up in East London. In the 1960s and 1970s Brodie was a photojournalist on the staff of *The Times* and *Sunday Times*; he worked predominantly on the newspapers but also had his pictures run in the *Sunday Times Magazine*.

Former *Sunday Times* editor Harold Evans remembers Brodie as a 'terrific photographer'.[15] He assigned Brodie to coordinating the picture desk as he knew his tough stance would ensure that the dispatched photographers would deliver on their promises made at news conferences. Brodie worked closely with photographers Ian Wright, Bryan Wharton, Michael Ward, Peter Dunne and Frank Herrmann at the height of the *Sunday Times*' investigative powers. His work covered numerous conflicts – the India-Pakistan War (1965), the Six-Day War (1967) and the Troubles in Northern Ireland – and was chosen for the *Sunday Times Magazine*'s cover, including for the one-year memorial in 1975 of the Turkish Airlines Flight 981 plane crash. Brodie also developed colour features on, for instance, Spanish bullfighters on horseback and warriors of the Khyber Pass.

Closer to home, Brodie's assignments took him to The Beatles recording at Abbey Road studios (1963) and to the Kray Twins' mother's front room in Valance Road, Bethnal Green (1965), working on the latter alongside *Sunday Times* crime correspondent Cal McCrystal. Those who met Brodie described him as 'blunt' and 'burly', but Steve – as he was known to his friends – was complex, incisive and a straight talker. Brodie's Soho observations show the massive contrast between night and day in the area. He brings us routine street scenes, wry portraits of locals, strip club exteriors, and great work from nights out with the police or with charities as they conducted raids or rescue missions. These images give a real sense of drama in which the Soho criminal underworld becomes palpable.

Brodie accompanied late-night police teams looking for under-17s and school absconders in back alleys and grotty cellar clubs, where they were removed from illegal sex work. For a photographer with experience of war reporting, this was relatively safe, and Brodie merged into the shadows to capture the story at close quarters. These Soho 'sweeps' were made in a converted school bus – windows barred – by the West End Central police. Brodie's work from these forays was raw. The so-called 'clean-up' was only ever temporary. Investigative reporter David Leitch, who worked on the *Sunday Times* Insight team, spoke of 'the legendary Brodie, who felt no assignment had been properly wrapped up until blood was spilt, or a door booted in at the least'.[16] The original prints and negatives from Brodie's Soho, crime-focused work often bear on their reverse the words 'Not to be used unless face covered!' to protect identities. This work has remained unseen since it was first published.

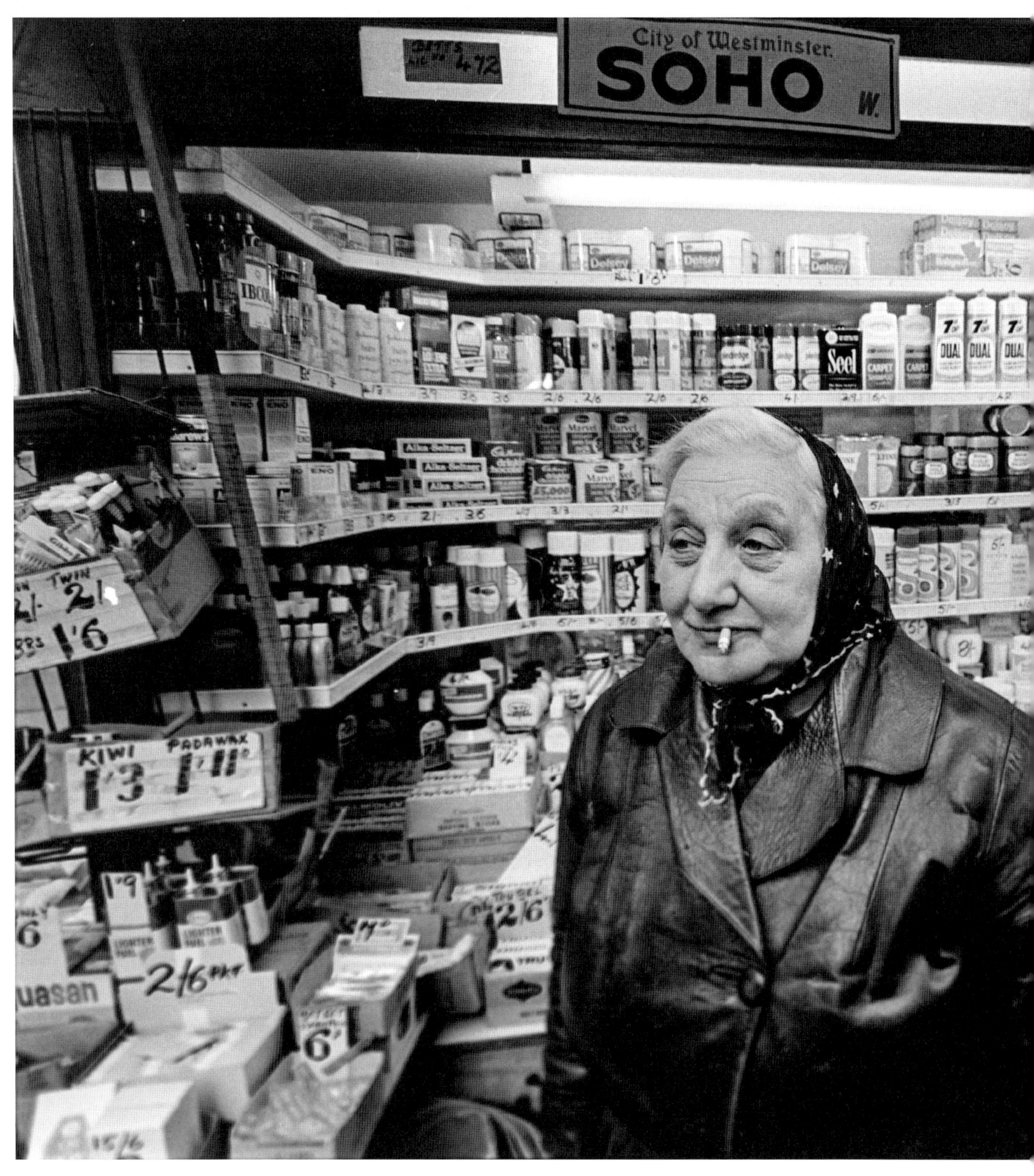

All images are from ‘Passport to Soho’, a selection of which were published in the *Sunday Times Magazine*, 21 January 1968.

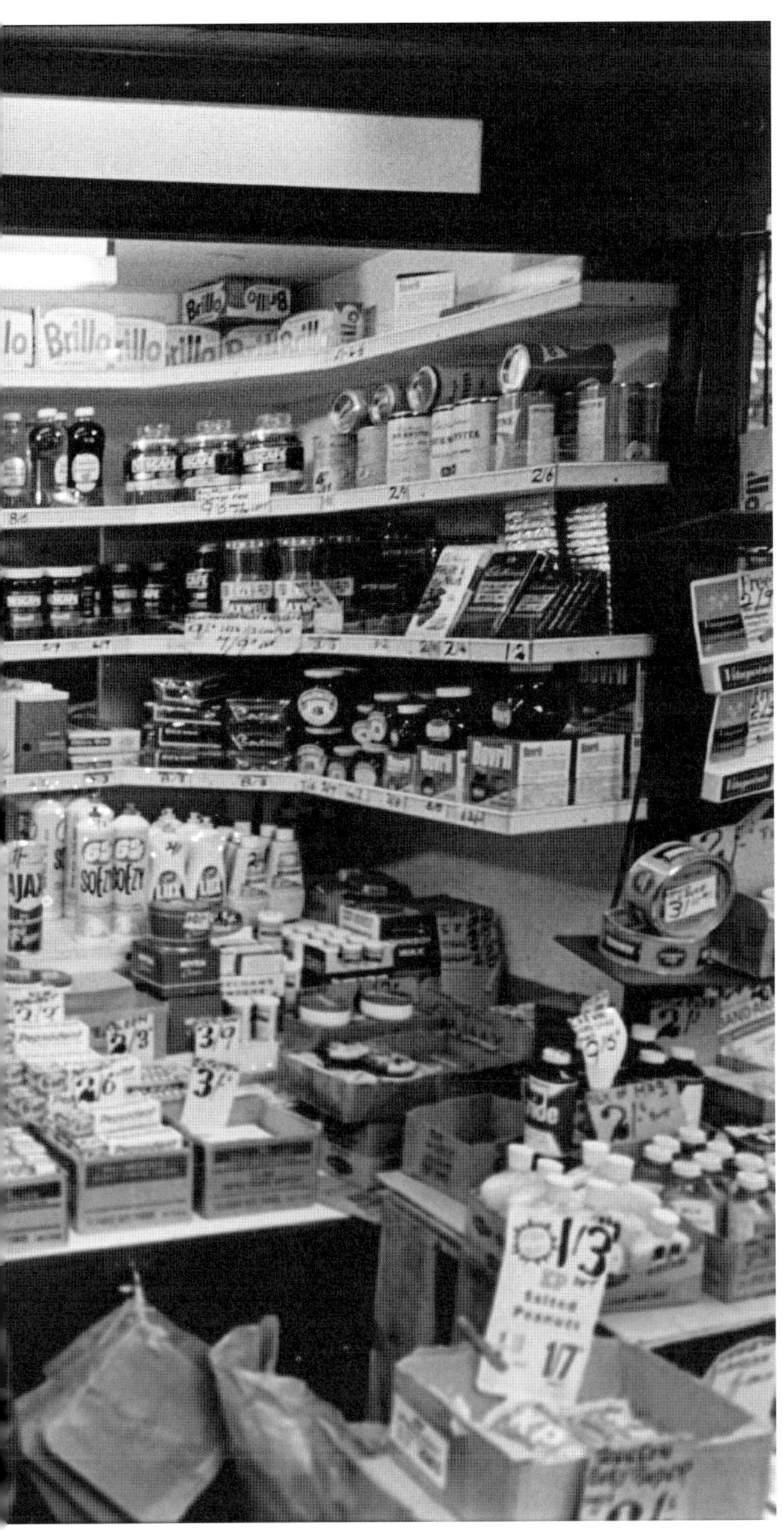

Brillo
Bovril
AJAX
1/3
Salted Peanuts

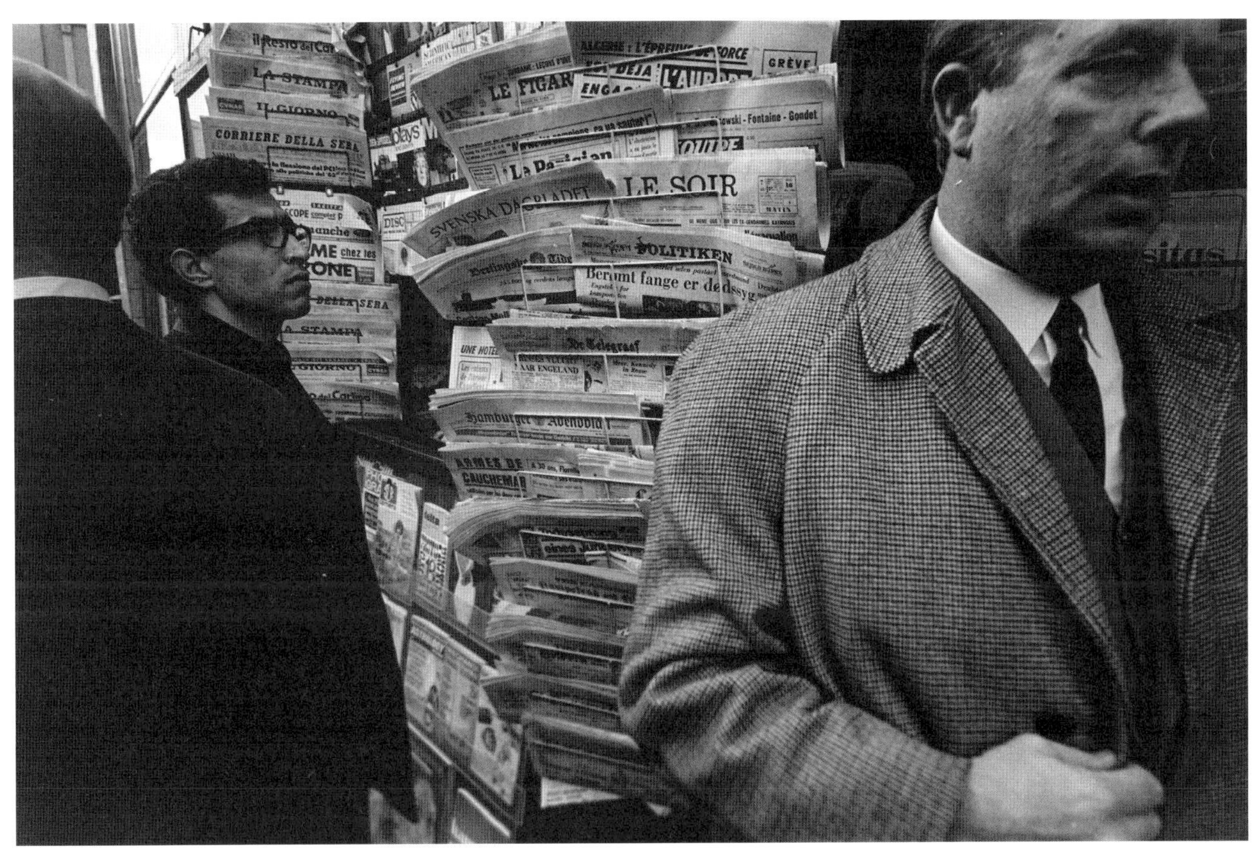
LA STAMPA
CORRIERE DELLA SERA
LE SOIR
POLITIKEN
GRÈVE
AAR ENGELAND

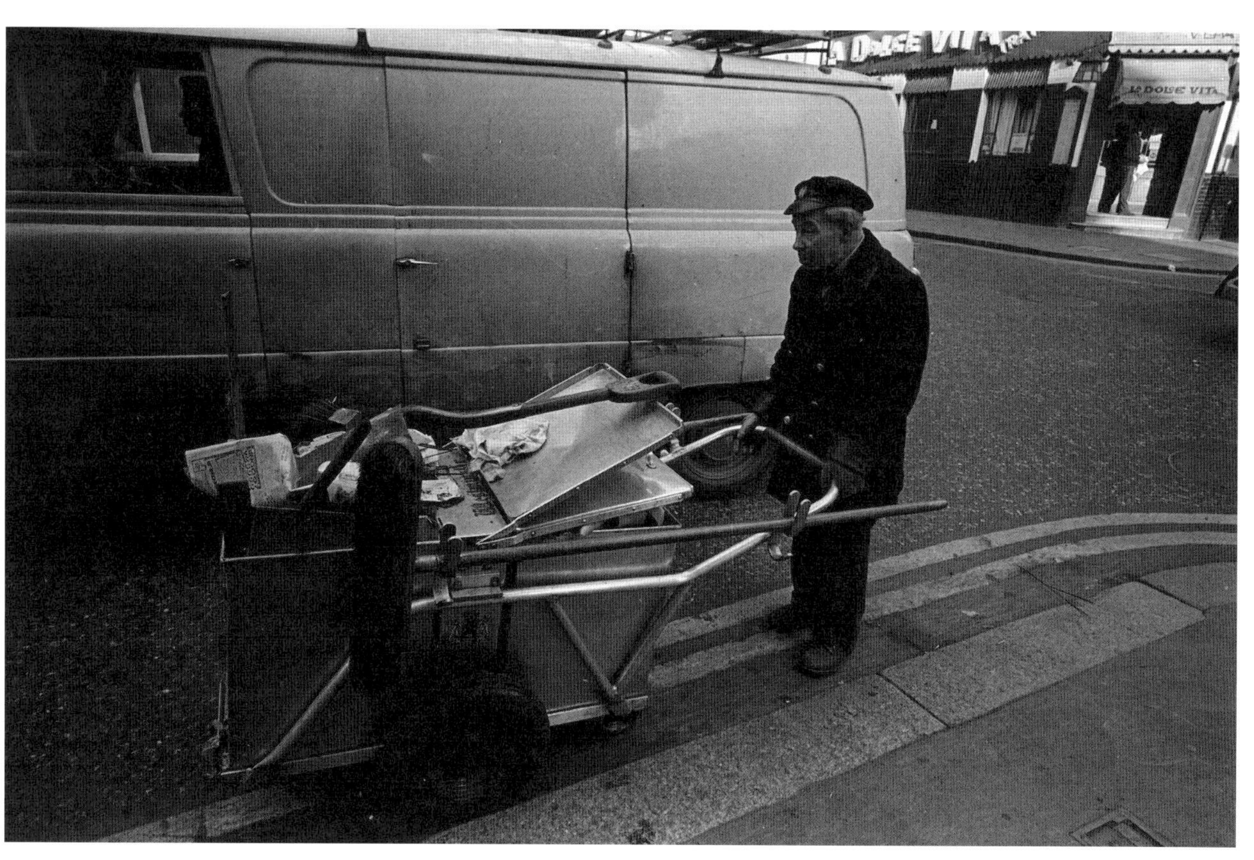
LA DOLCE VITA

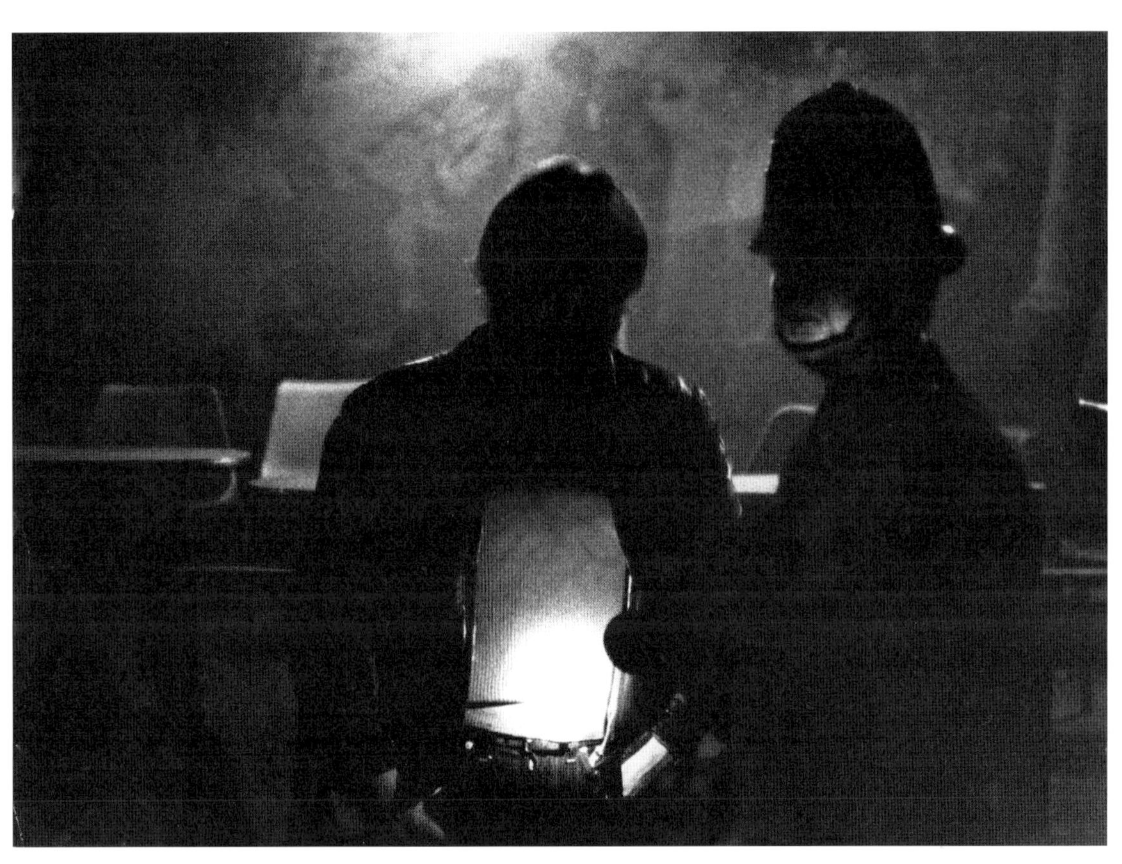

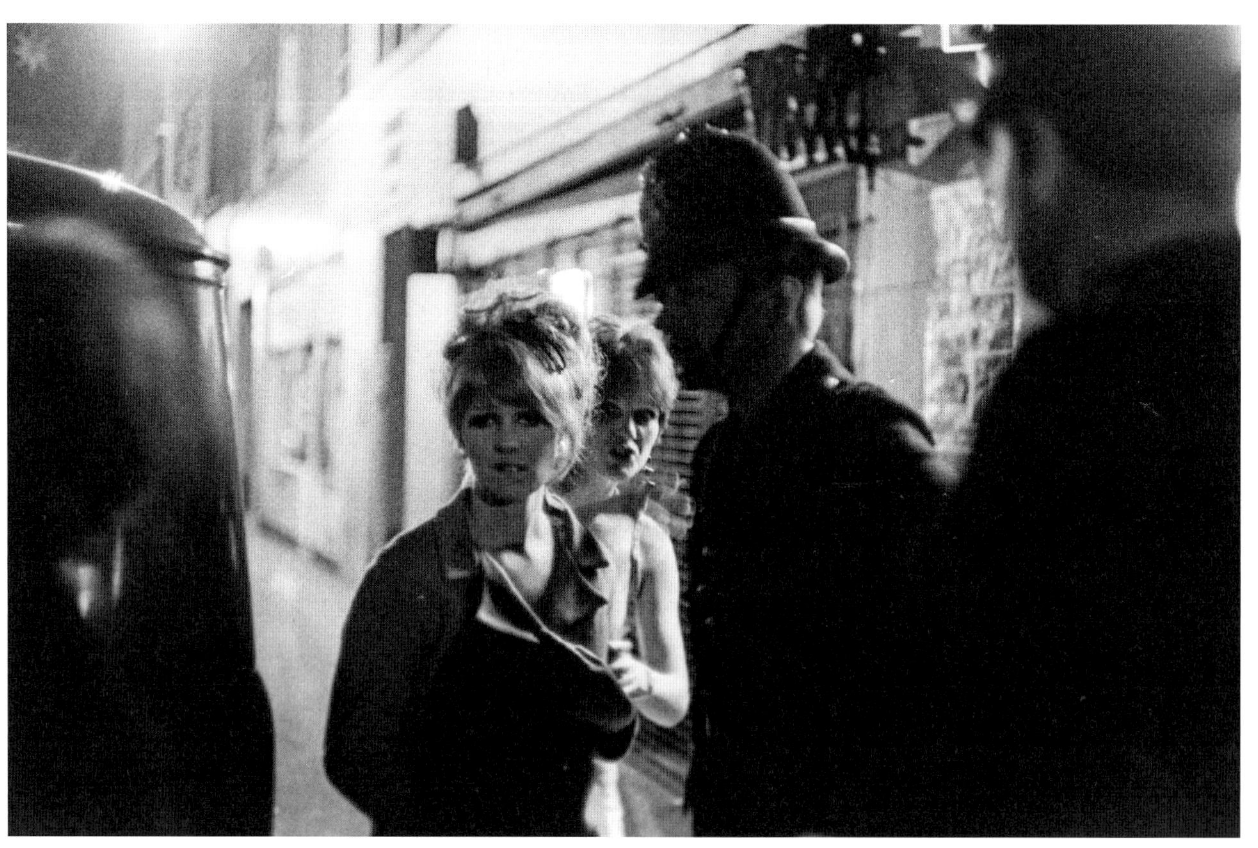

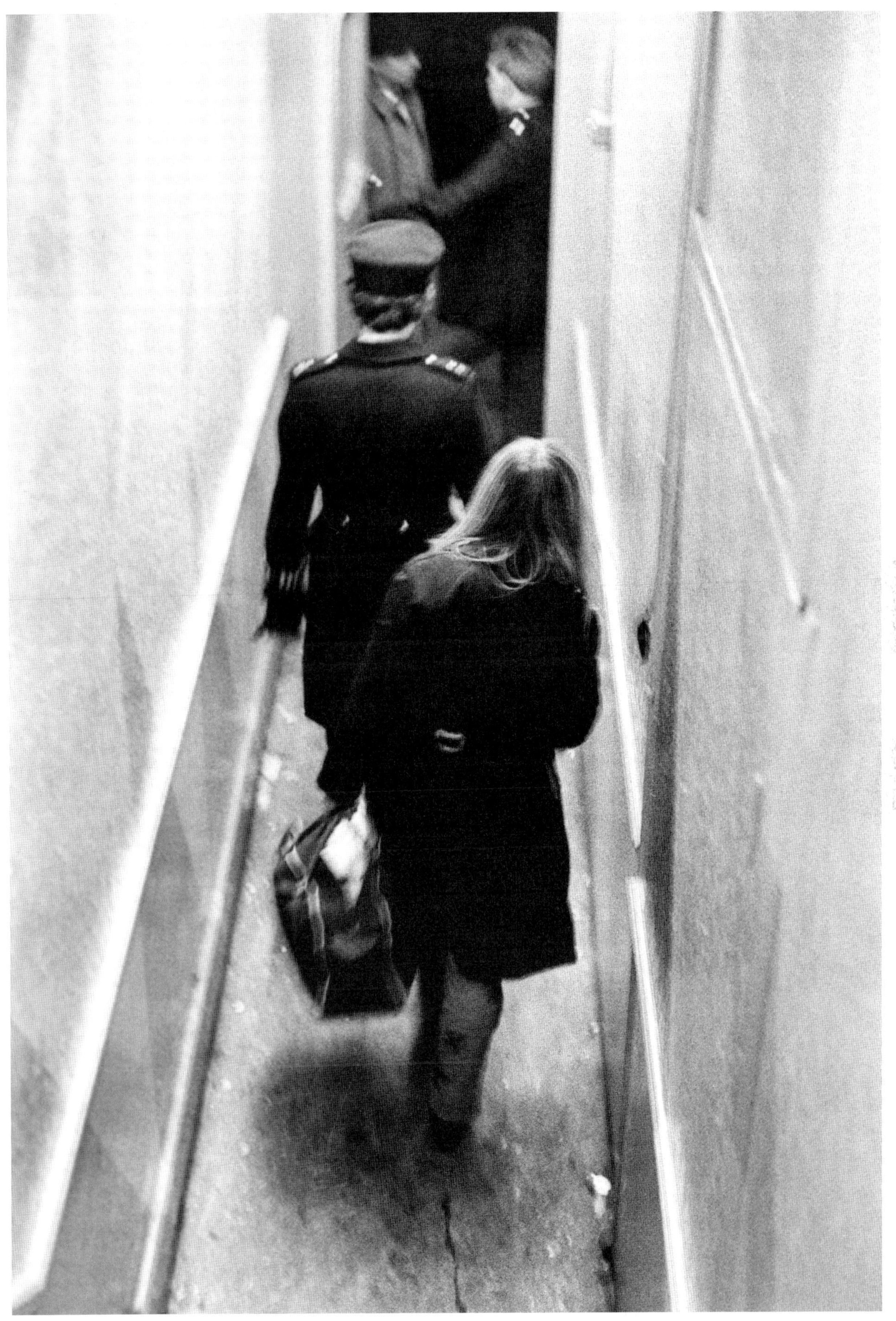

Brodie documented a police operation in the area under the direction of Inspector Elizabeth Reid.

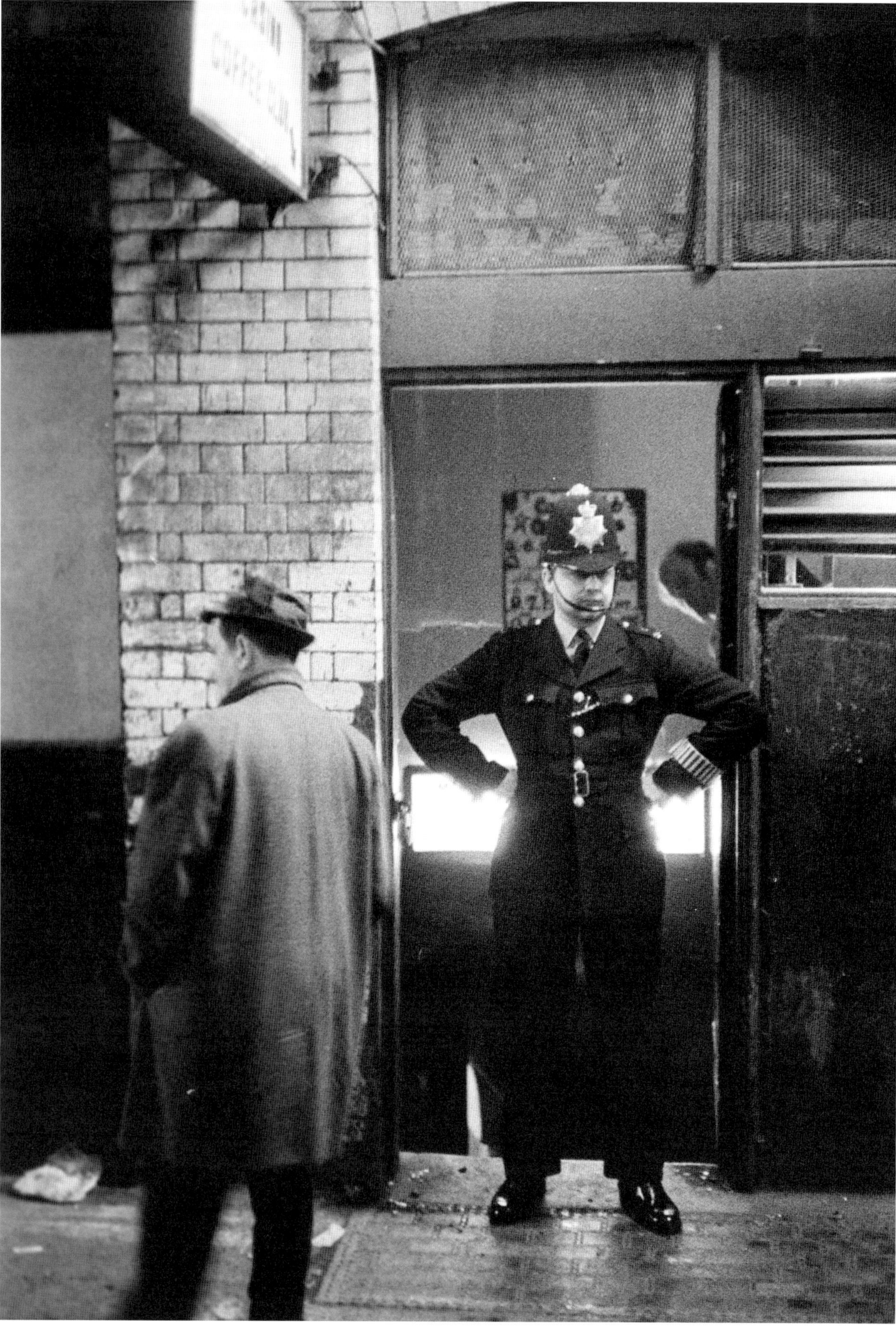

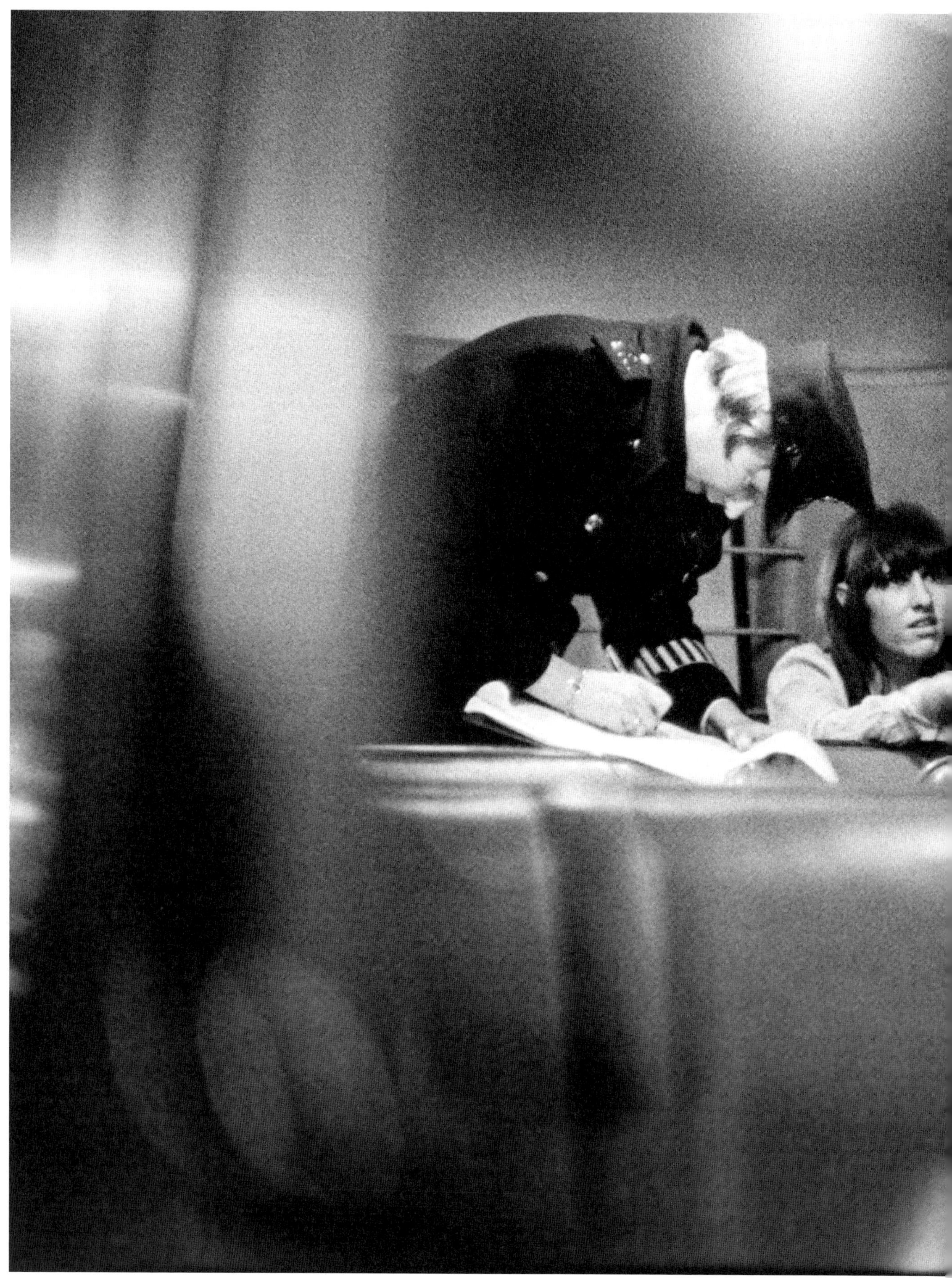

 Vulnerable adolescents were rounded up and questioned.

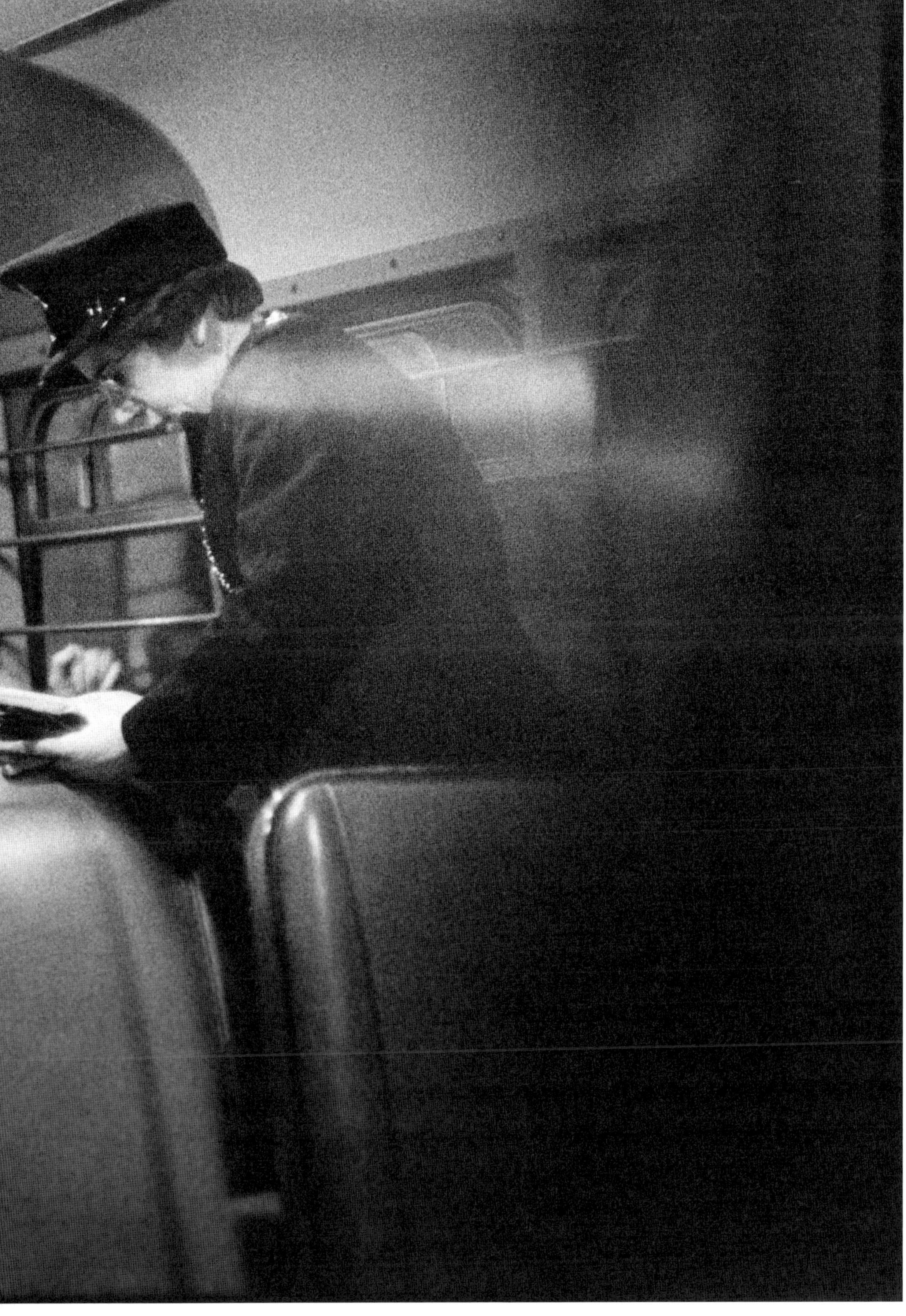

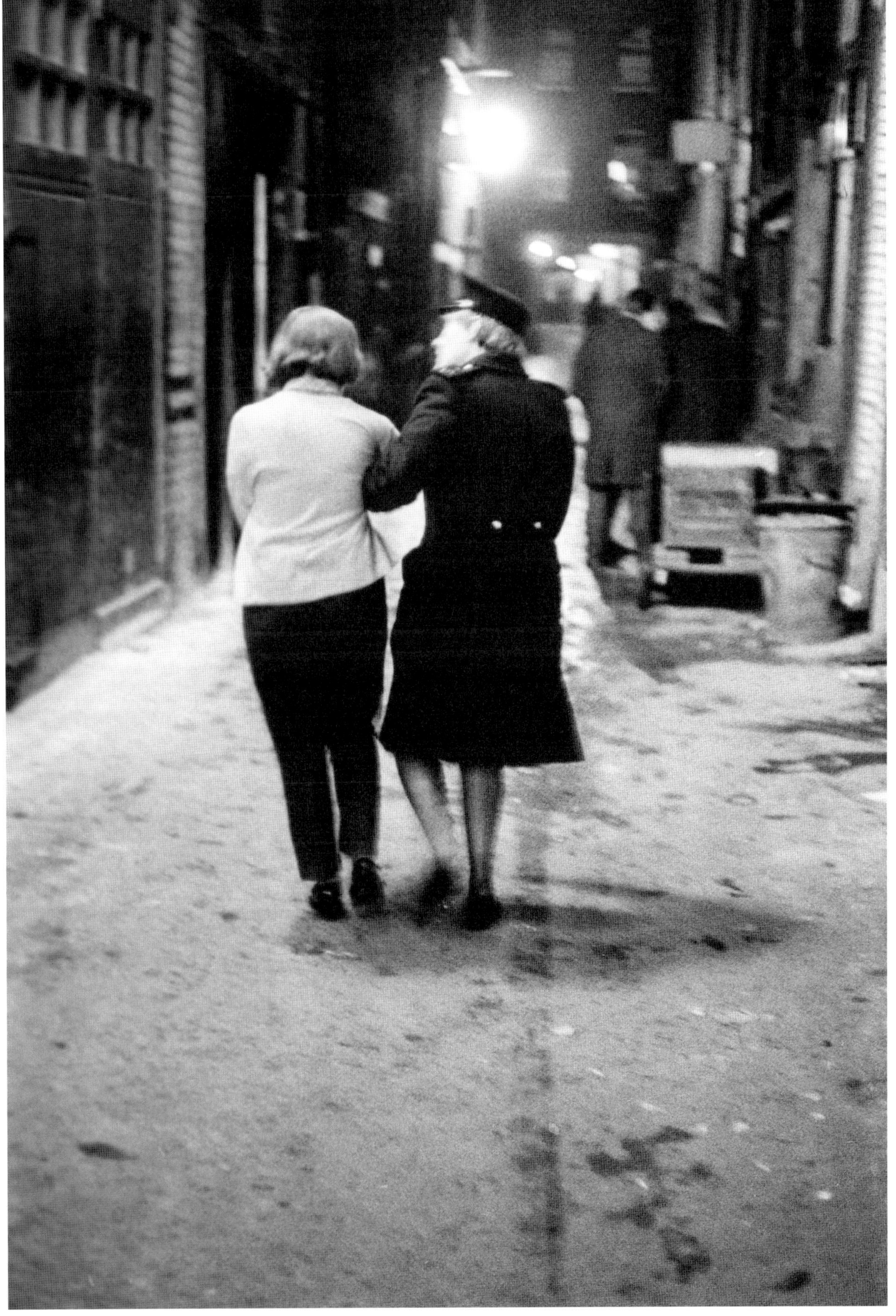

CORINNE DAY

Corinne Day (1962–2010) started her career as a fashion model, and it was during this period, while travelling for work, that she began taking intimate shots of her friends. She later stated, 'as soon as I started taking photographs, I loved it. I felt I'd found my feet.'[17] On the suggestion of a photographer friend she showed her work to Phil Bicker, art director at *The Face* magazine. The feature that resulted from that meeting, 'The 3rd Summer of Love', launched not only Day's career but also the career of the sixteen-year-old model she cast: Kate Moss. The shoot took place on the beach at Camber Sands, East Sussex, and was published in the magazine in July 1990. For both Day and Moss this moment was a game-changer; indeed, it also announced the fashion spirit of the new decade. Day's raw, pared-back photographs ran in opposition to the highly produced images that dominated high fashion editorials at the time. Day valued everyday friendships, mundane happenings and unglamorous locations, all of which shaped both the content and form of her photography.

What is perhaps little known is that the bulk of Day's personal and editorial work was shot in her flat on Brewer Street, Soho. She and her partner Mark Szaszy, a photographer and filmmaker, lived at the epicentre of the creative media world – surrounded by the multiple model agencies, fashion PR offices, photo processing labs and magazine offices that made up the cogs of the fashion editorial machine. Their well-lit flat was on the top floor of a 1930s block; the Raymond Revuebar and a 'Girls, Girls, Girls' neon sign could be seen from the window. As well as being their home, the space doubled as a site for meetings and as a working photography studio. After shoots, the flat would continue into the night as a gathering venue for a steady stream of friends and visitors. Since the rest of the building was non-residential, music could be played loudly throughout the night.

Day's Soho work gives us a fascinating insight into the lives of those in her circle. In the Brewer Street images, Day allows the viewer unfiltered access to the comings and goings of friends and models: we see them dancing, drinking and crashing out on sofas as the photography shoots morphed into nights of excess and hungover mornings. For Day, professional models and friends were often one and the same, so that in her images the clothes become almost incidental. We look in on these lives as if catching a passing glimpse into her flat through a window. Day's Soho work remains unparalleled as a document of that particular creative moment – a compelling snapshot of the uninhibited 1990s – while also evoking the casual intimacy of those domestic spaces in which we spend our formative years.

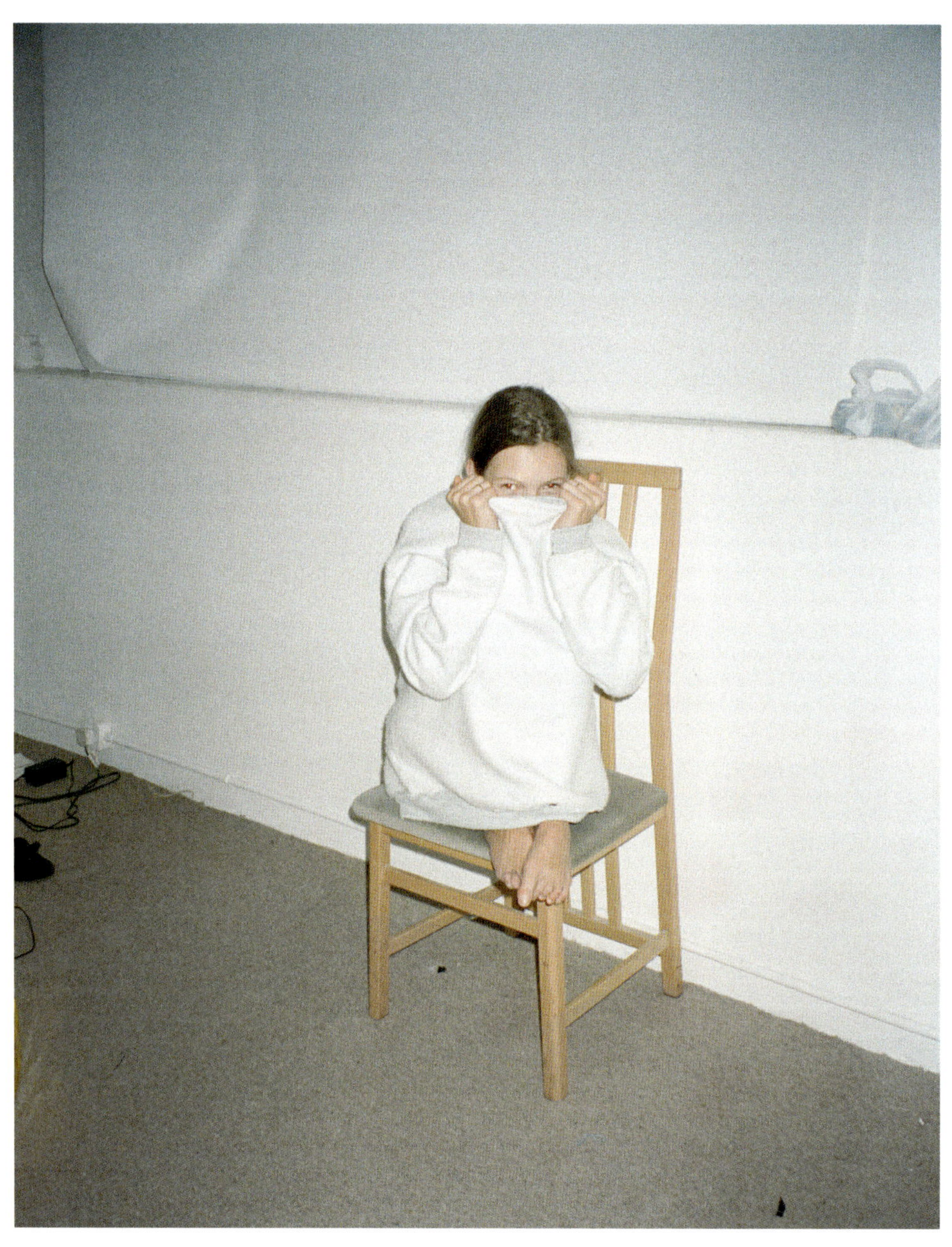

‘Kate Moss Waking Up’, Brewer Street, c. 1990.

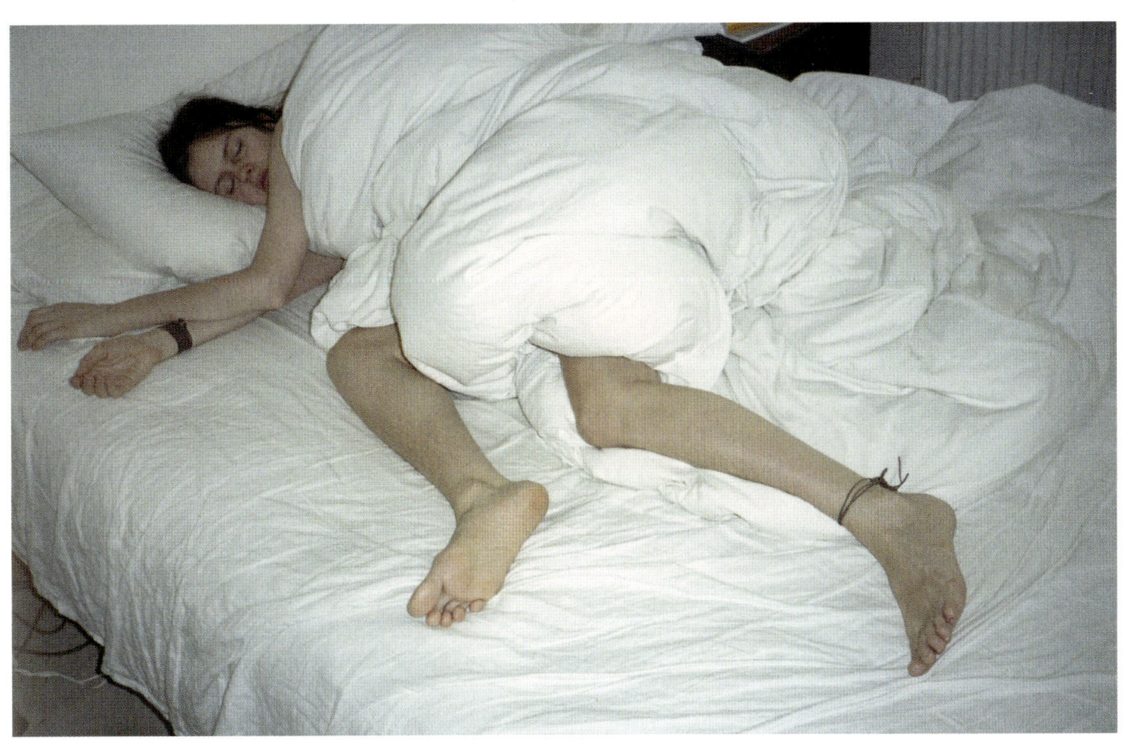

‘Corinne at Home’, Brewer Street, c. 1999.

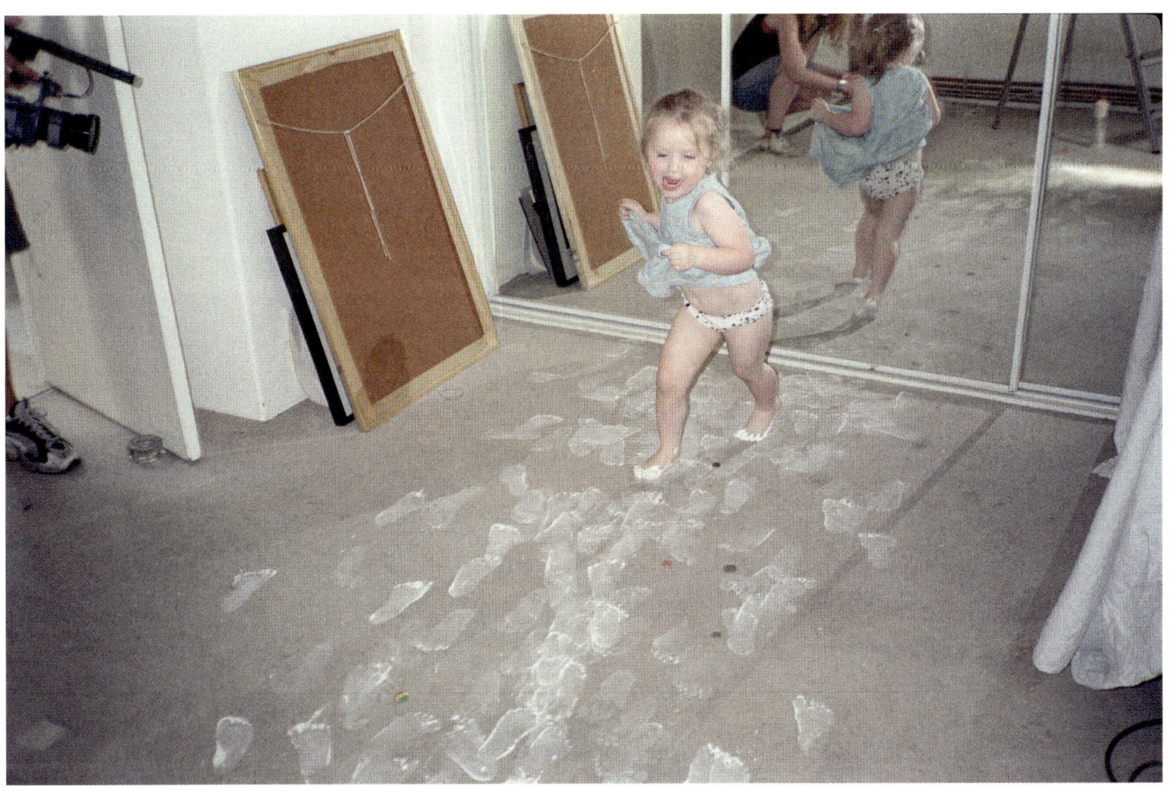

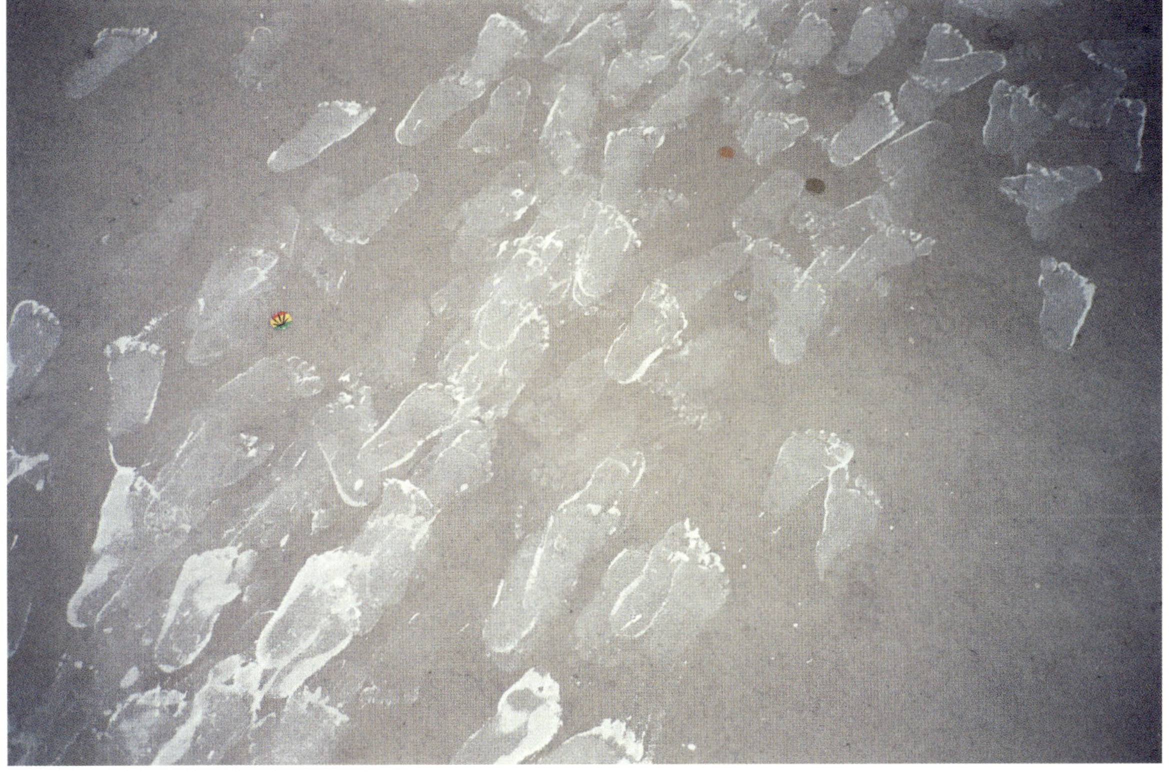

'Mia and her Footprints', Brewer Street, c. 2001.

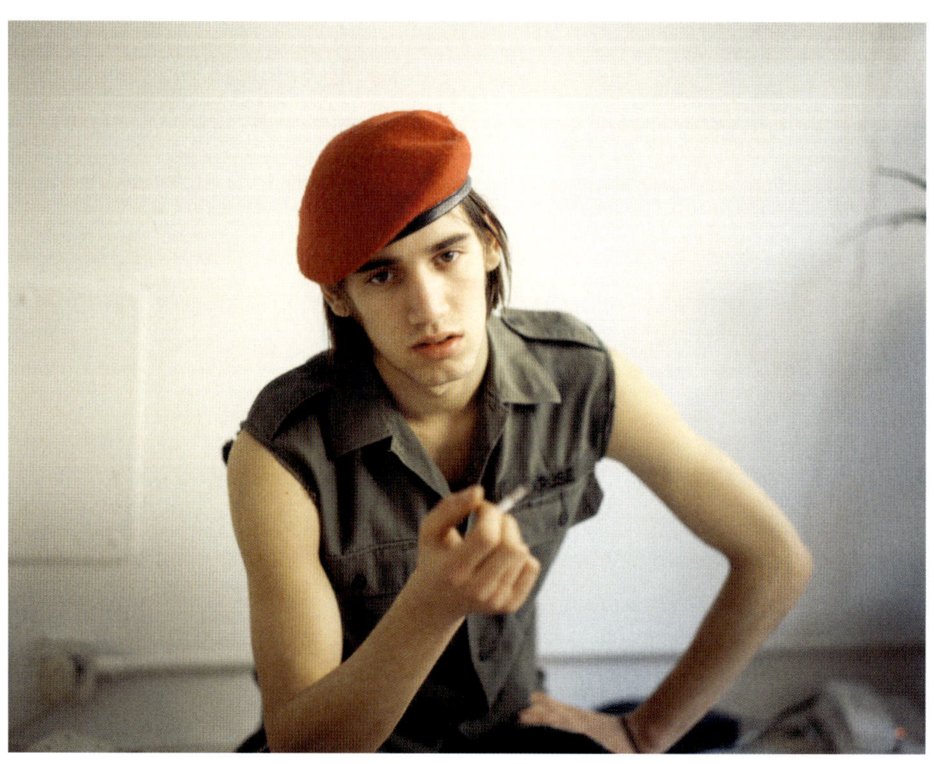

'George in Red Beret', outtake from the feature 'Goths on Acid' for *Ray Gun* magazine, June–July 1995.

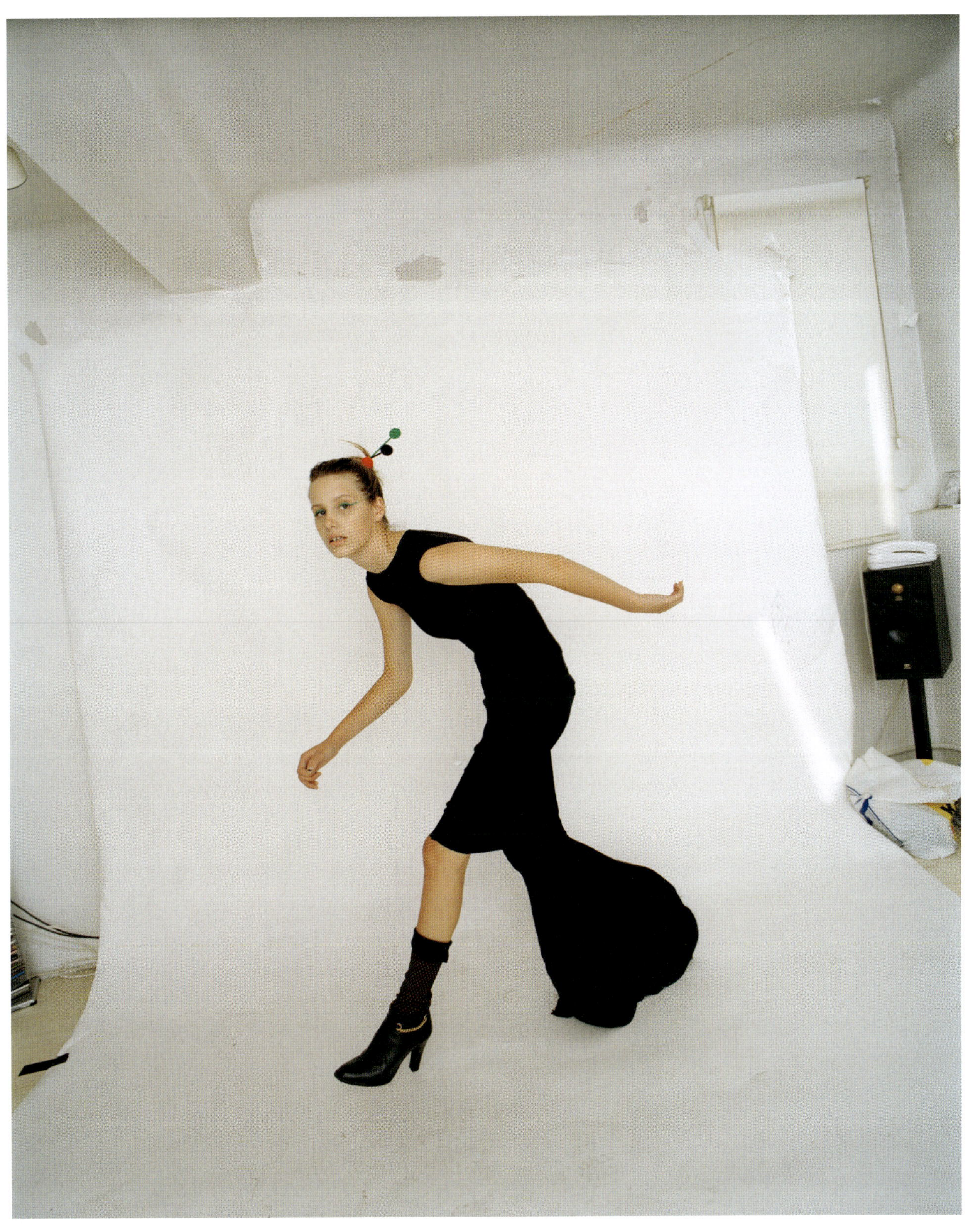

'Georgina Cooper in the Living Room', from 'That Imaginary Line', *Interview* magazine, January 1996.

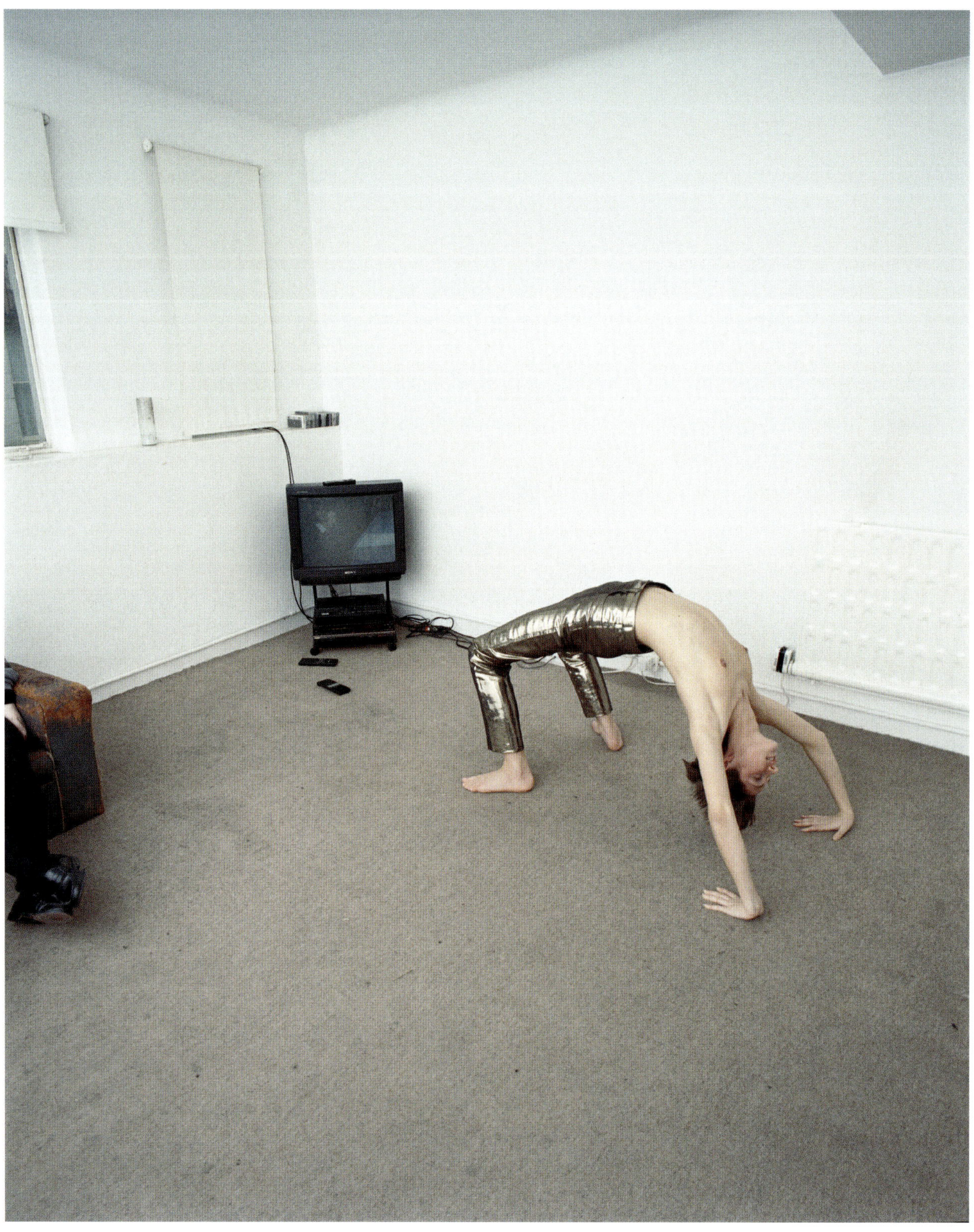

 'Rose in the Living Room', outtake from the 'England's Dreaming' editorial for *The Face* magazine, August 1993.

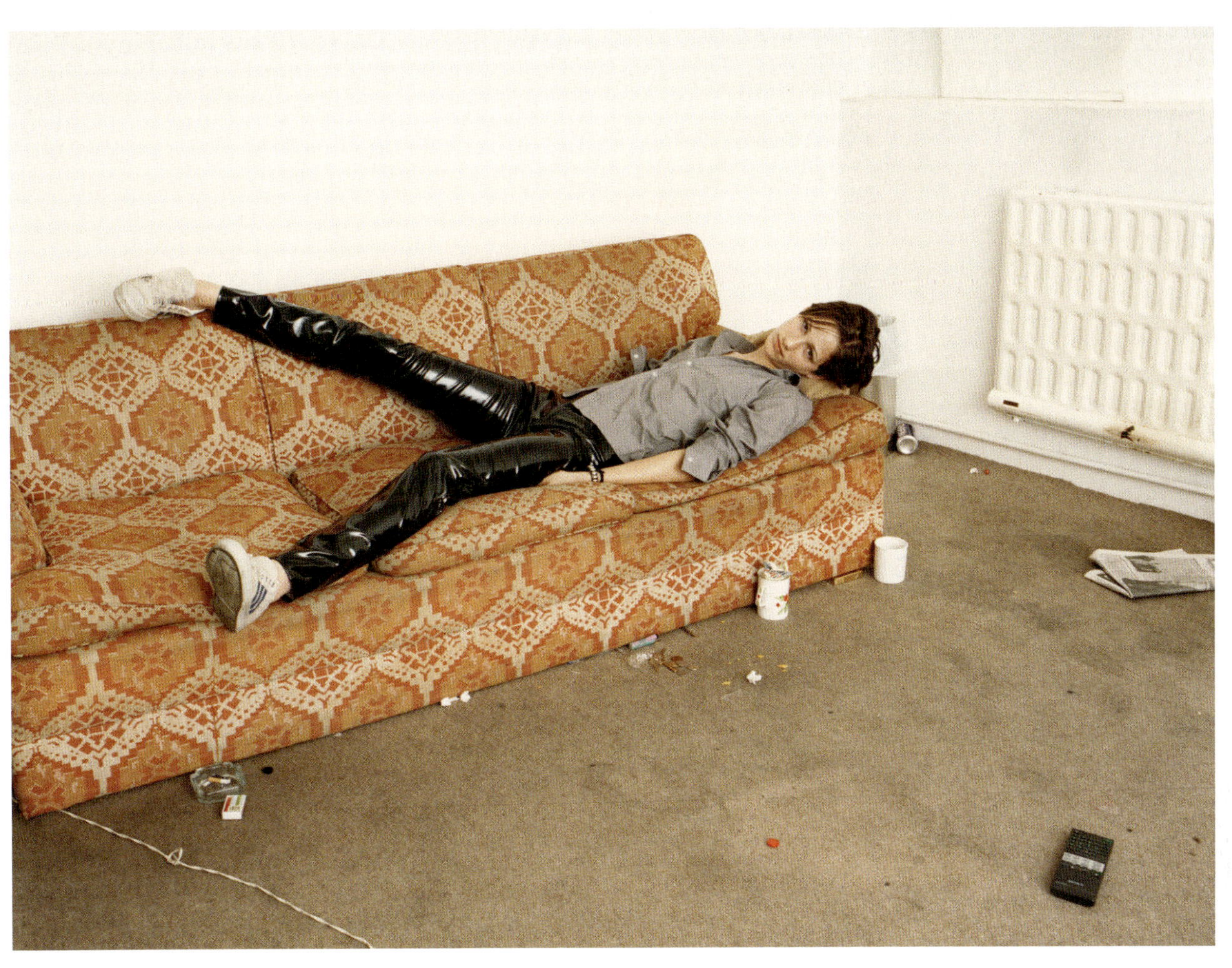

‘Rose on Orange Sofa’, from ‘England’s Dreaming’, *The Face*, August 1993.

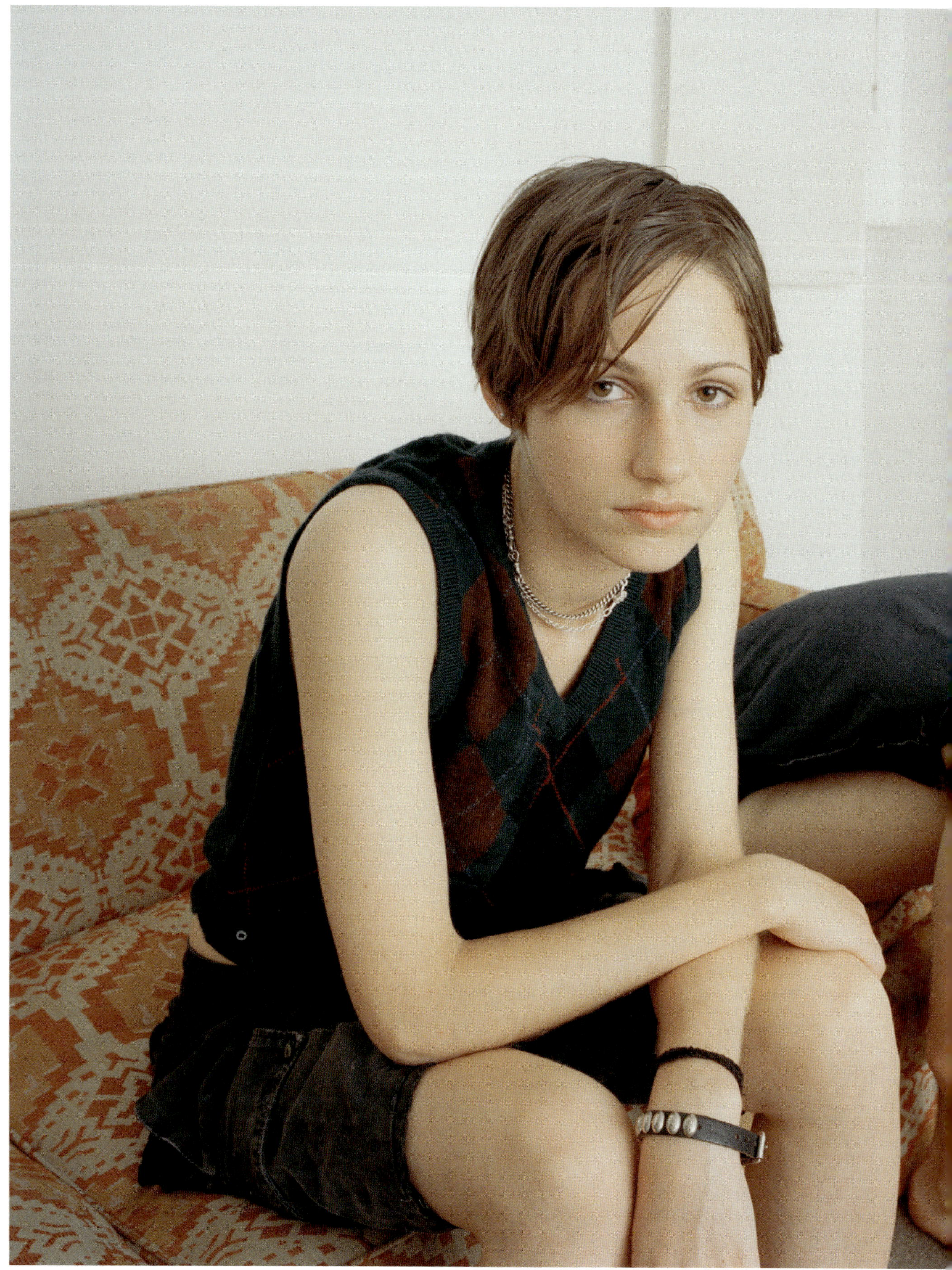

 'Rose and George Skinning Up', Brewer Street, c. 1994.

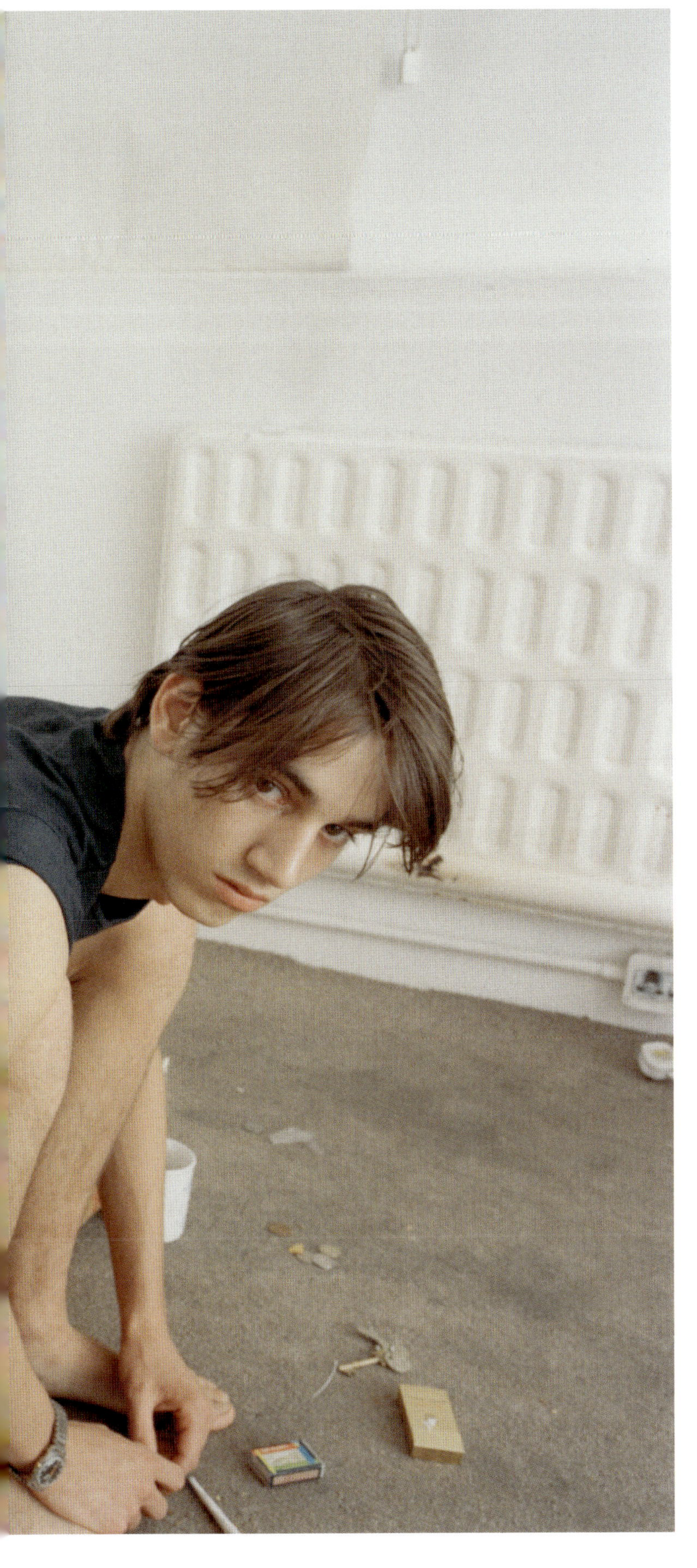

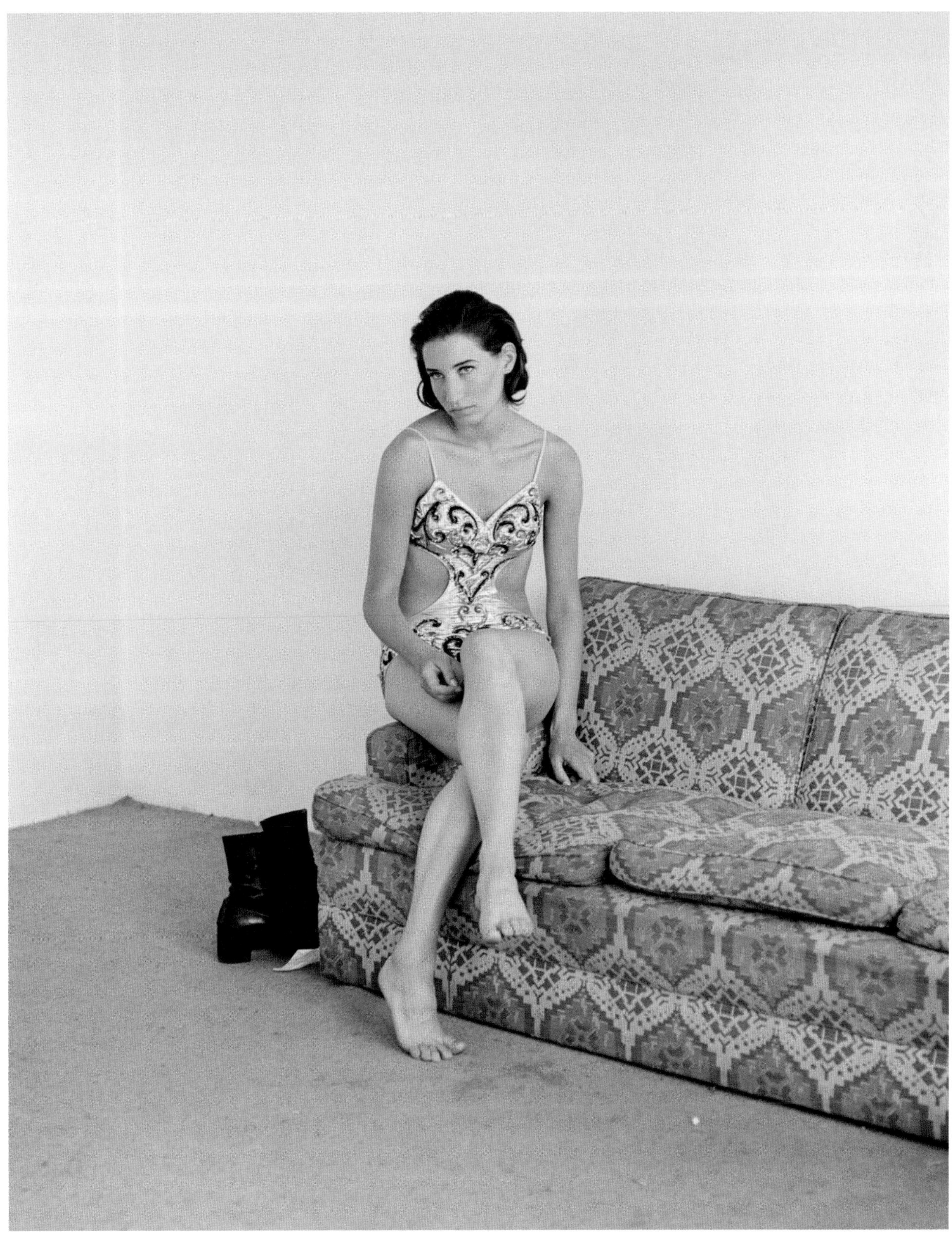

‘Sarah Murray on the Orange Sofa’, *Ray Gun* magazine, c. 1994.

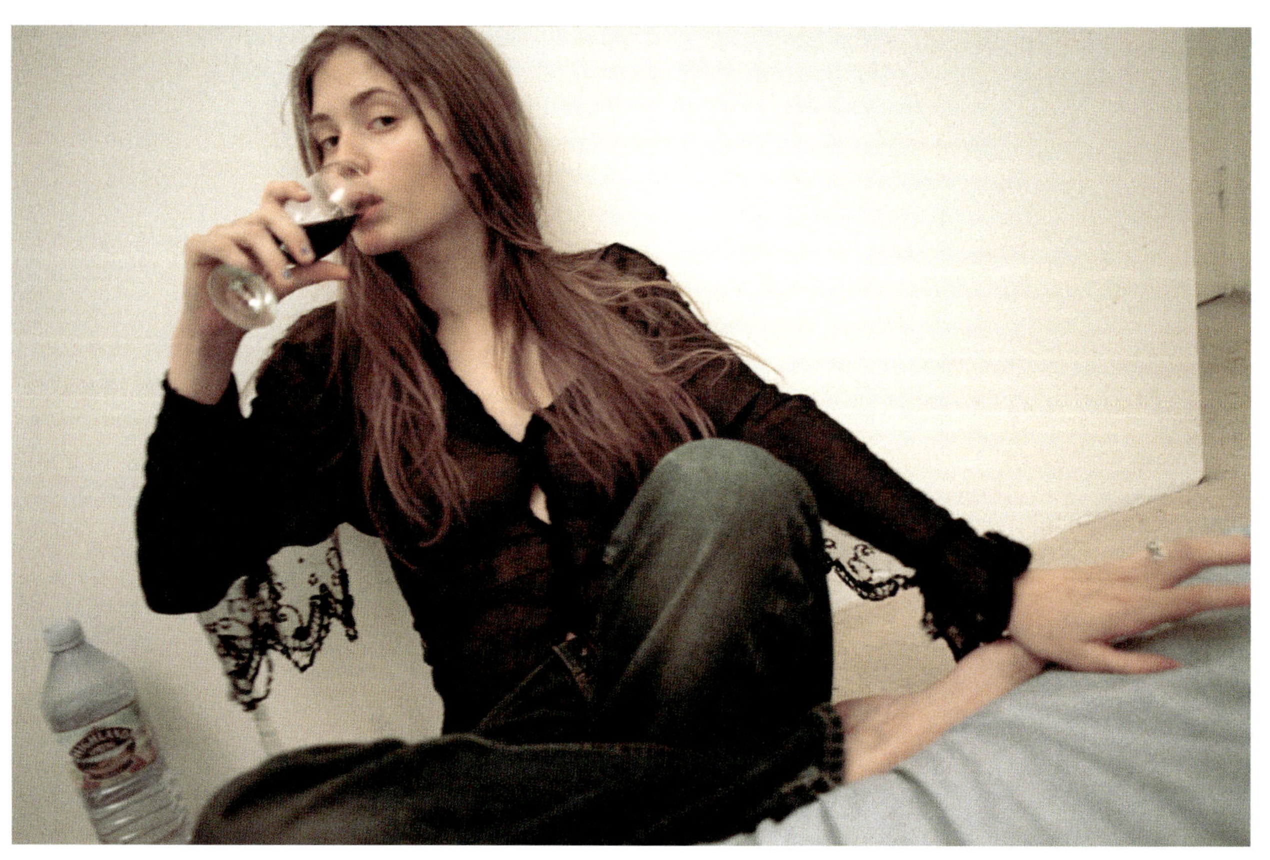

 ‘Little Emma with Red Lips’, Brewer Street, c. 2003.

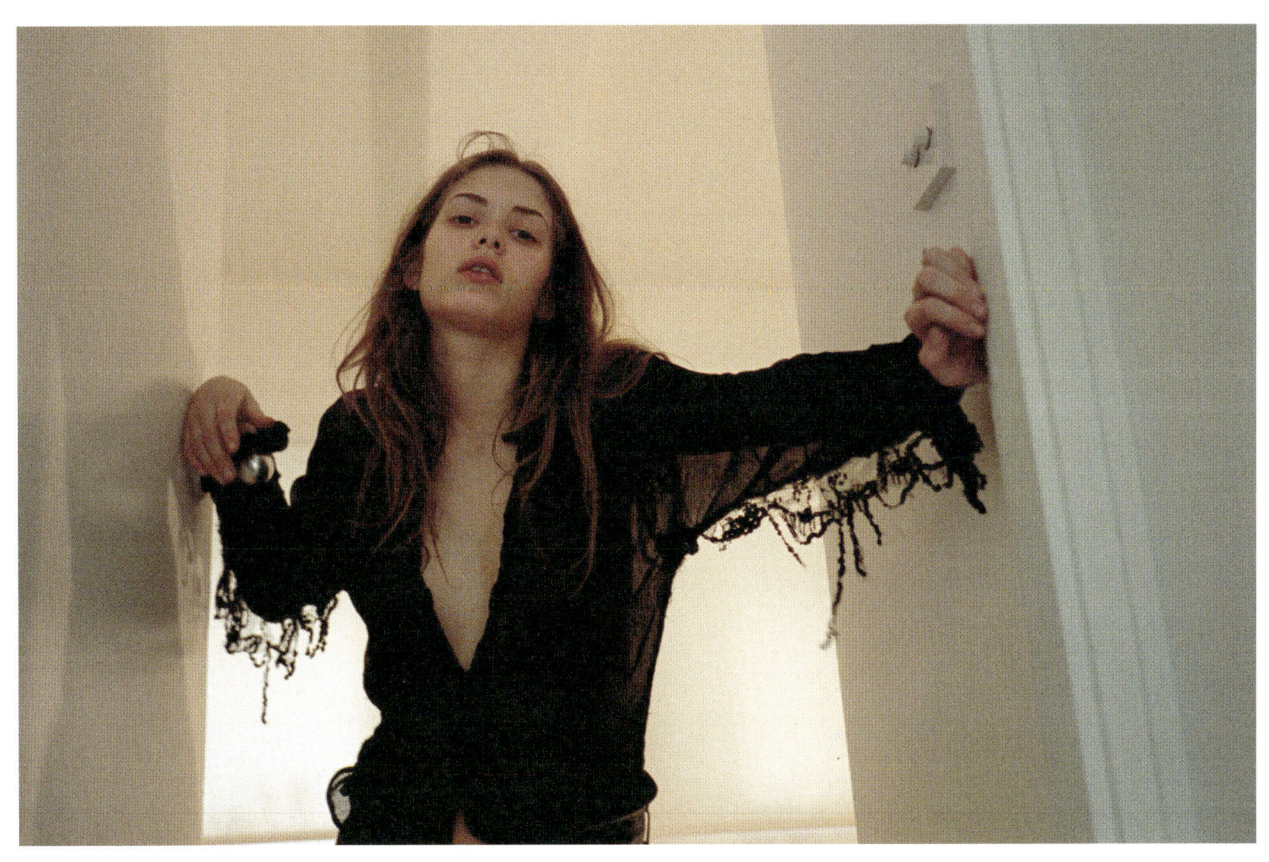

‘Little Emma’, Brewer Street, c. 2003.

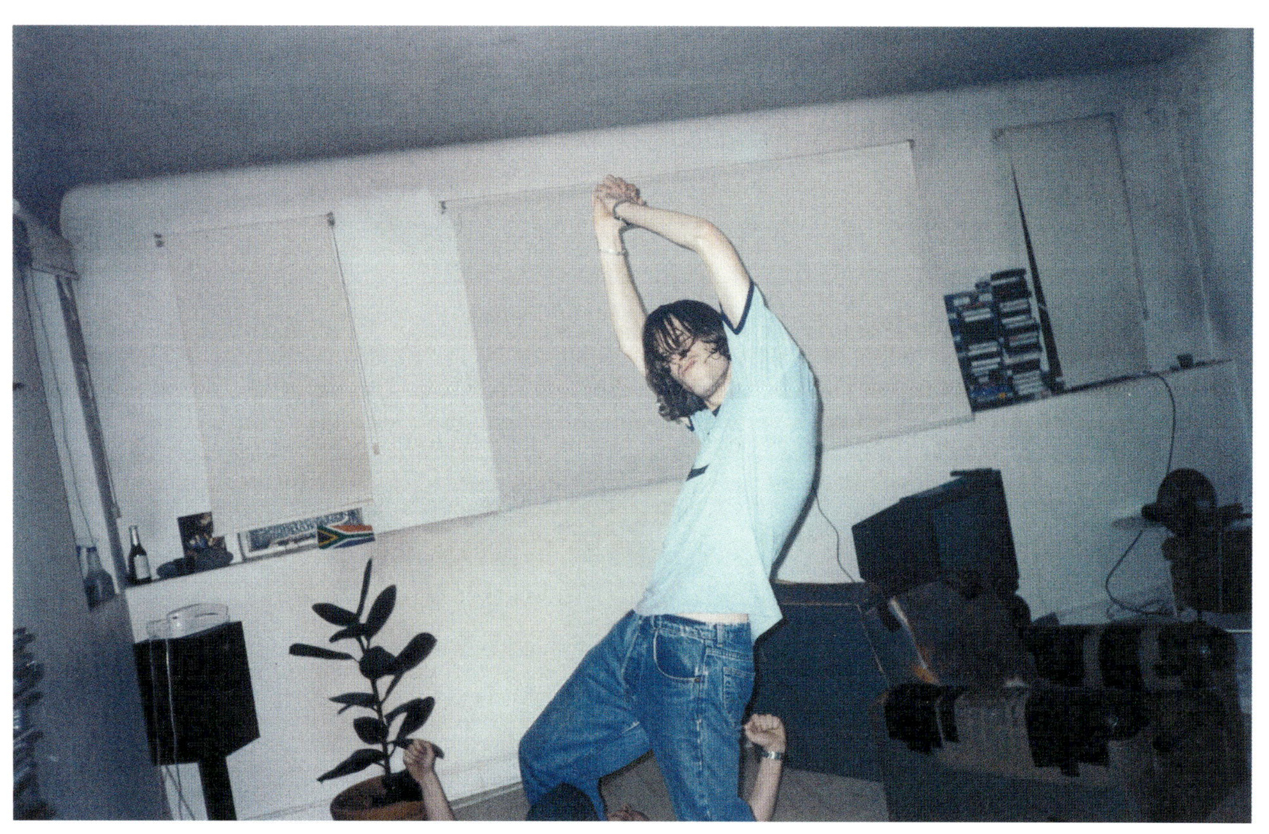

 ‘Andy and Greg Dancing’, Brewer Street, 1995.

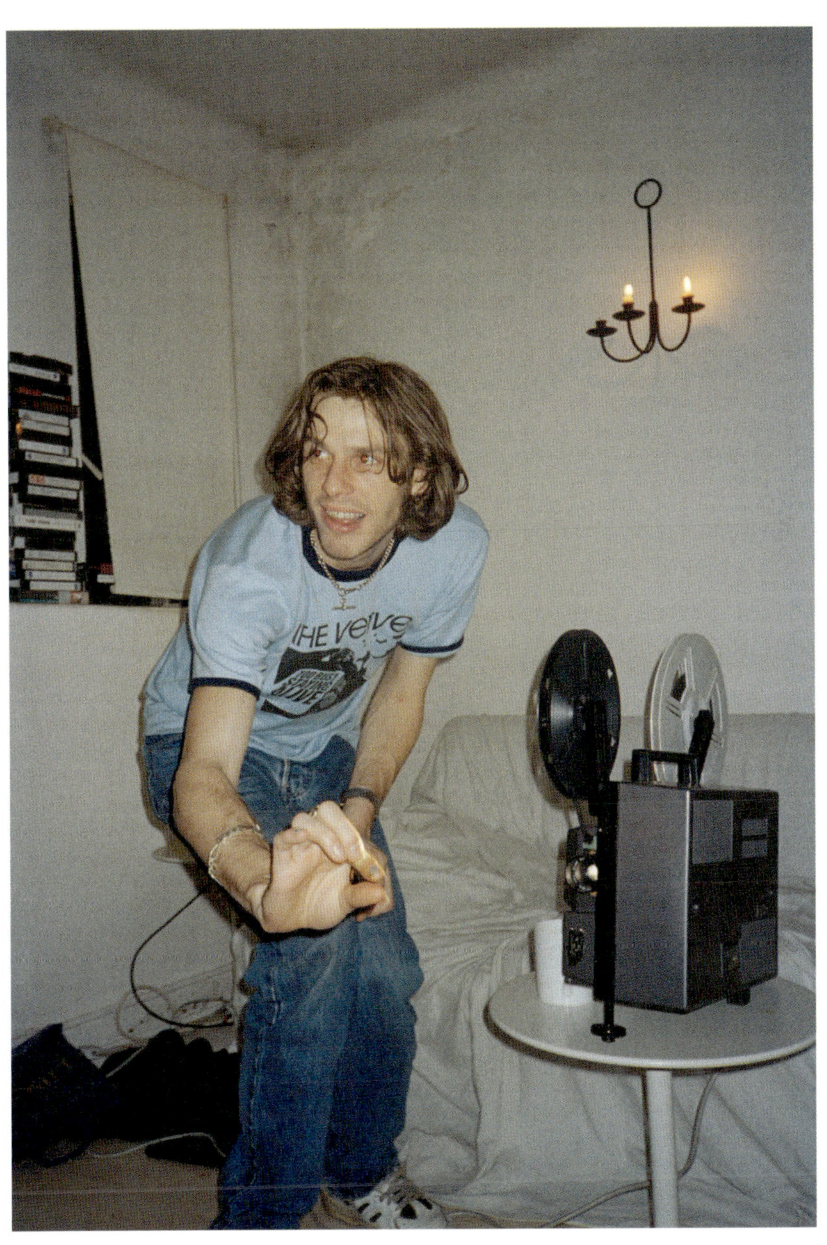

‘Andy Making Shadows on the Wall at Night’, Brewer Street, 1995.

CLANCY GEBLER DAVIES

Clancy Gebler Davies (b. 1966) is a photographer, printmaker and journalist based in London. She photographed the Colony Room Club, Soho's most celebrated private members' club, between 1999 and 2000, and these photographs have sat mostly untouched since.

The club was opened in 1948; the artist Francis Bacon, one of its first members, was paid £10 a week by the proprietor to lure in the big spenders. By the late 1990s, Young British Artists including Damien Hirst, Sarah Lucas, Gavin Turk and Tracey Emin were all regulars, as were noted writers, journalists, art dealers and musicians. Gebler Davies rightly resists seeing the work as a 'who's who' of a particular moment in the club's history: that would suit neither her ethos nor that of the club itself. She didn't always know or care who was 'notable', and neither did the other patrons. It was not important who you were – simply that you weren't boring.

The members-only club was above a trattoria on Dean Street, with the walls and ceilings painted a thickly coated, bilious green. The drinking was industrial and smoking and swearing were seen as amiable – talking business would get you thrown out, sometimes forcibly. Gebler Davies's first attempt to enter was when a friend bet her £5 that she wouldn't get past the threshold; her friend lost the bet. After she first charmed her way in, she became a regular and was made a member soon after. Sometime later the club's then-proprietor, Michael Wojas, approached her regarding her enormous unpaid bar tab. To pay off the bill she started working shifts behind the bar and thus became a familiar fixture.

In theory, taking pictures in the Colony Room was strictly forbidden, but Gebler Davies had become friends with Wojas. He had sufficient trust in her motivations as well as in her ability to handle herself if confronted by anyone unhappy with having their photo taken. Now with permission from the boss, Gebler Davies shot nearly a hundred rolls of black-and-white film. The fact that she worked behind the bar and was female were, she feels, advantages to her – mostly because nobody thought the pictures would be any good. If she was questioned as to what she was planning to do with the photographs, she would answer honestly: she didn't know.[18] Very few people saw any of the prints and for the most part she was accepted as simply part of the place. Her approach was neither subtle nor clandestine – she was always forthright about using the camera. Indeed, with her pretty brutal flash gun, big SLR and even bigger personality, there was simply no chance of her fading into the background.

The club was quite a confined space, and Gebler Davies's photographs capture an almost claustrophobic atmosphere. The exuberance of the place and performativity of the guests are palpable and very much match the club's legendary reputation. What is more surprising – but just as present in the work – is how often moments of tenderness cut through the volume in this fabled and unique drinking den.

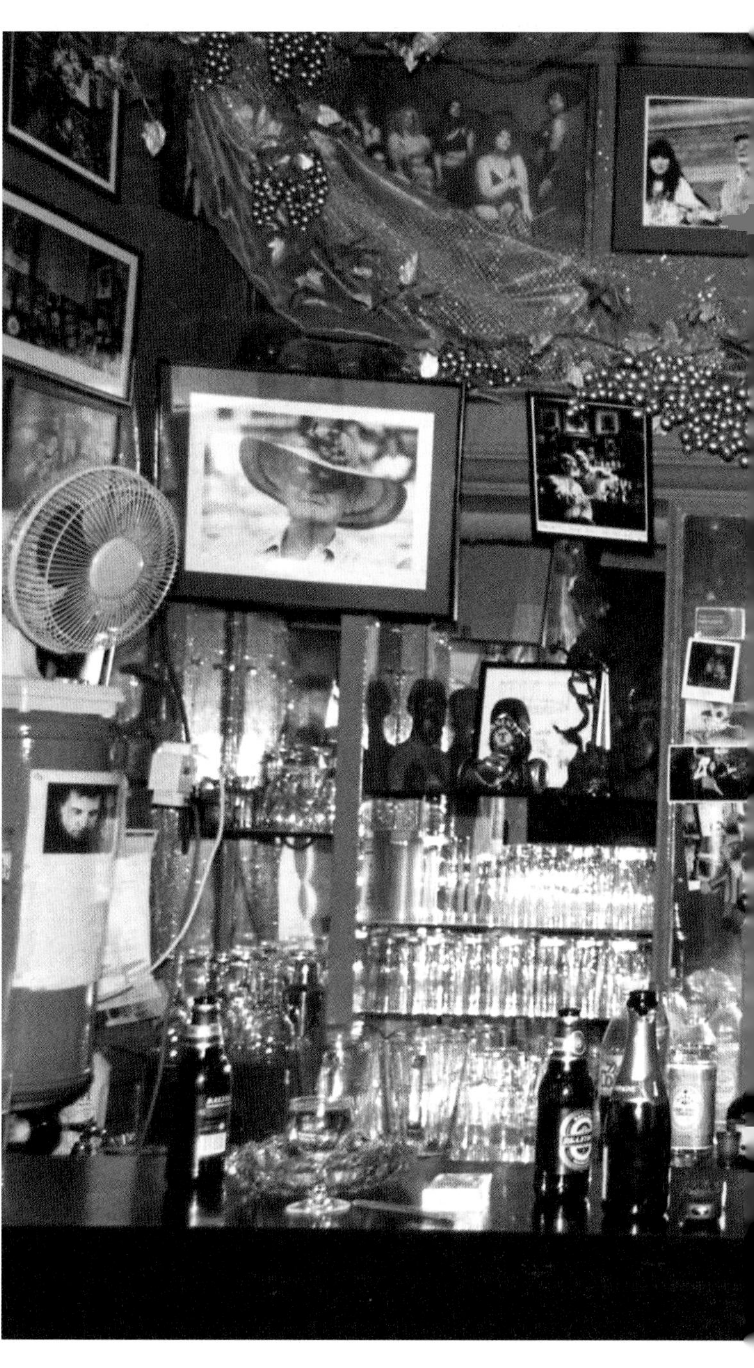

All images are from the series *The Colony Room Club*, 1999–2000.

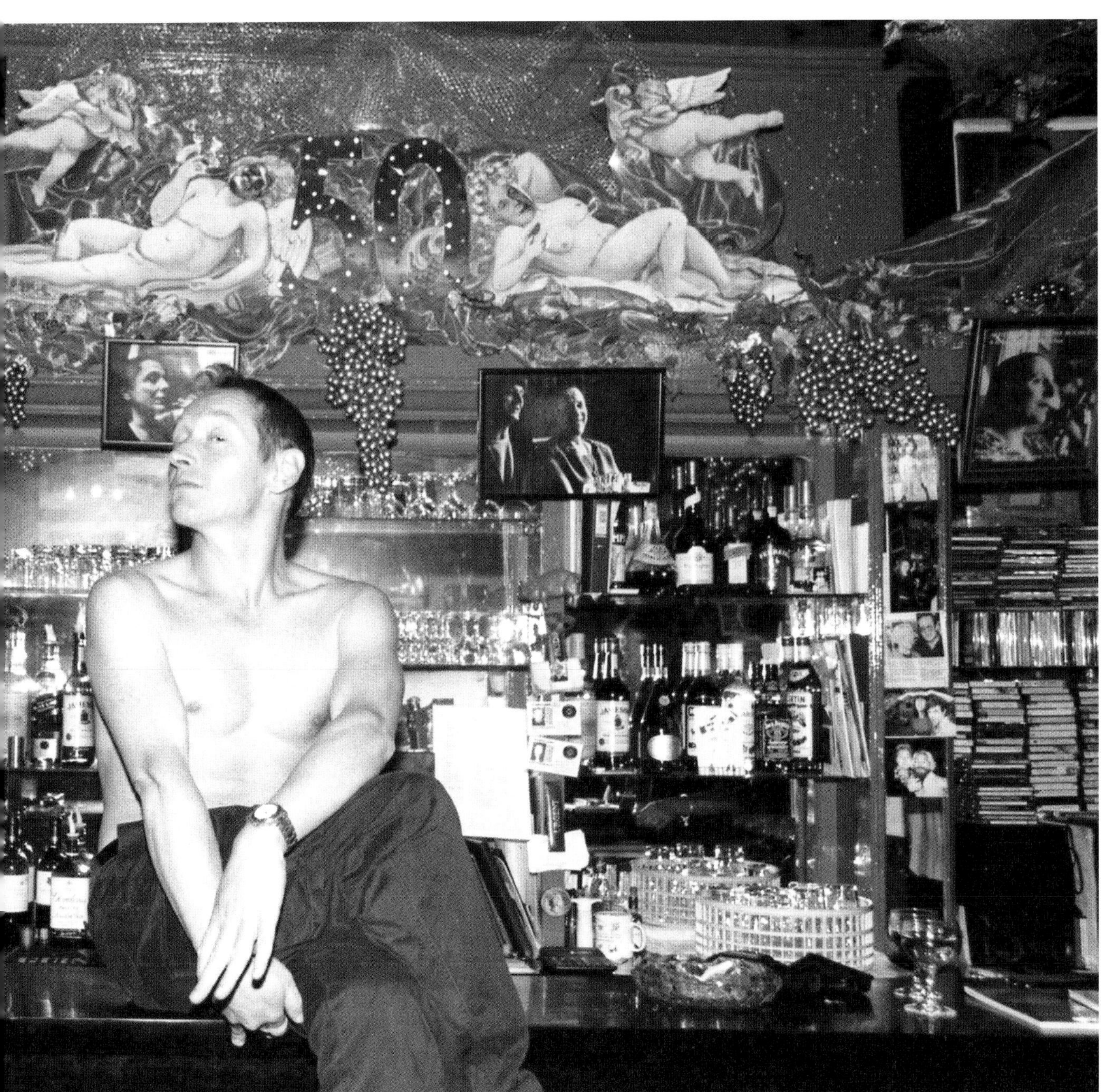

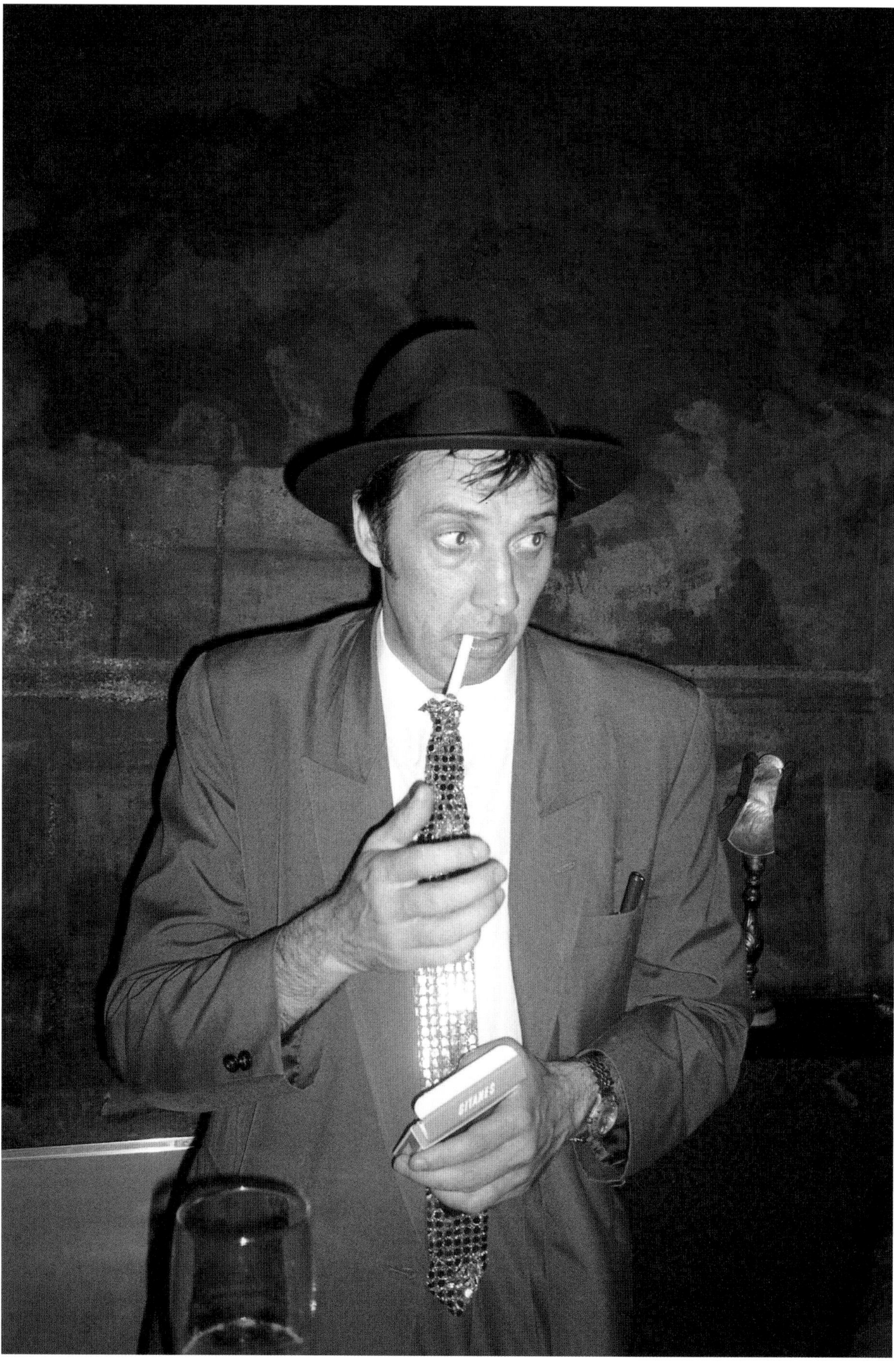

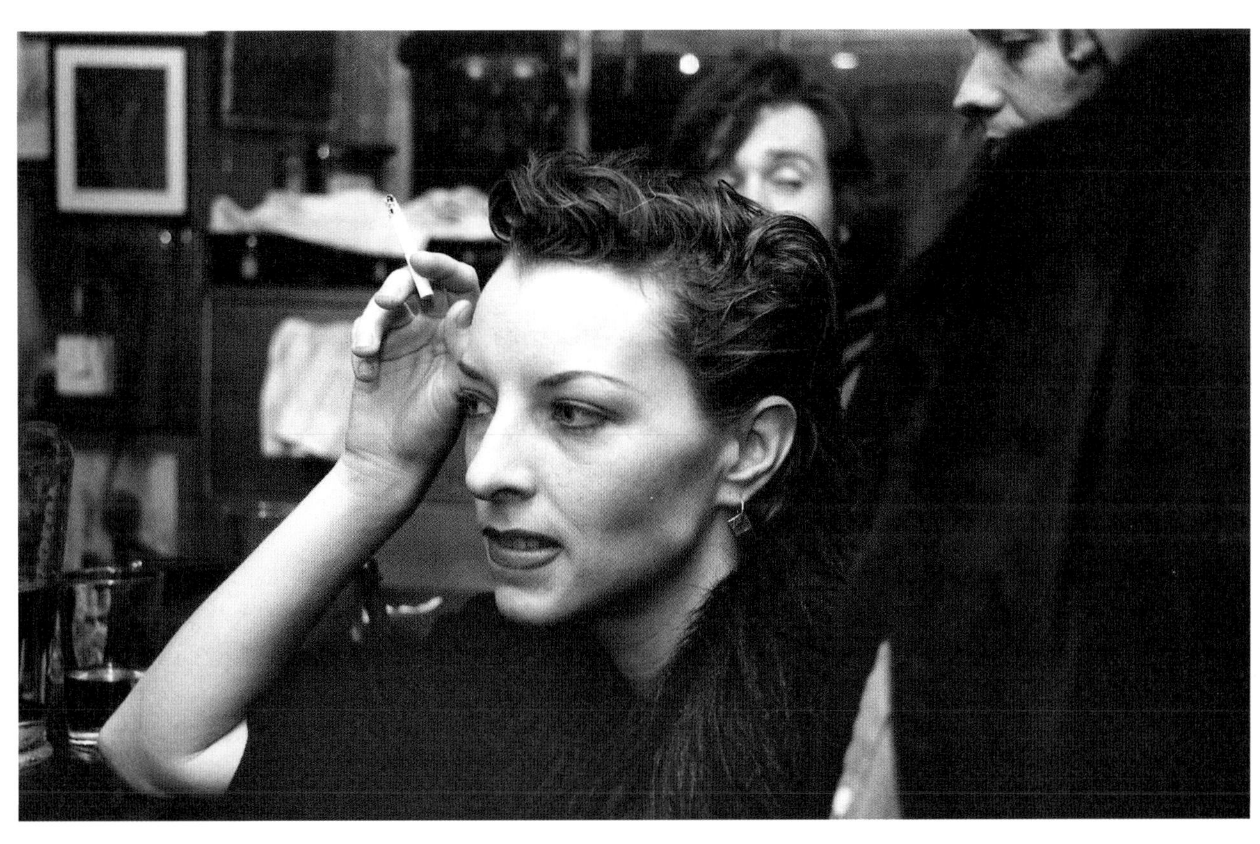

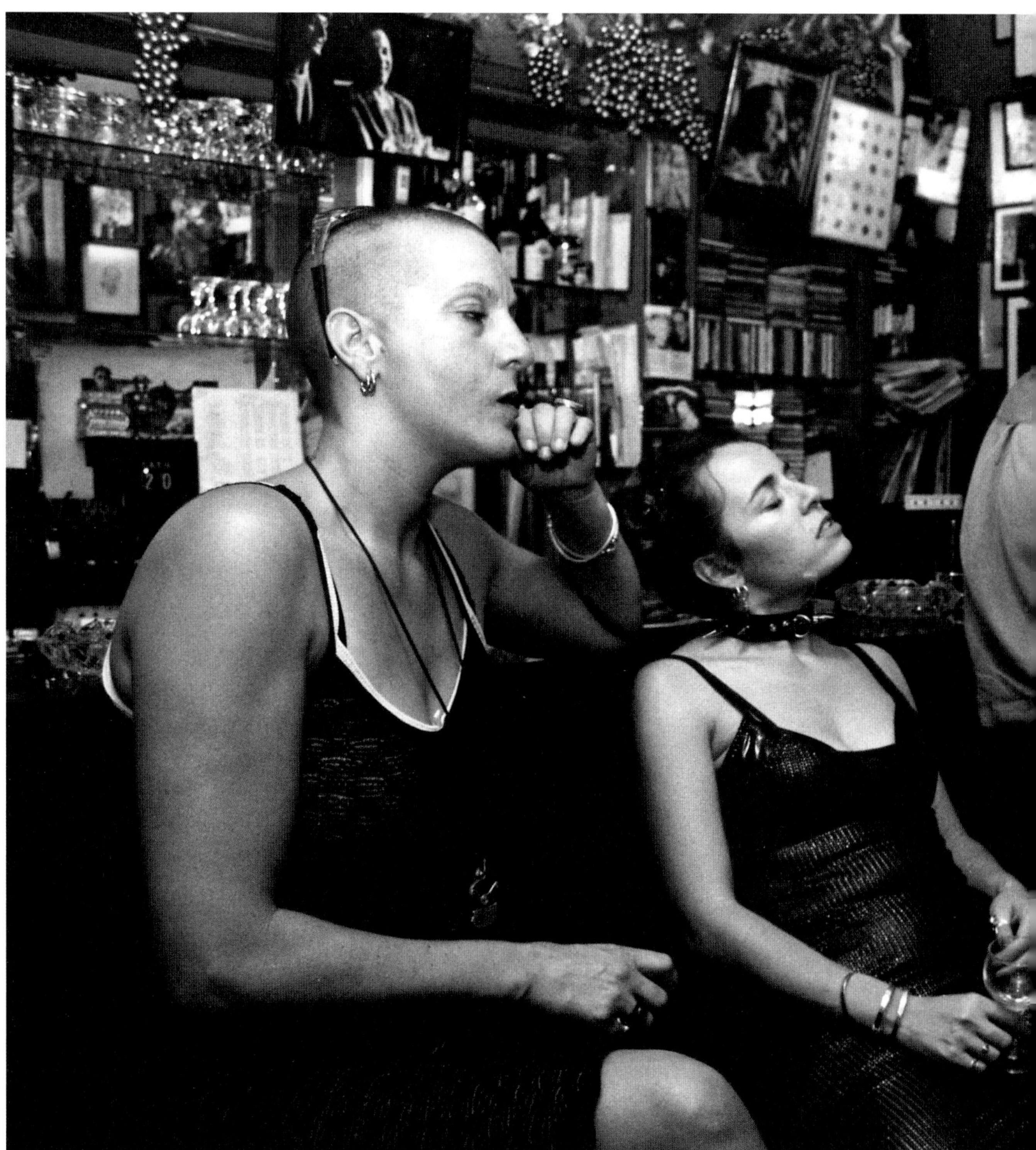

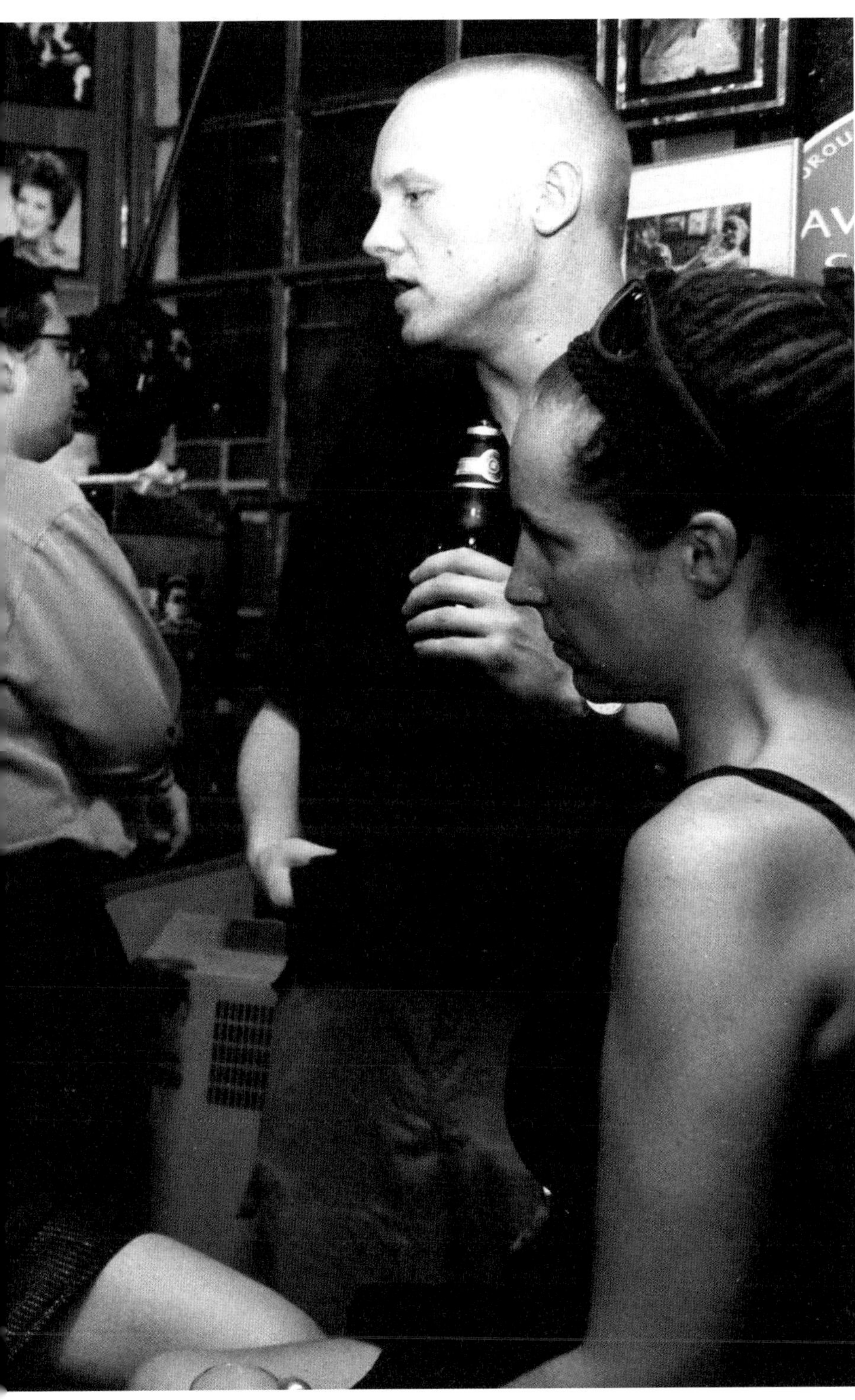

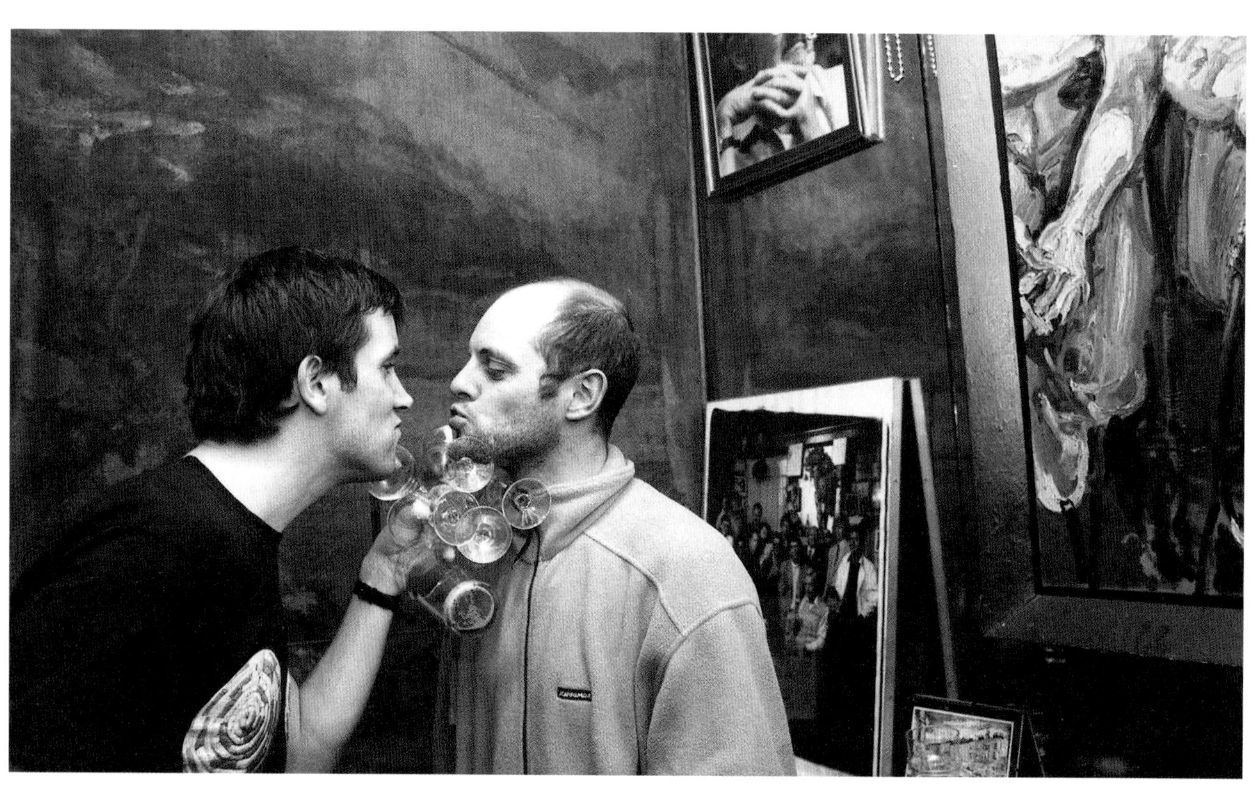

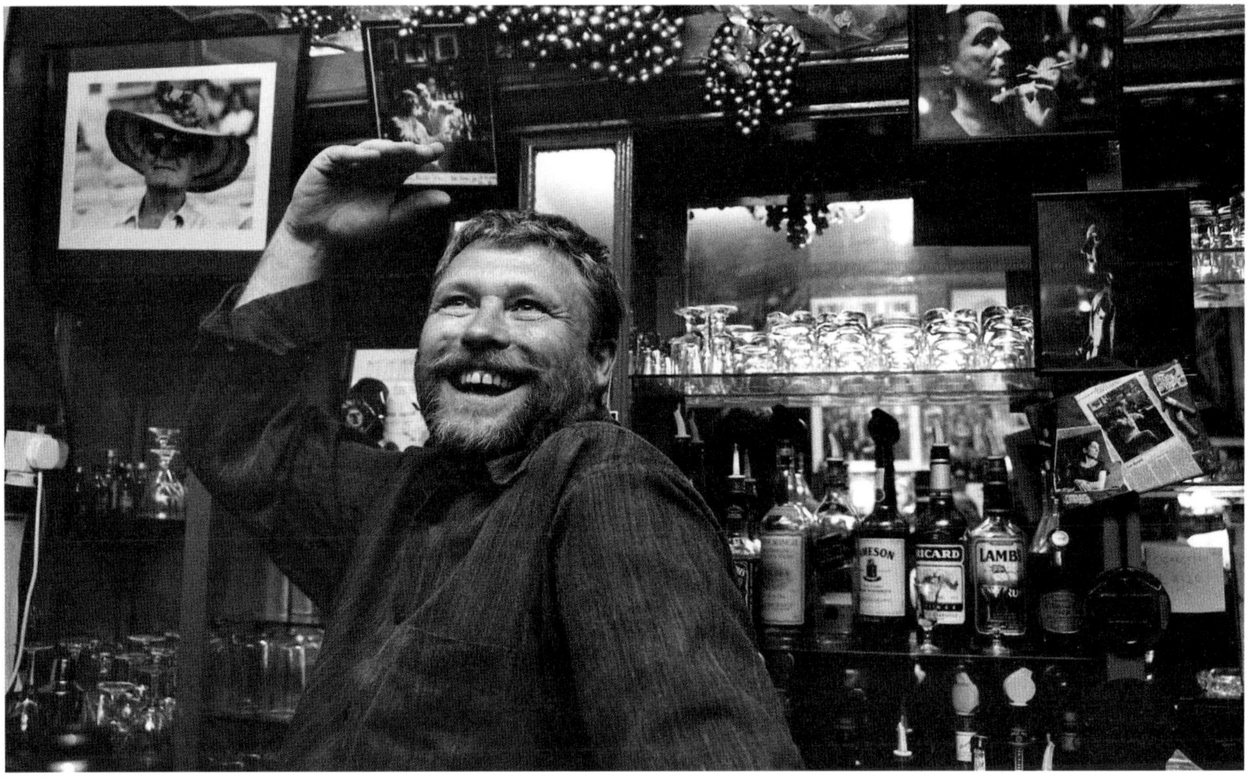

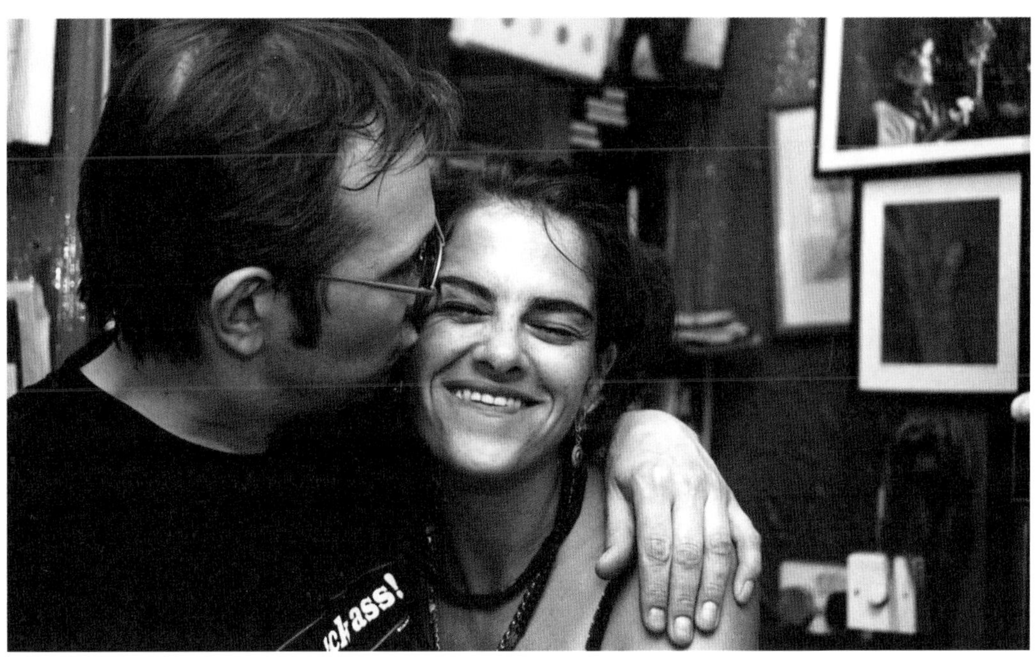

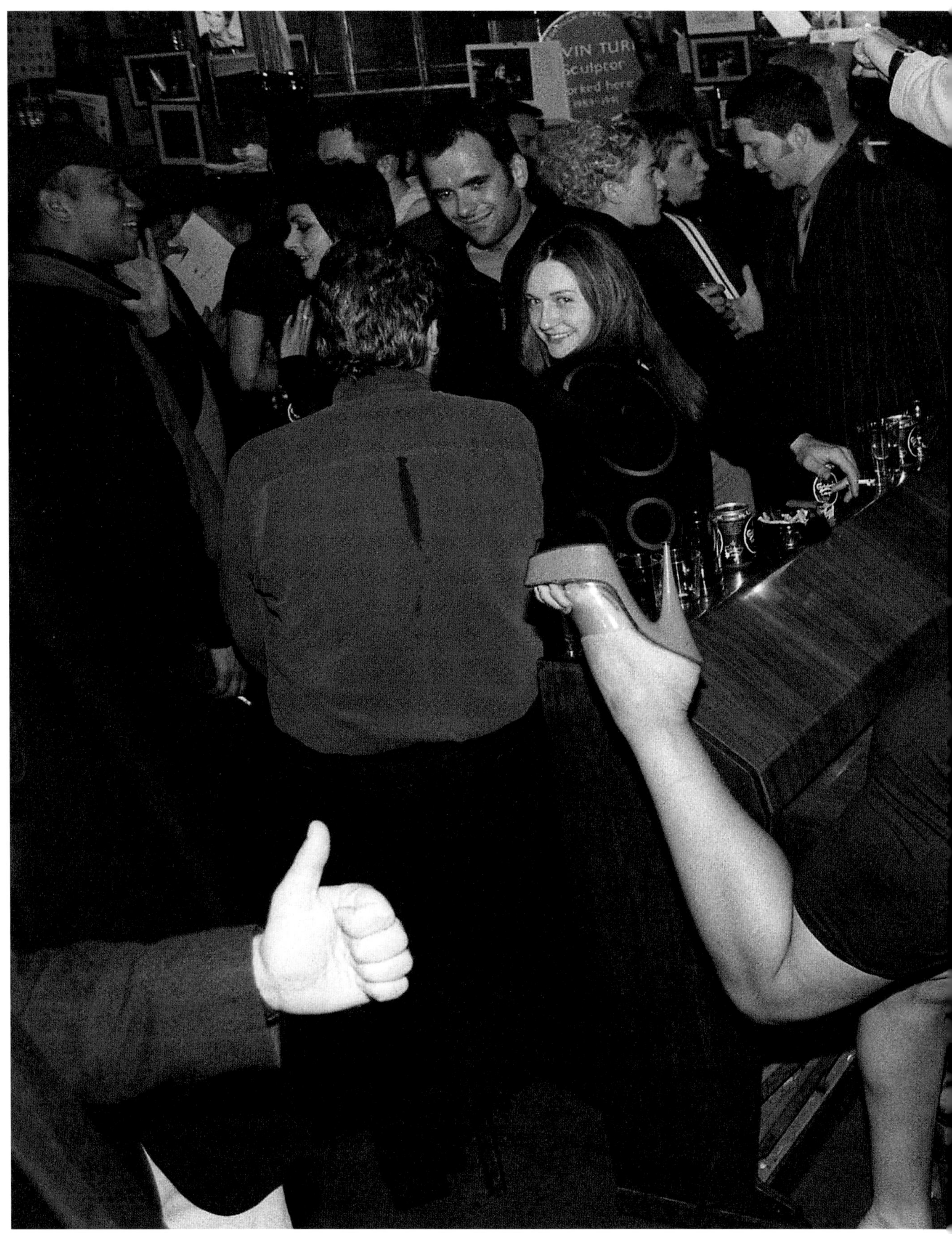

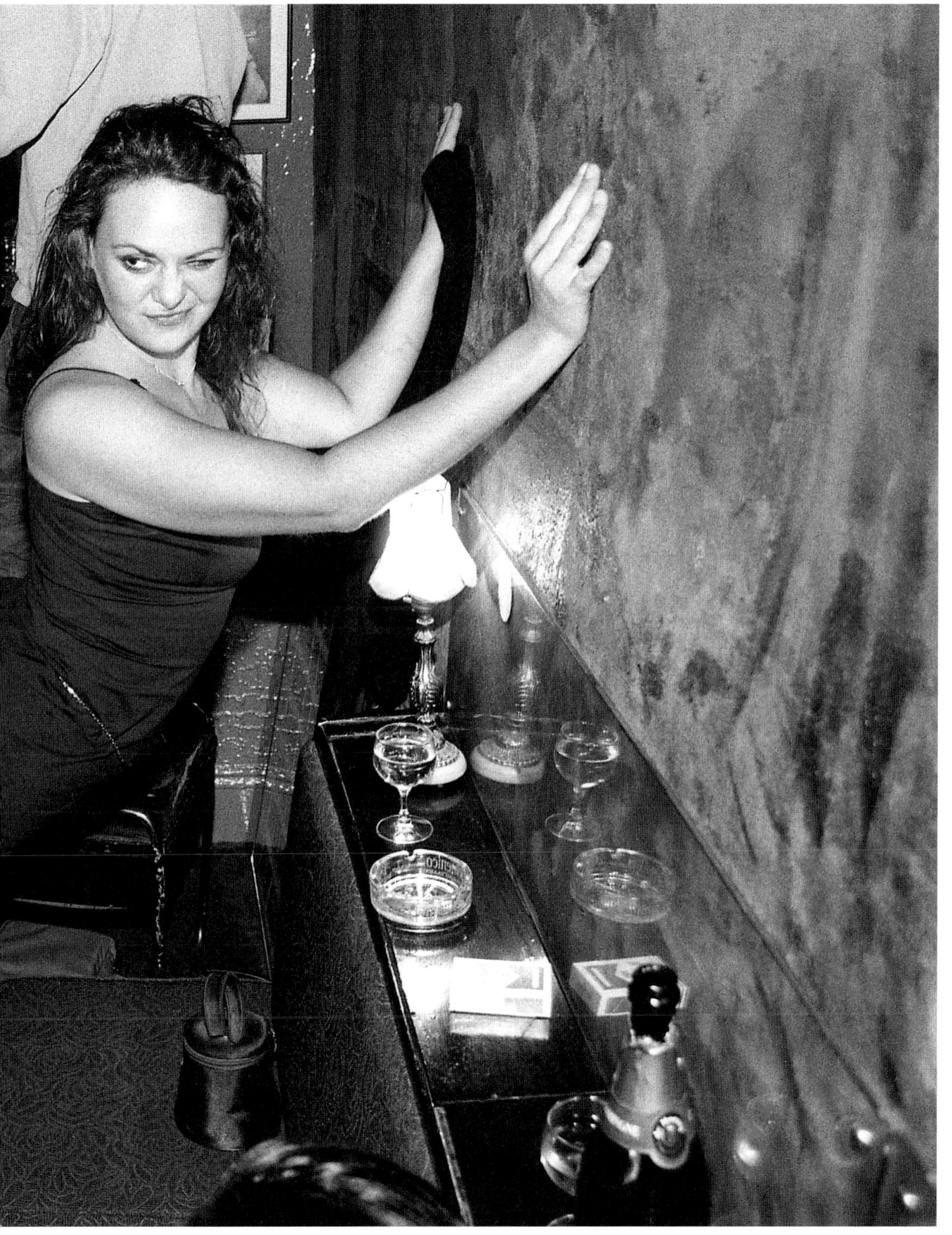

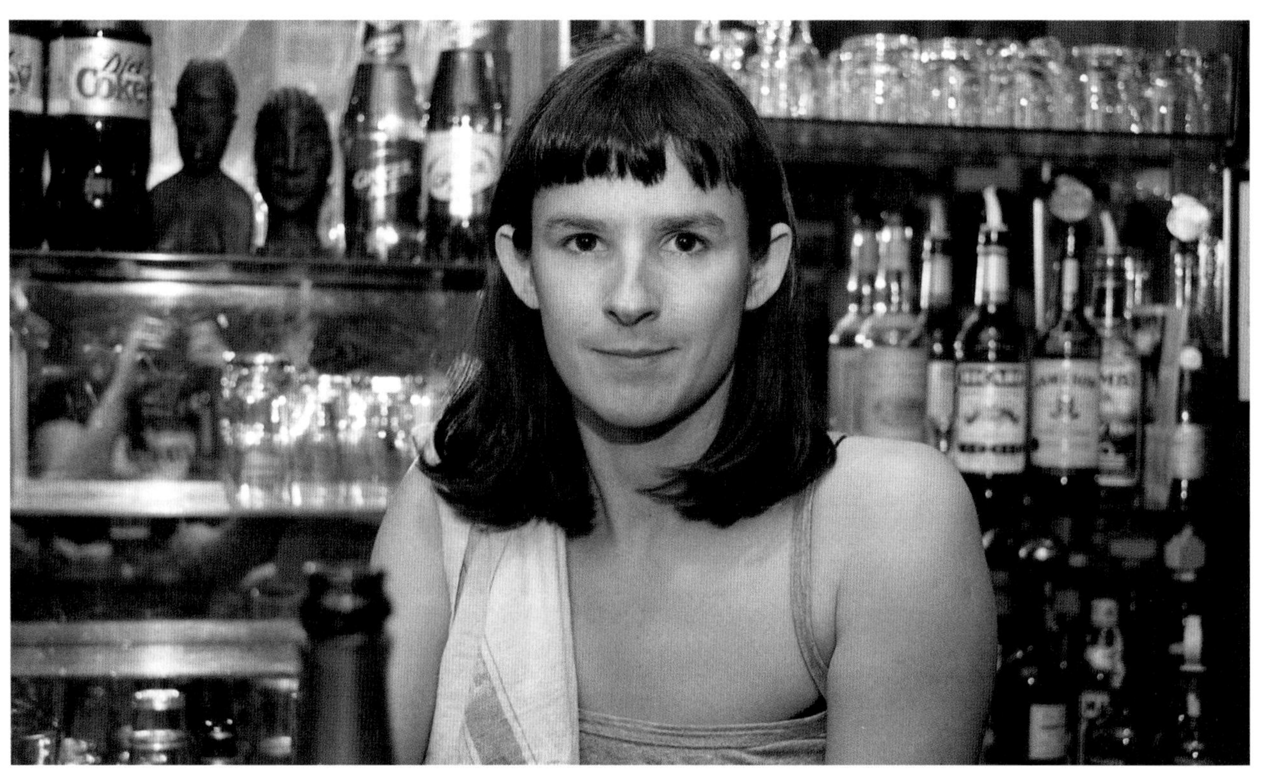

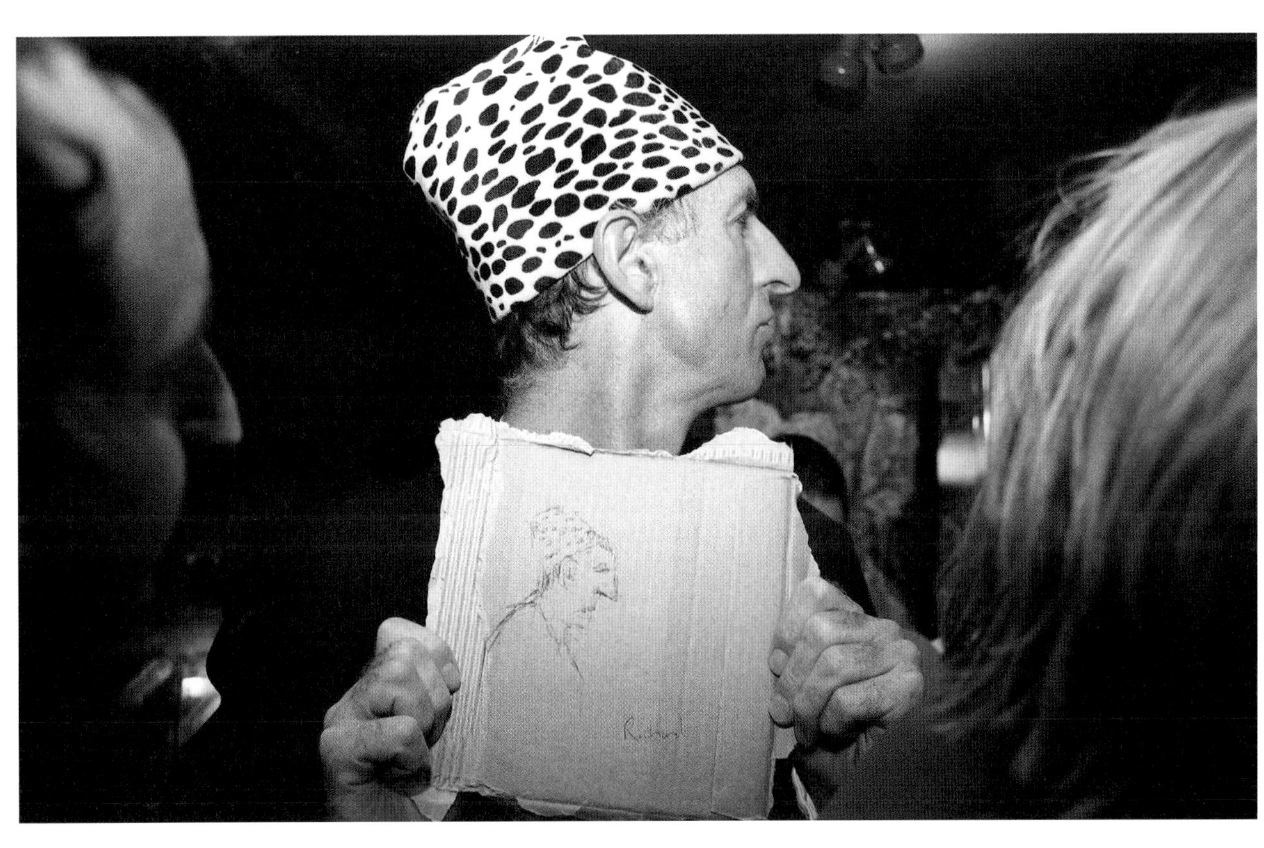

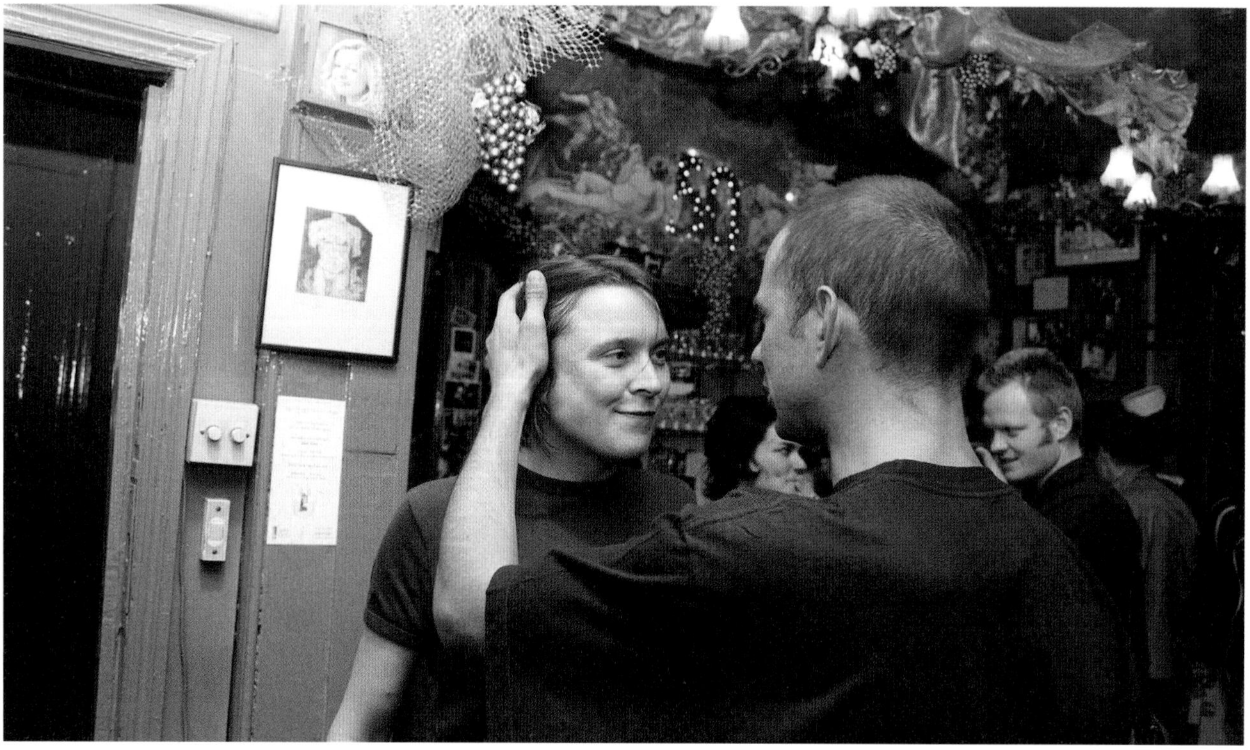

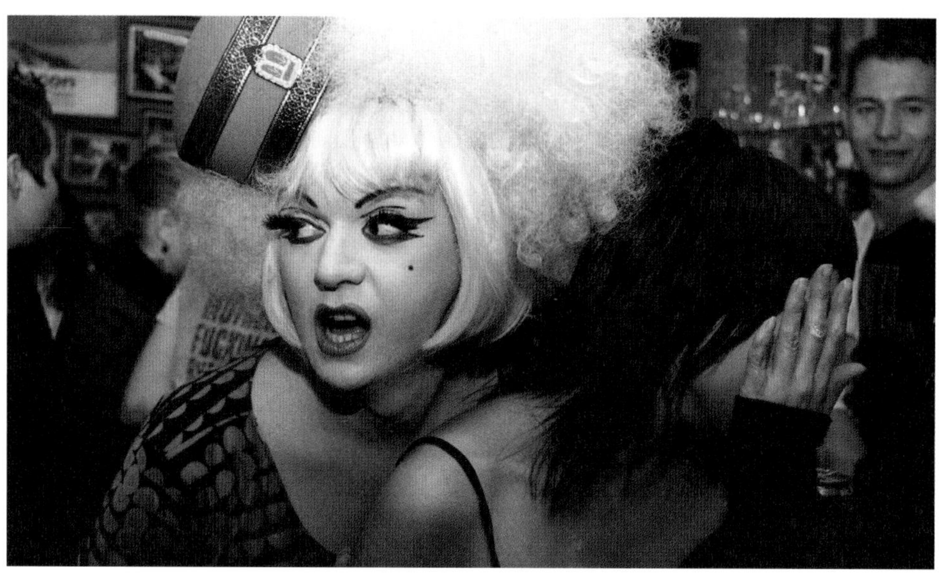

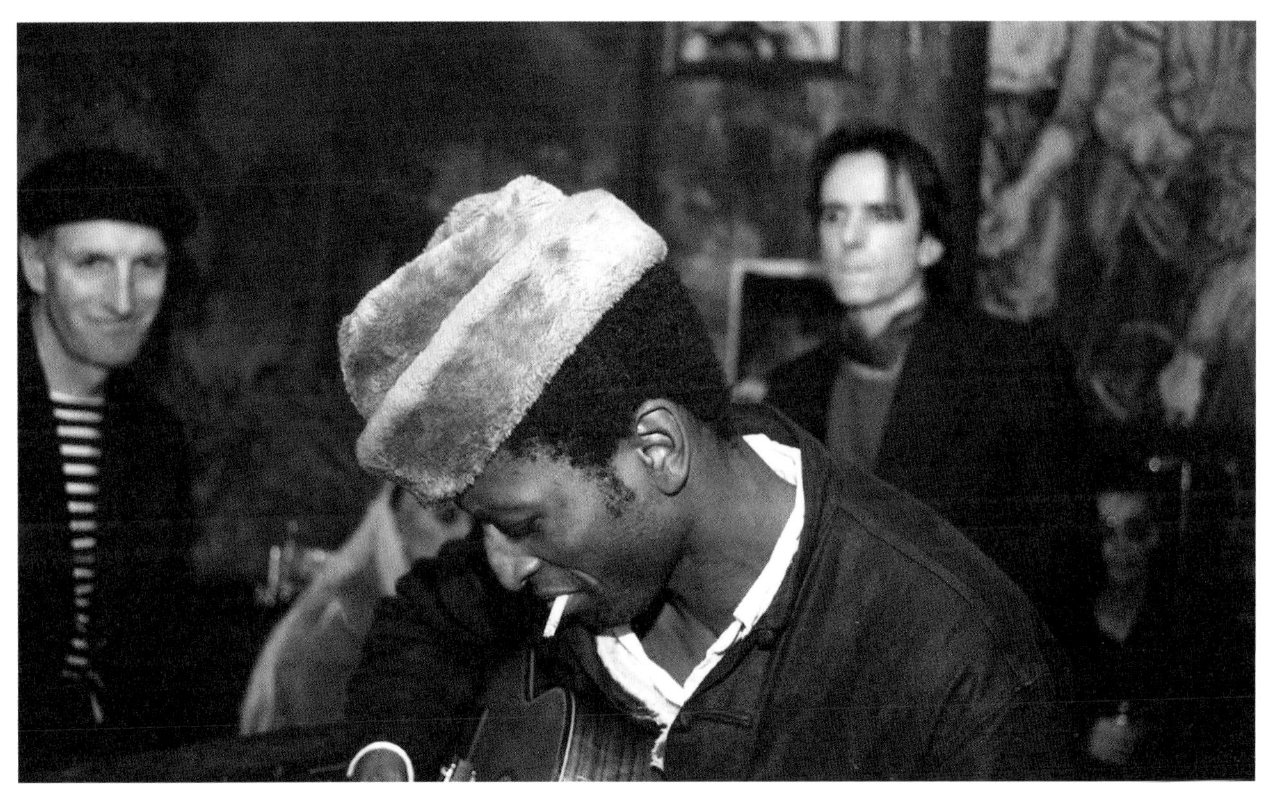

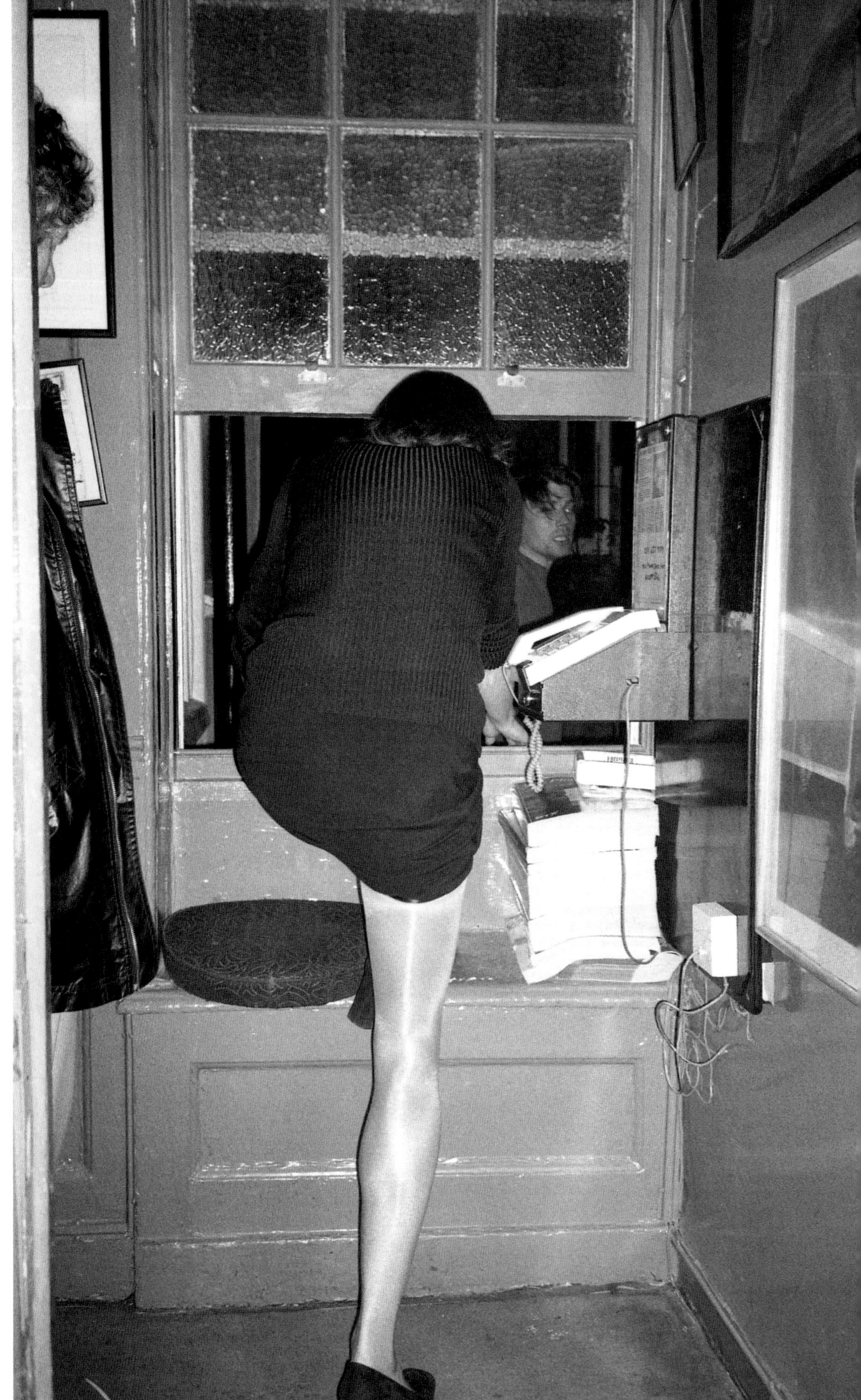

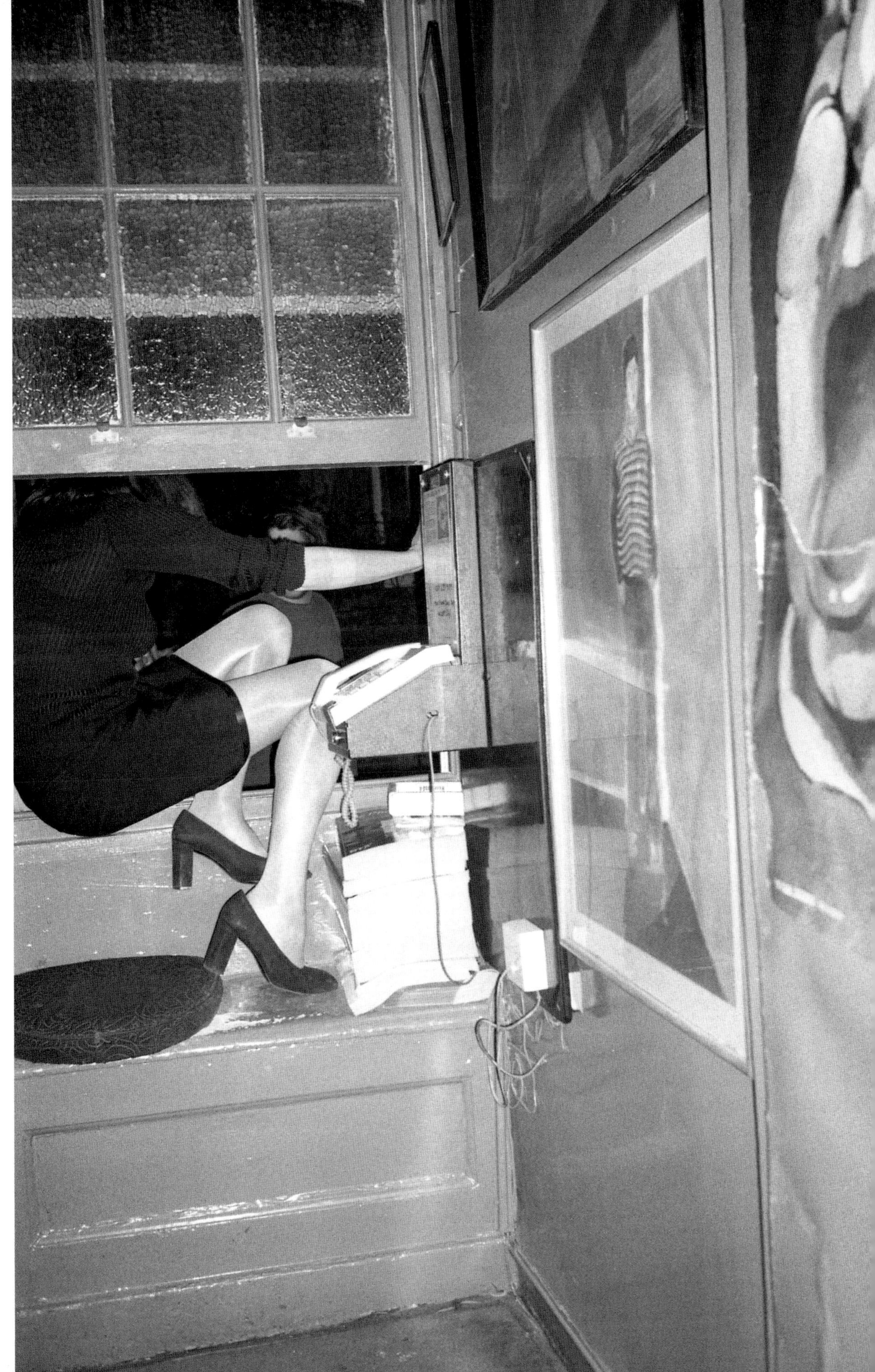

JOHN GOLDBLATT

Born in Manchester, John Goldblatt (1930–2009) emigrated to South Africa in 1955. By 1956 he had started to develop his photography, working on the streets of Johannesburg and visiting townships – the latter of which was illegal. Goldblatt opposed apartheid and was sensitive to its painful inequalities, using his time off from a corporate job as a copywriter to produce human interest stories. His trips to photograph marginalised people living under the regime required considerable courage. He photographed everything from charitable outposts feeding impoverished children to political demonstrations and dancing on the streets. South Africa produced many gifted photographers in the same period, many of whom were also working in response to apartheid, including Peter Magubane, Alf Kumalo, Bob Gosani and David Goldblatt (coincidentally also born in 1930). Between 1958 and 1961 John Goldblatt had his work published in the *Rand Daily Mail*, the *Golden City Post* and *Drum* magazine – the latter of which brilliantly formulated an issue-based photographic approach that became synonymous with highlighting political struggle.

On his return to the UK, Goldblatt worked as a freelance photographer for the *Sunday Times Magazine*, the *Jewish Chronicle*, *The Guardian*, *The Observer* and as a photographer and picture editor for Greenpeace (1988–92). He also interviewed prominent African writers and was a writer himself.

Goldblatt's photo-essay 'The Undressing Room' for the influential *Creative Camera* magazine was developed speculatively and taken over four consecutive evenings at a Soho strip club. He was welcomed by the performers and management and in a short space of time produced a set of incisive and tender images that seem to reflect on race and the impact the performers' job had on their family and their private life – all garnered within the very tight space of the dressing room. Goldblatt had a natural flair for choosing the right moment and spotting thought-provoking details. The only trouble he faced while creating the work was one encounter with a bouncer: 'In taking a day shot of the more photogenic exterior of another club [Naked City, Dean Street], through my viewfinder, I saw [the bouncer] ... coming out of the club towards me. I shot him, then he swiped at me. Pow! Glasses broken in the gutter. Head full of noises and bright flashes.'[19] The set of images did not sell well but was featured in *Creative Camera* in October 1968 between work by the great John Heartfield and Tony Ray-Jones.

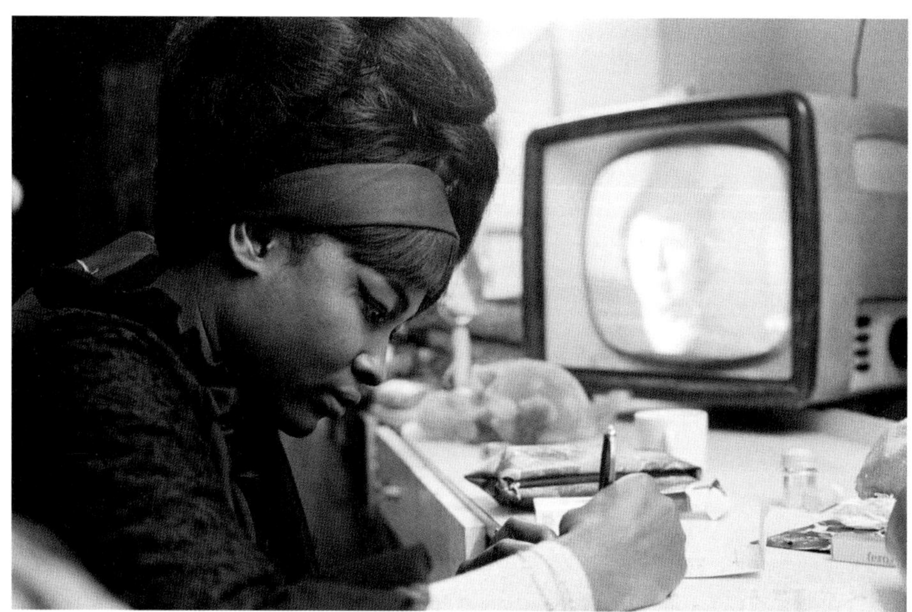

 All images are from 'The Undressing Room', a selection of which were published in *Creative Camera*, October 1968.

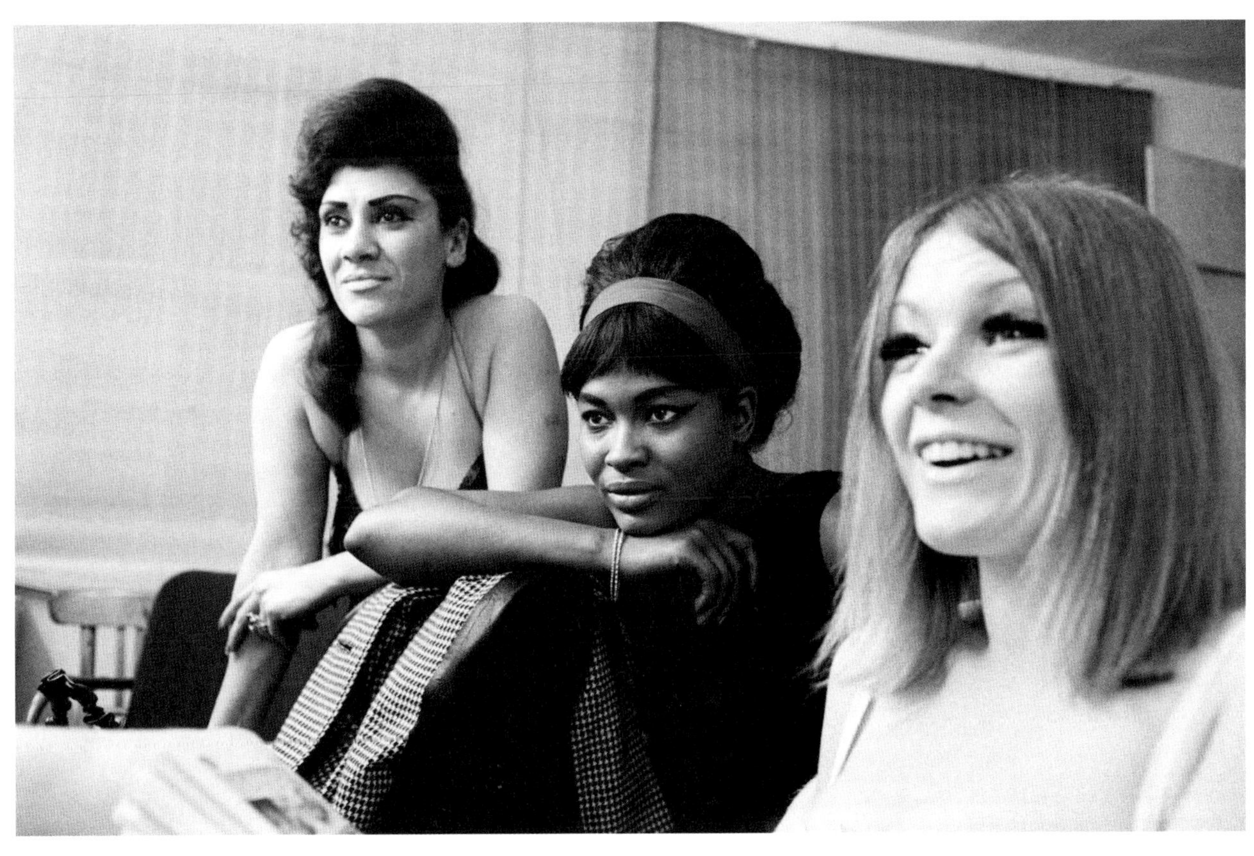

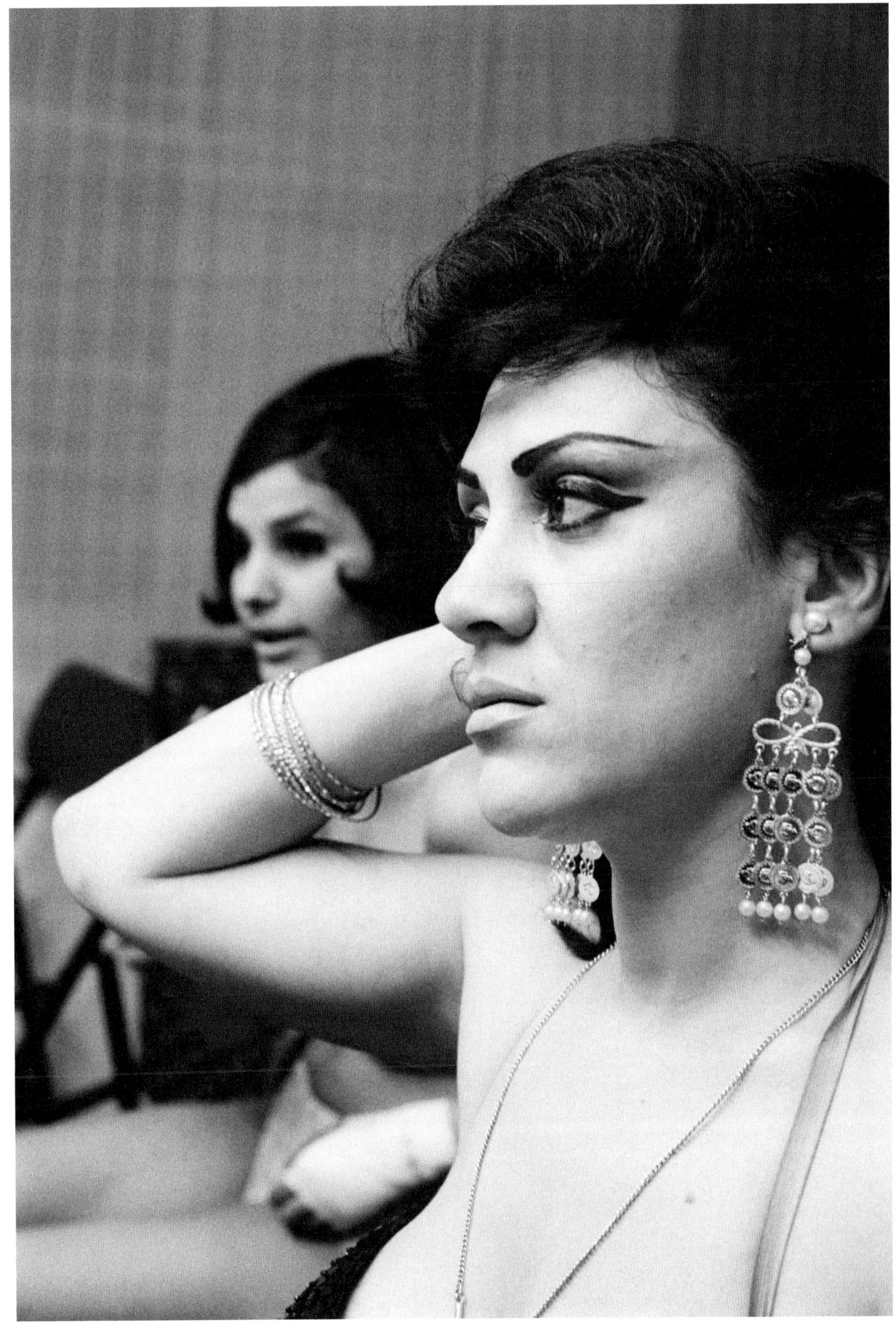

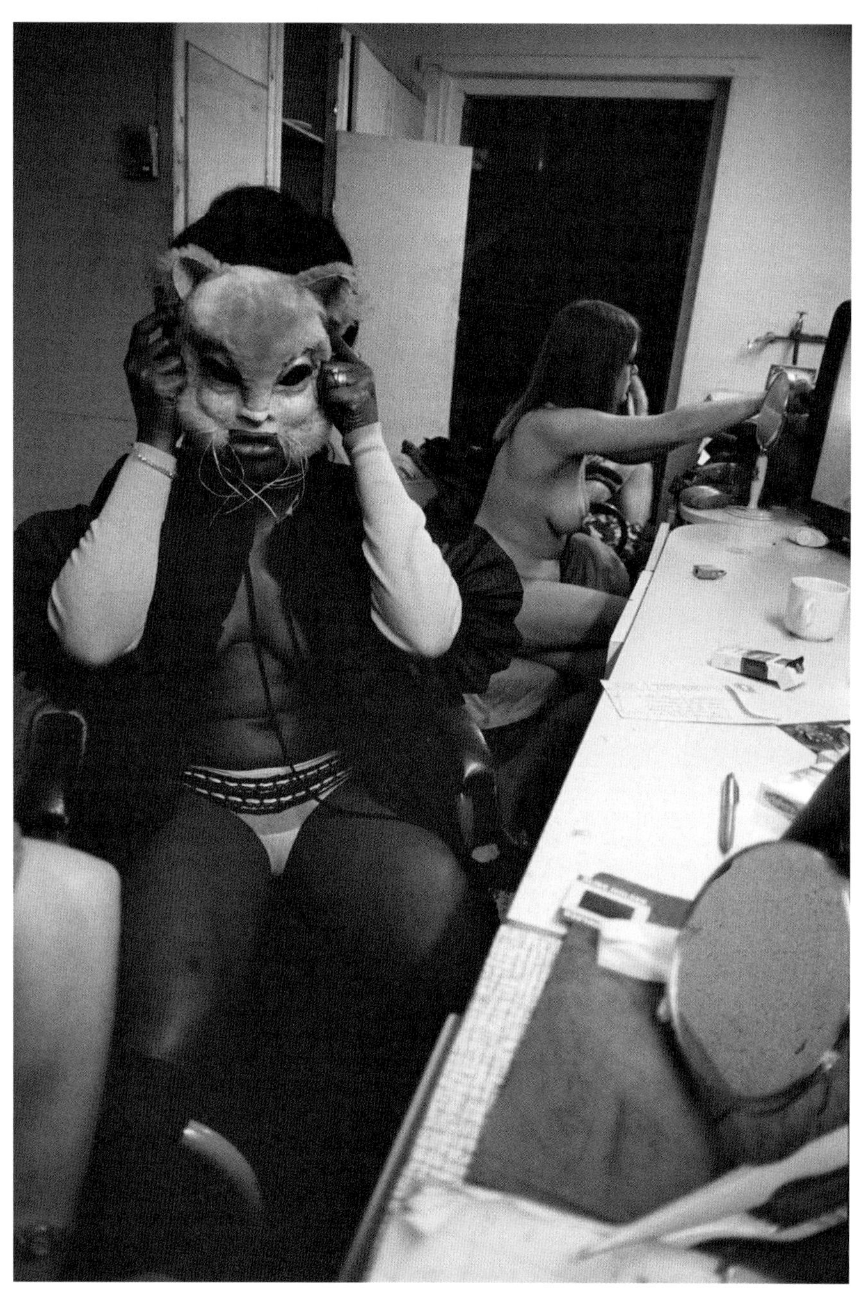

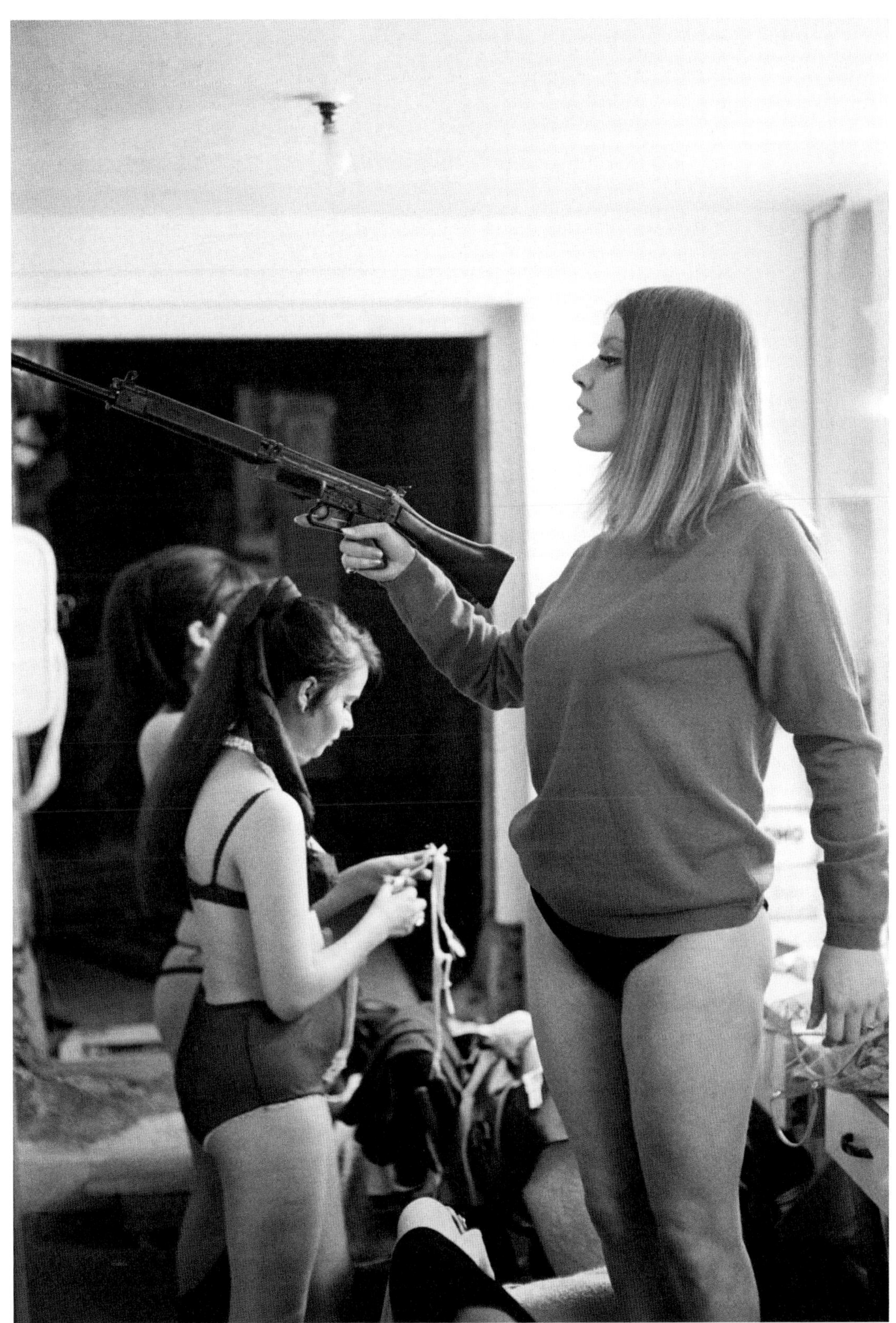

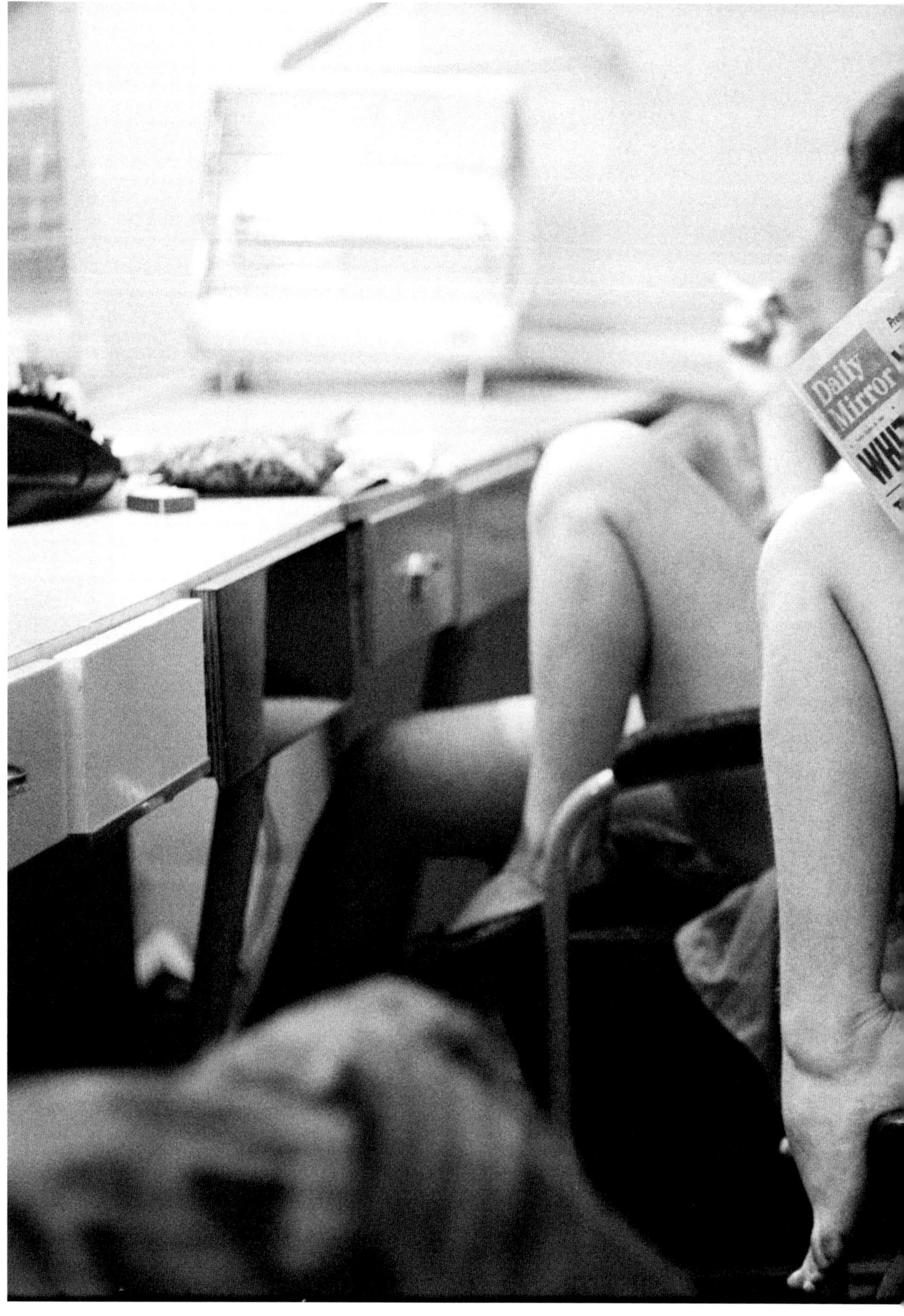
Daily Mirror

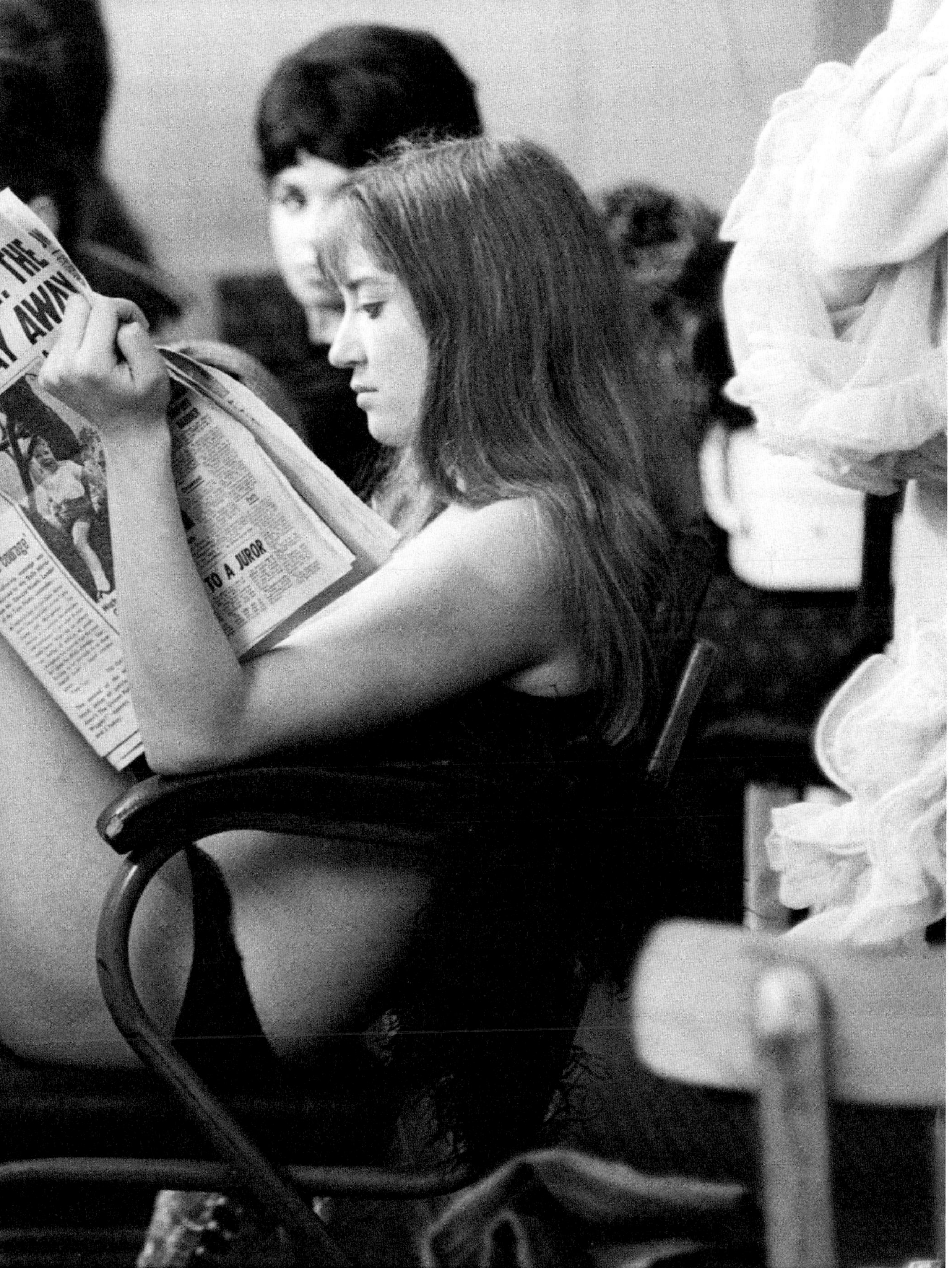

THE
TO A JUROR
courage

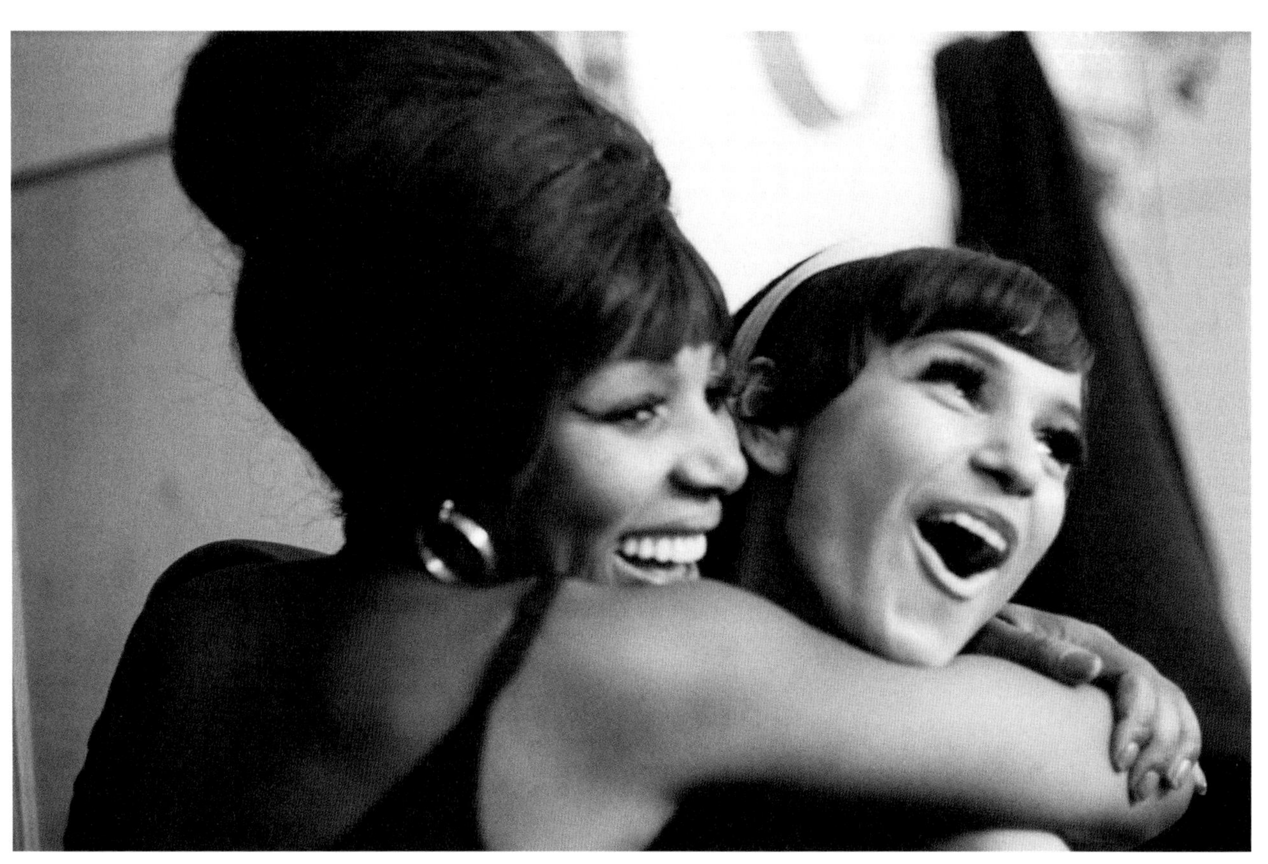

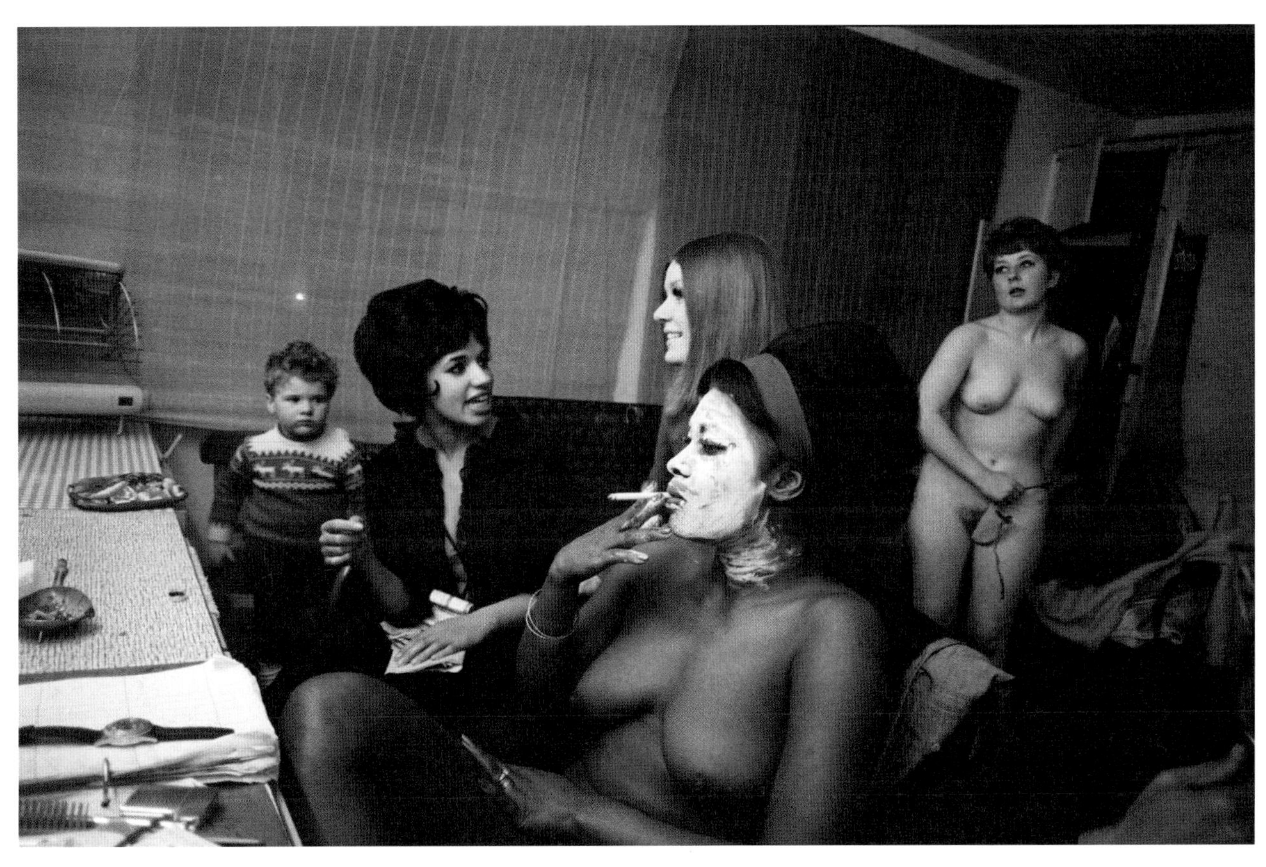

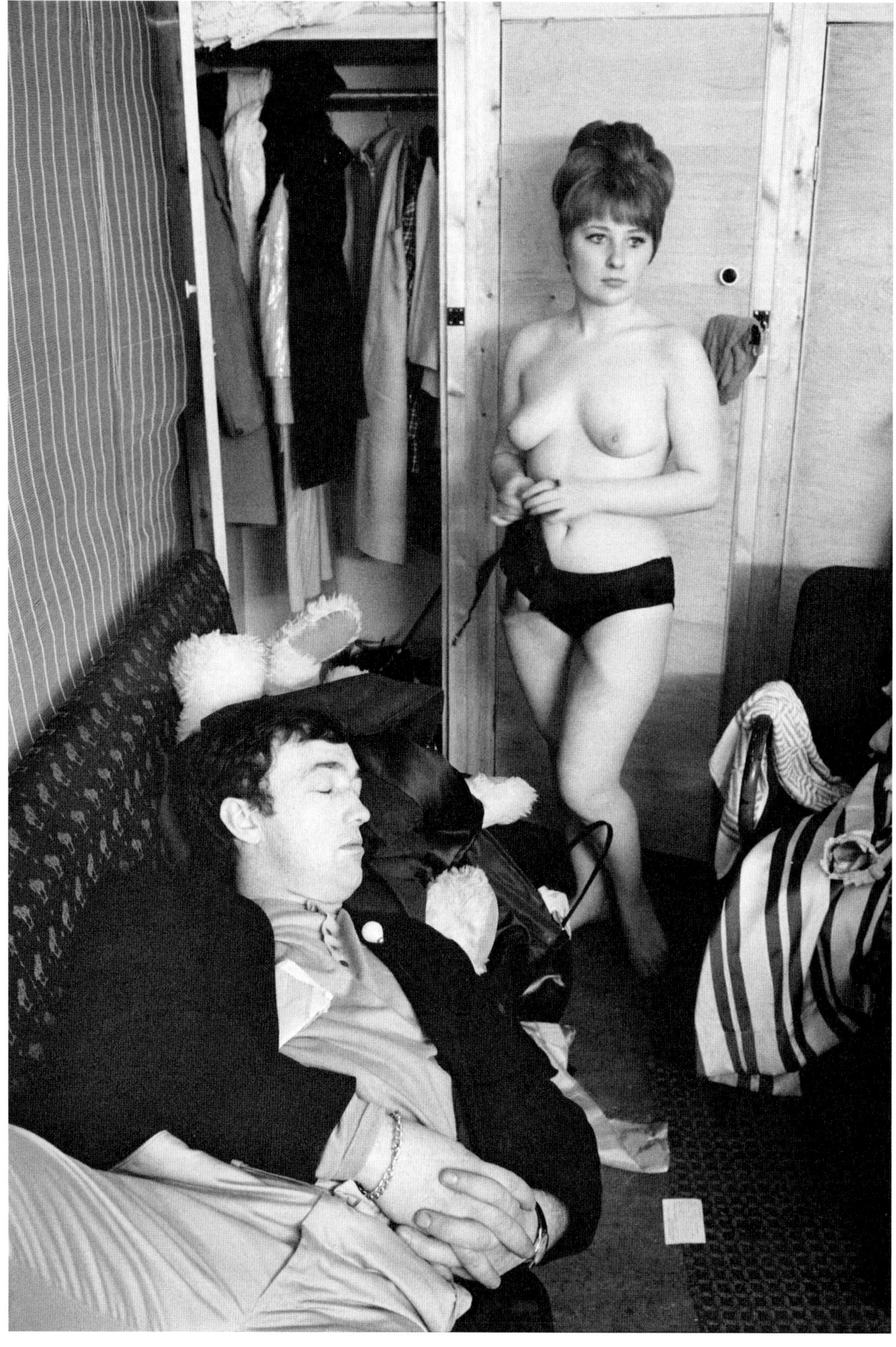

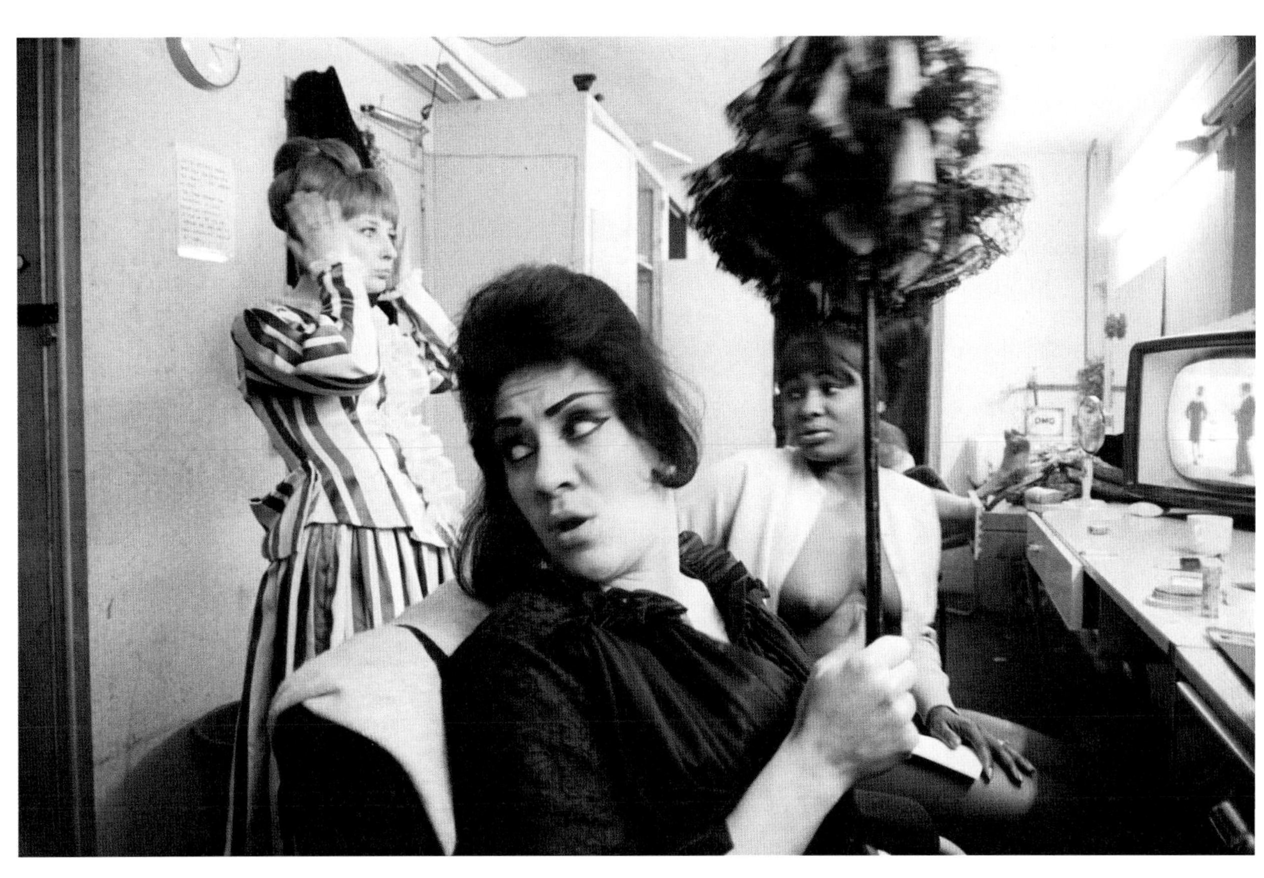

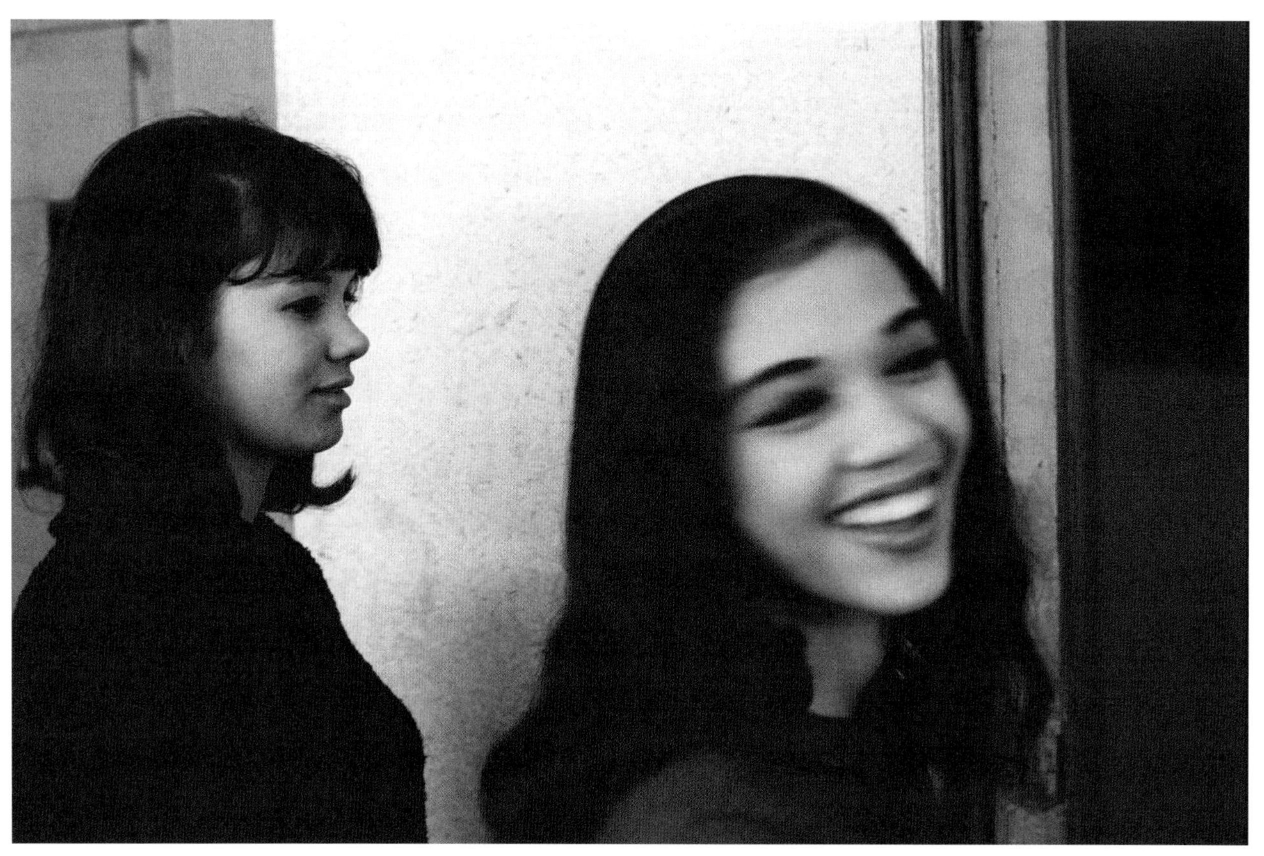

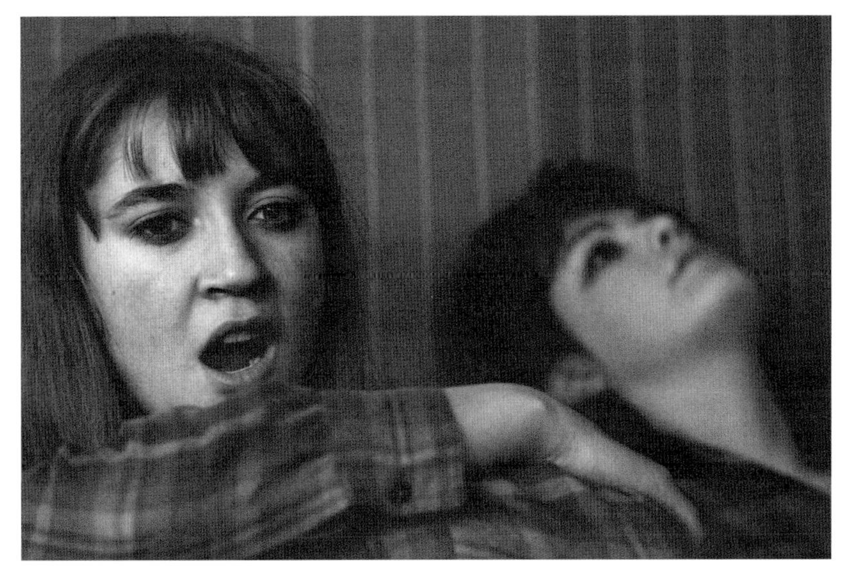

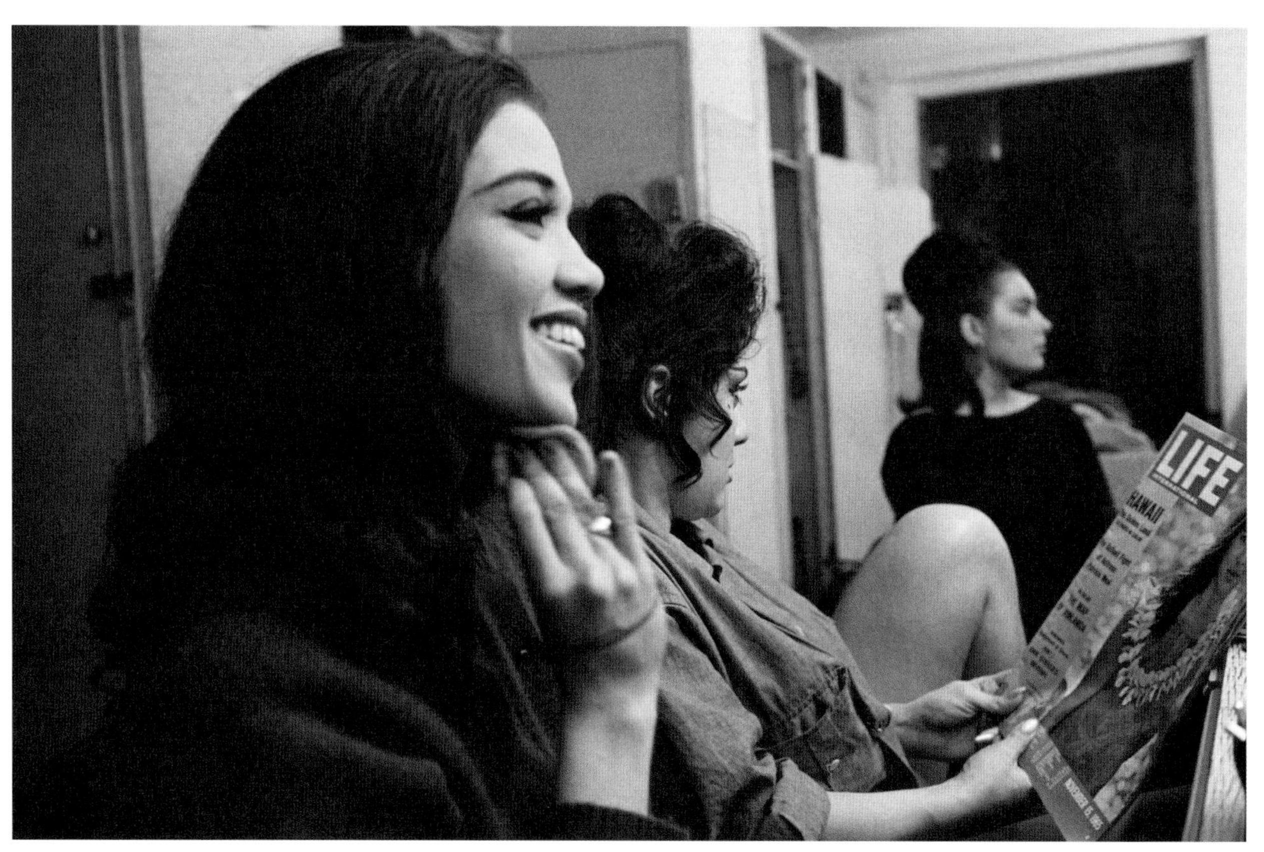
LIFE
HAWAII

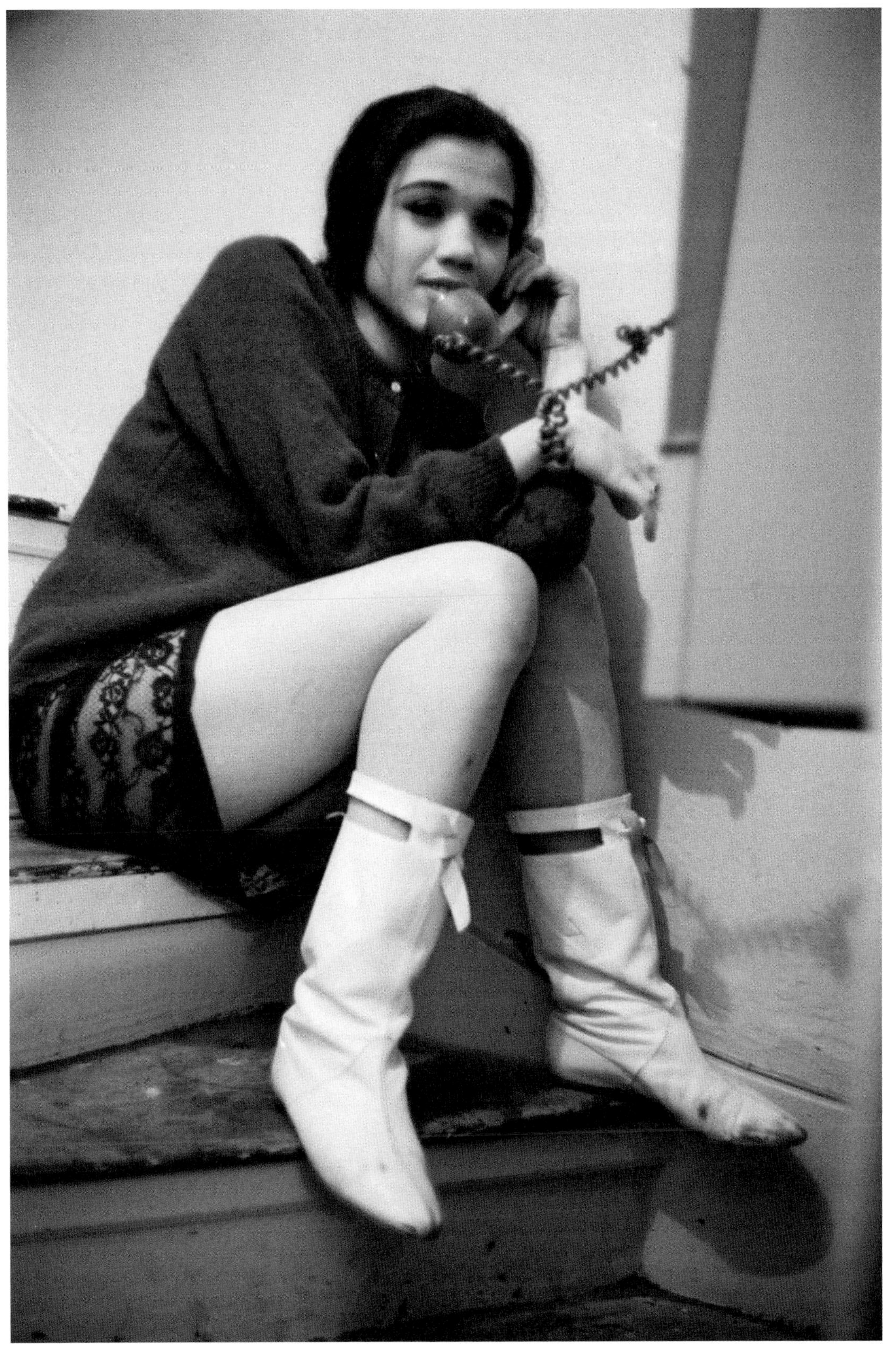

WILLIAM KLEIN

William Klein, born in 1928 in New York, has been a controversial moderniser ever since his breakthrough book *New York* was published in Paris in 1956. Klein's vision of New York was somewhere between paranoiac and contemptuous, the New York publishers he approached telling him: 'This isn't New York. It looks like a slum.'[20]

His approach was influenced by fellow Hungarian emigrés László Moholy-Nagy and György Kepes, who, like Klein, operated freely across artistic disciplines. Klein started as a painter, then quickly developed into a photographer and – after he mothballed his still cameras – started to produce films. His pop-abstract film *Broadway by Light* (1958), capturing the lights of Times Square, was followed later by a brilliant feature-length satire on the fashion industry, *Who Are You, Polly Maggoo?* (1966). Having worked for American *Vogue*, he had the necessary insider knowledge to produce an accurate critique of the industry.

Klein was responsible for instigating a movement towards expressionist documentary. Gary Winogrand, who followed in Klein's footsteps, summed it up well in his oft-quoted statement 'I take photographs to find out what something will look like photographed.' Klein later described his New York work as street 'looting', seeing it more as an 'exercise in style' and a way to 'let off steam'.[21] In part, the power of the work was driven by Klein's coming to terms with technical failures – blur, grain, errors in depth of field – elements which he found he could use to intensify the dramatic moment.

Klein's work was not just concerned with surface, however, and often included strong elements of political critique. In 1980 he returned to still photography, and by the *Sunday Times Magazine*'s 23 November 1980 issue, with its feature on Soho, he was back in full swing – up close, ferreting out details that resonated with the area's anti-establishment stance. This work has lain forgotten in Klein's own archive. The magazine's striking cover shows men hiding their faces as they emerge from a 'Sauna & Massage' establishment – which just happens to be at number 69. This is vintage Klein. The feature was billed back then as 'Soho's fight for survival' and was coupled with an excellent supporting story by Denis Herbstein (both the photographs and words have a life of their own, neither subservient to the other). Dynamic images include 'Christine, a French prostitute, surveys her workshop before opening for business' (as it was captioned), a cacophony of colour set off by Christine's turquoise tunic and the magenta bidet. Later in the sixteen-page feature we see punks on the street, the image used full-bleed for maximum effect. Paul Raymond, owner of the Windmill Theatre, is presented as the 'respectable' side of Soho's sex trade, while the Wilkes Brothers gunsmiths hark back to Soho's original craft-based businesses. Klein, ever the influencer, managed to get to what made Soho tick in super-quick time.

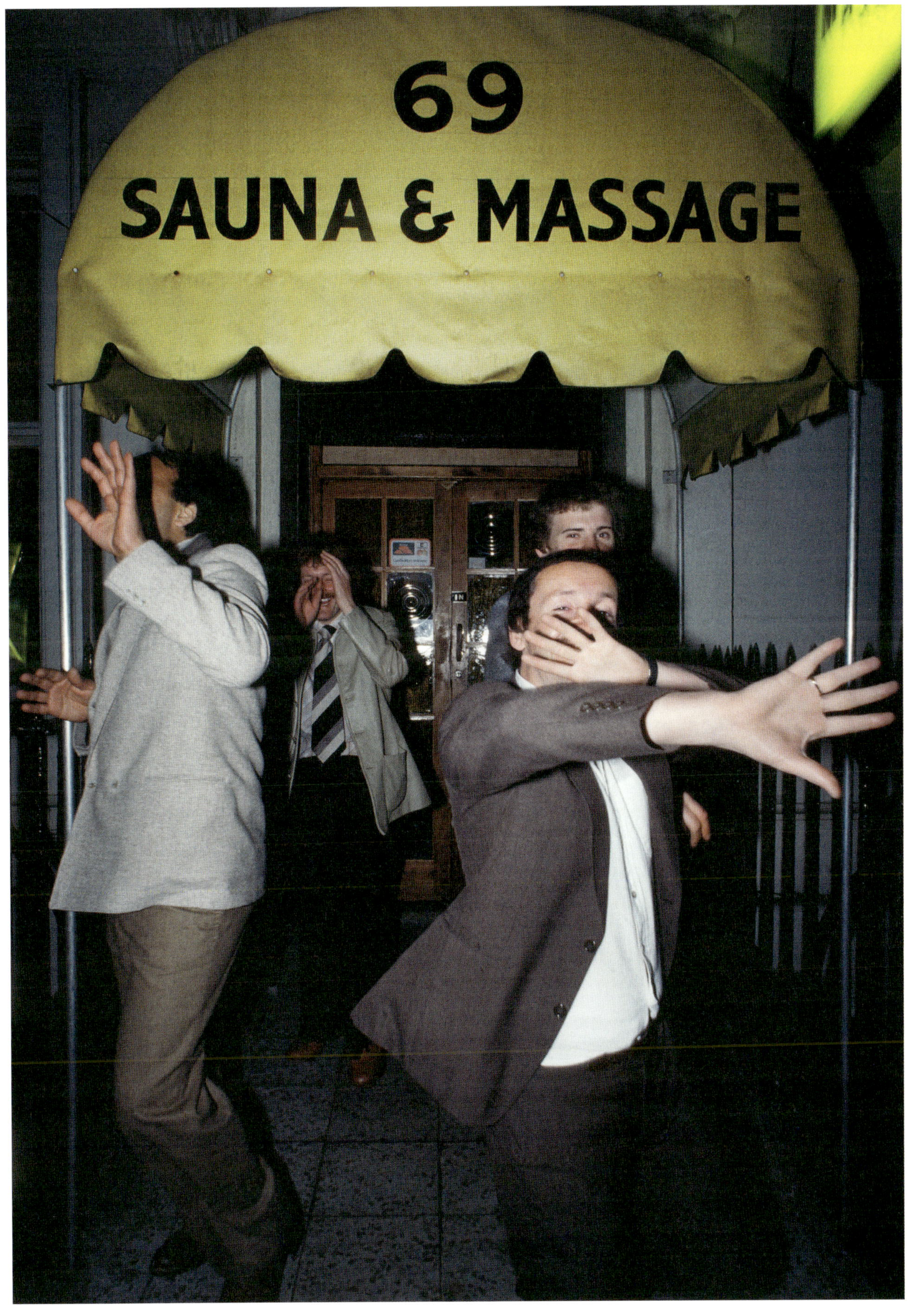

'Men hiding their faces as they emerge from a Sauna & Massage parlour.'

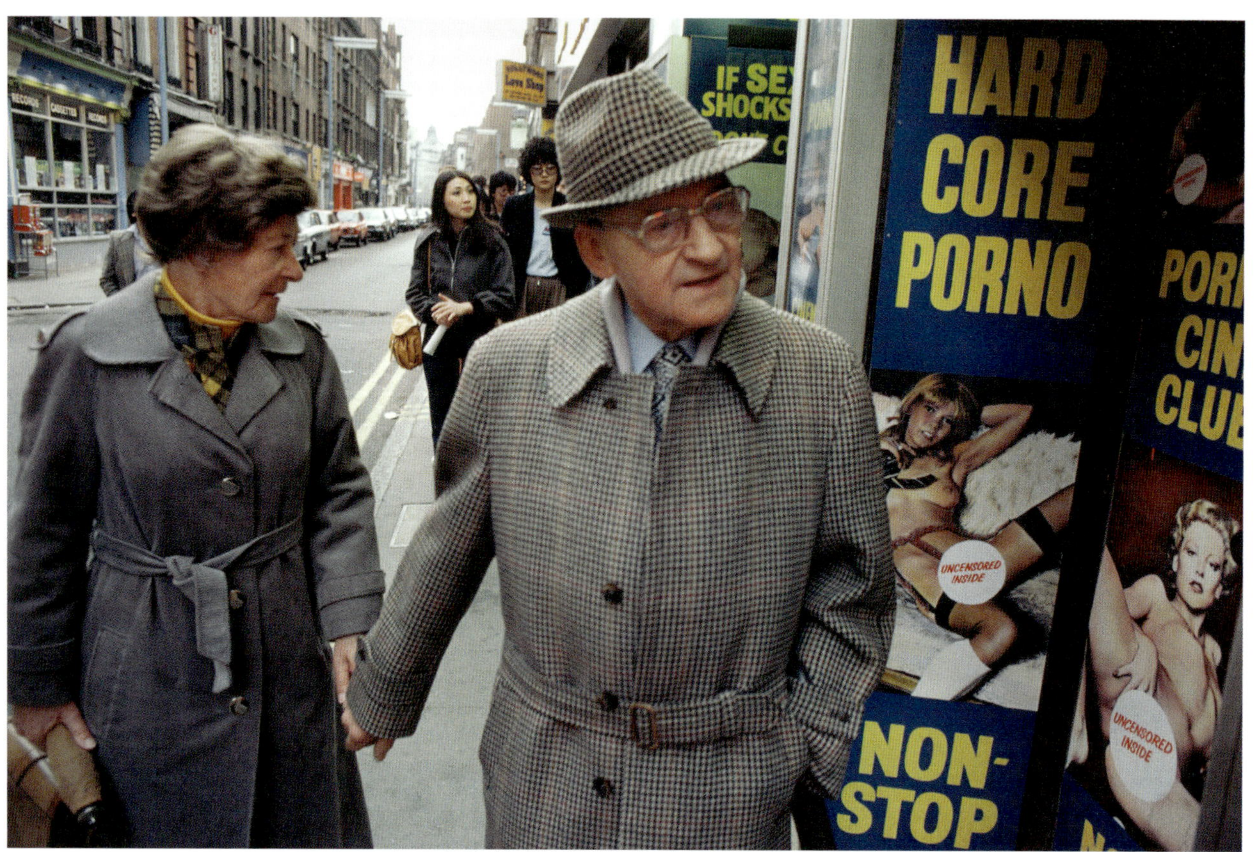

 'Porno joints are hard to ignore.'

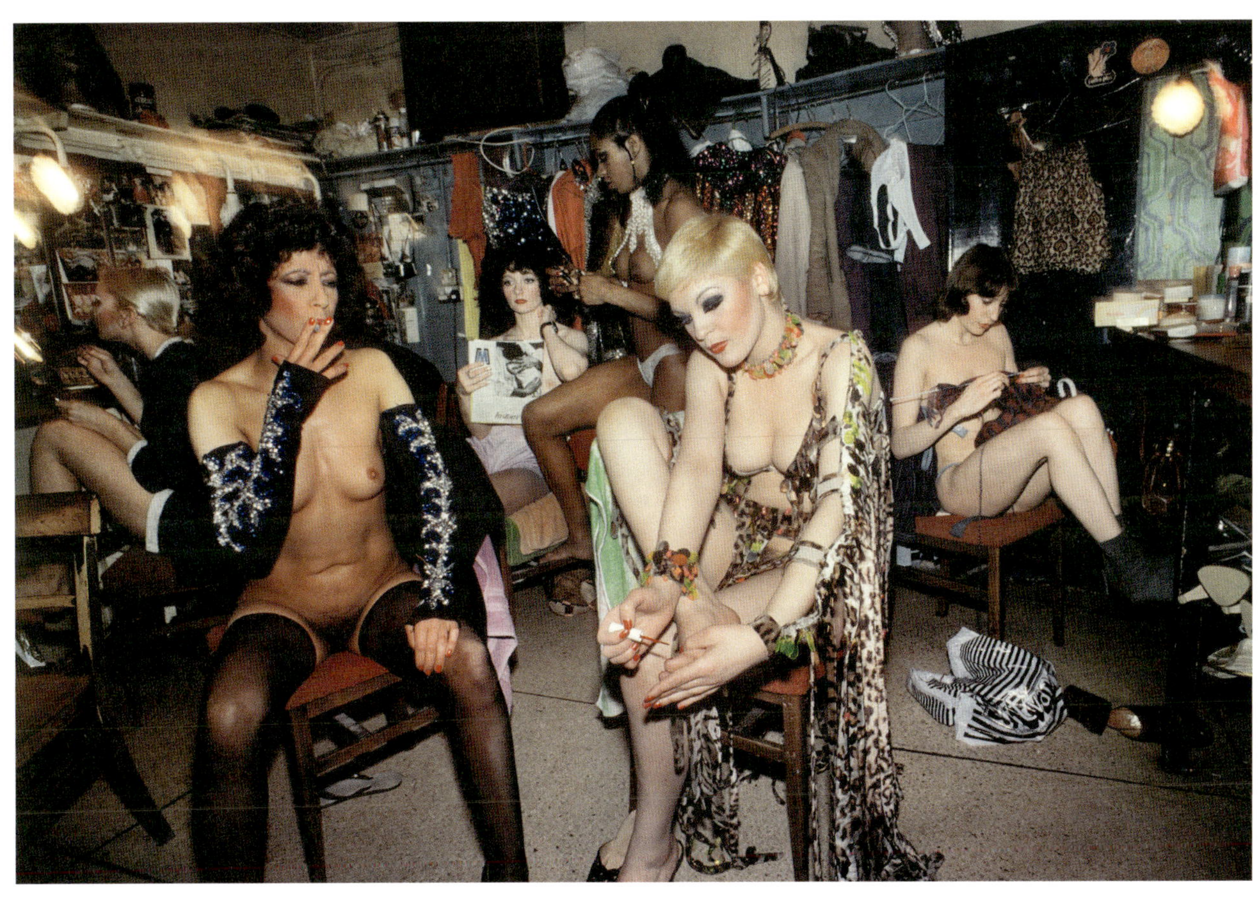

‘Backstage at the Revue Bar. A sign reads “The impression created by some of you is that you are totally disinterested in what you have just done on stage.”’

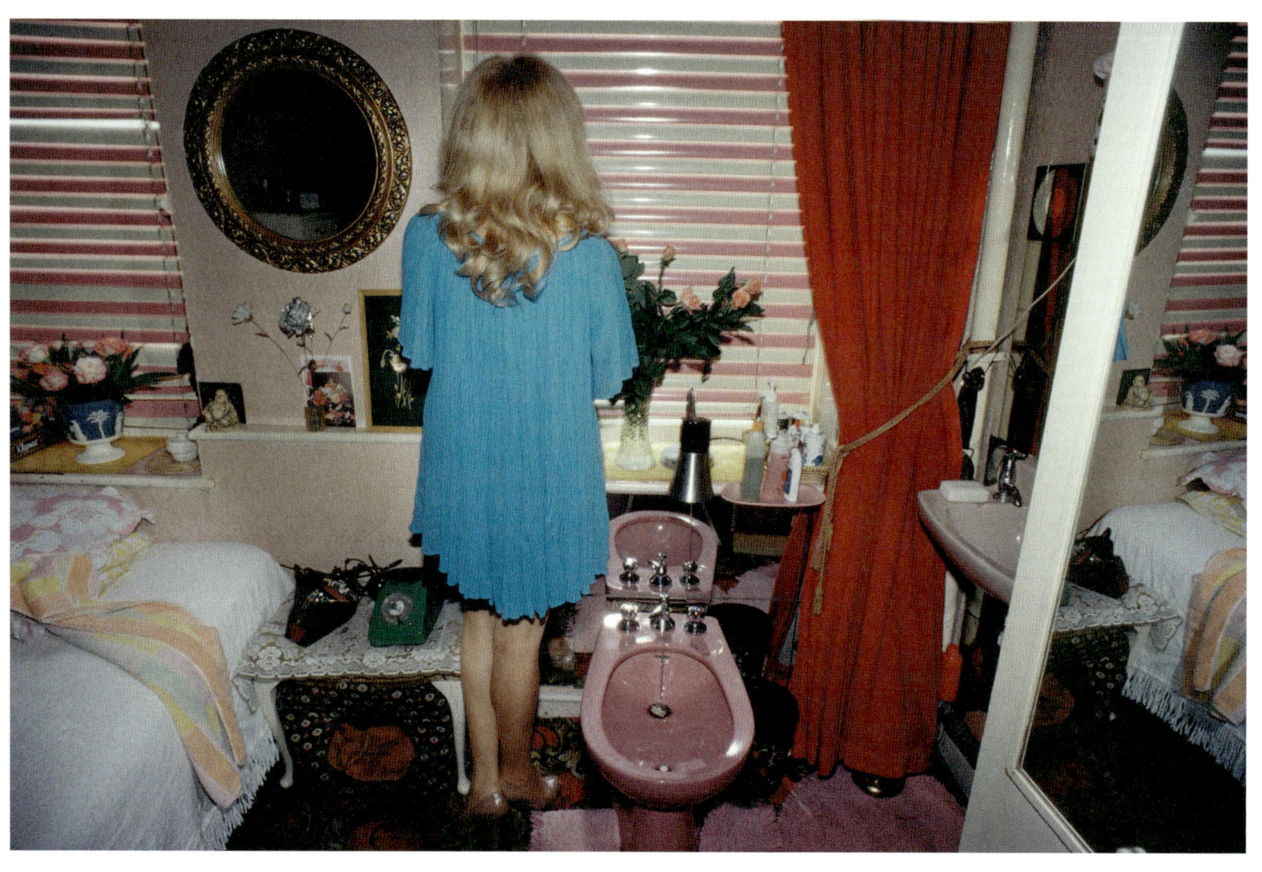

 ‘Christine, a French prostitute, surveys her workshop before opening for business.’

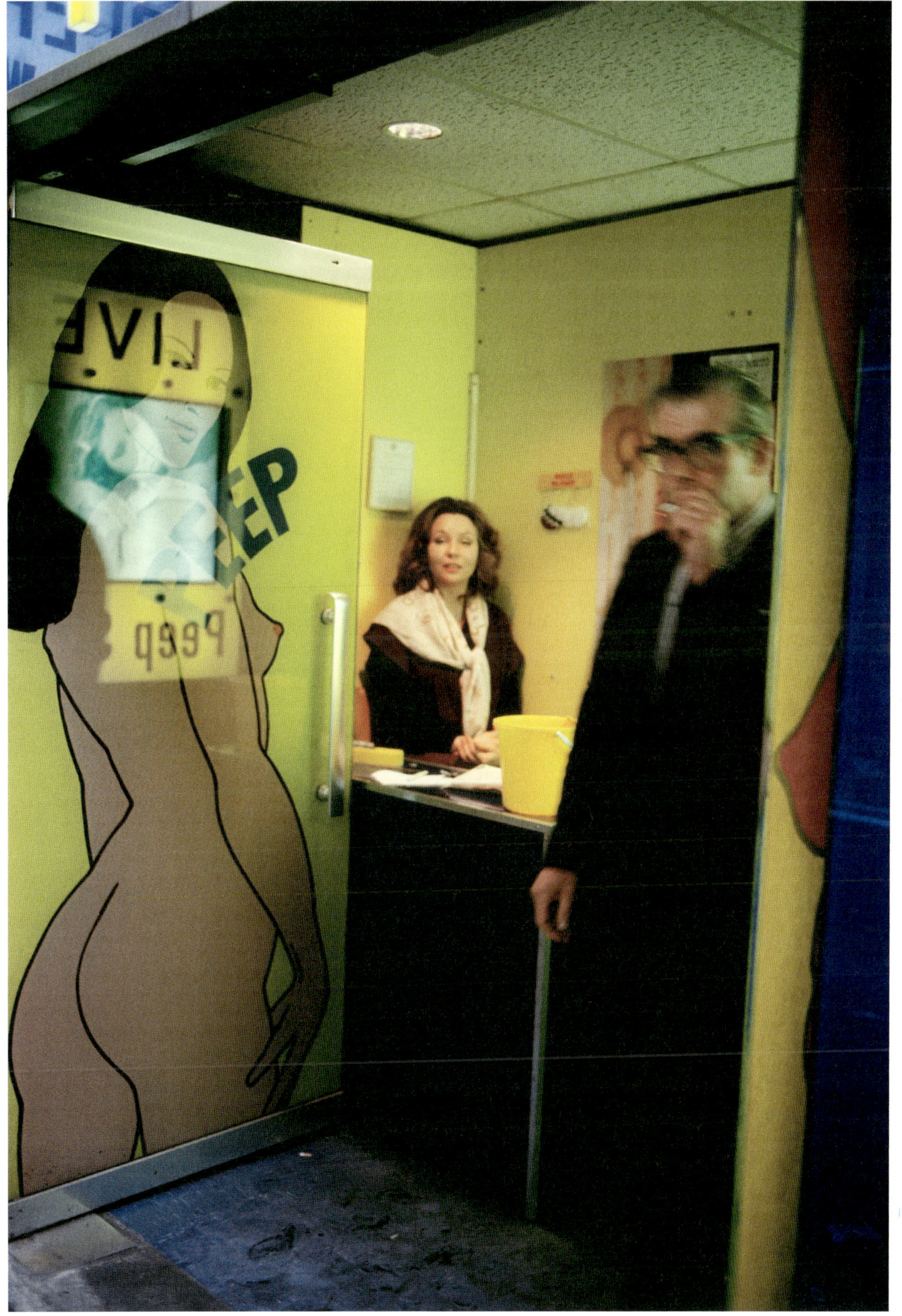

'Sex Shop entrance.'

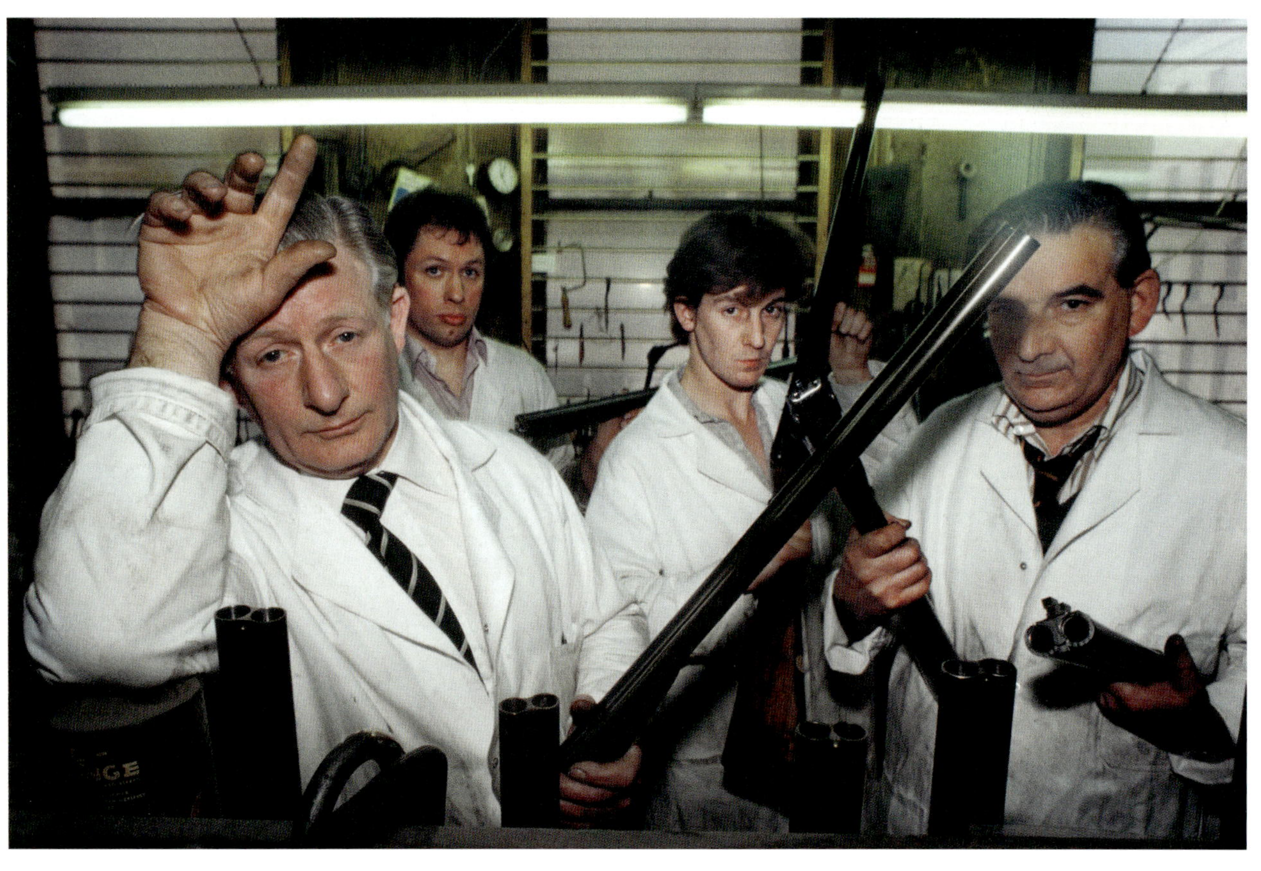

 'The Wilkes brothers, gunsmiths on Beak Street.'

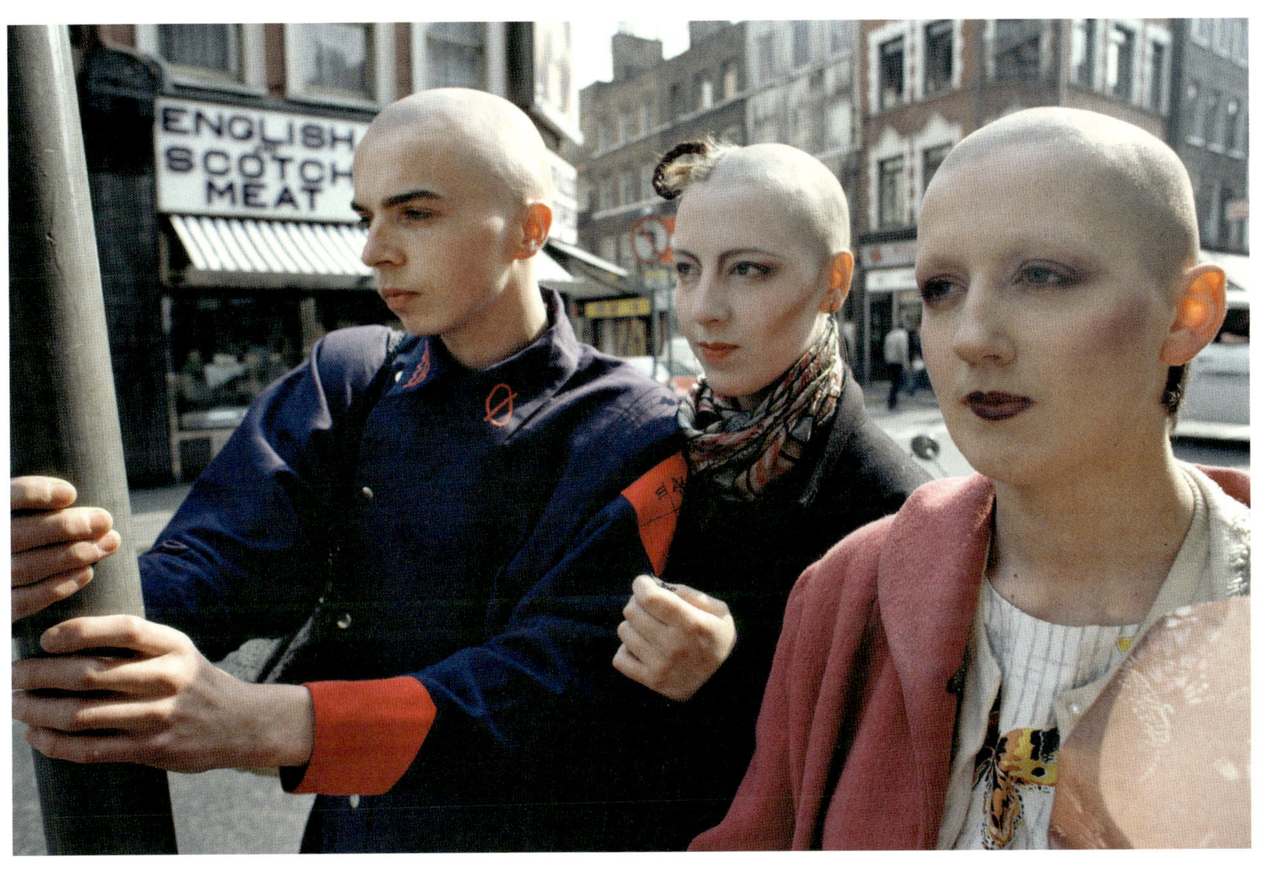

'Punks, young Brynners? Or maybe just day-trippers from Stevenage.'

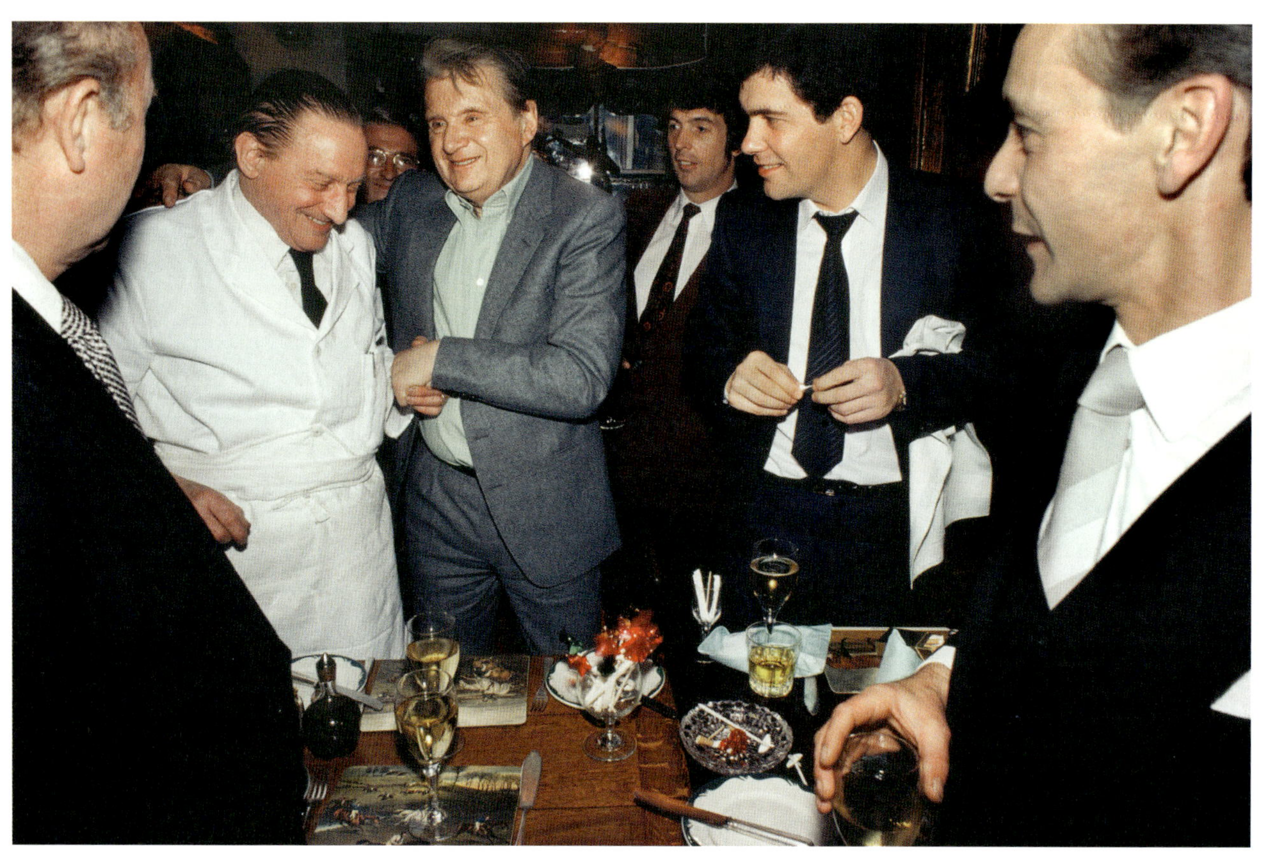

‘Francis Bacon at Wheeler’s Oyster Bar (est. 1929), Old Compton Street. Bacon once settled up a large bill at the restaurant with one of his paintings.’

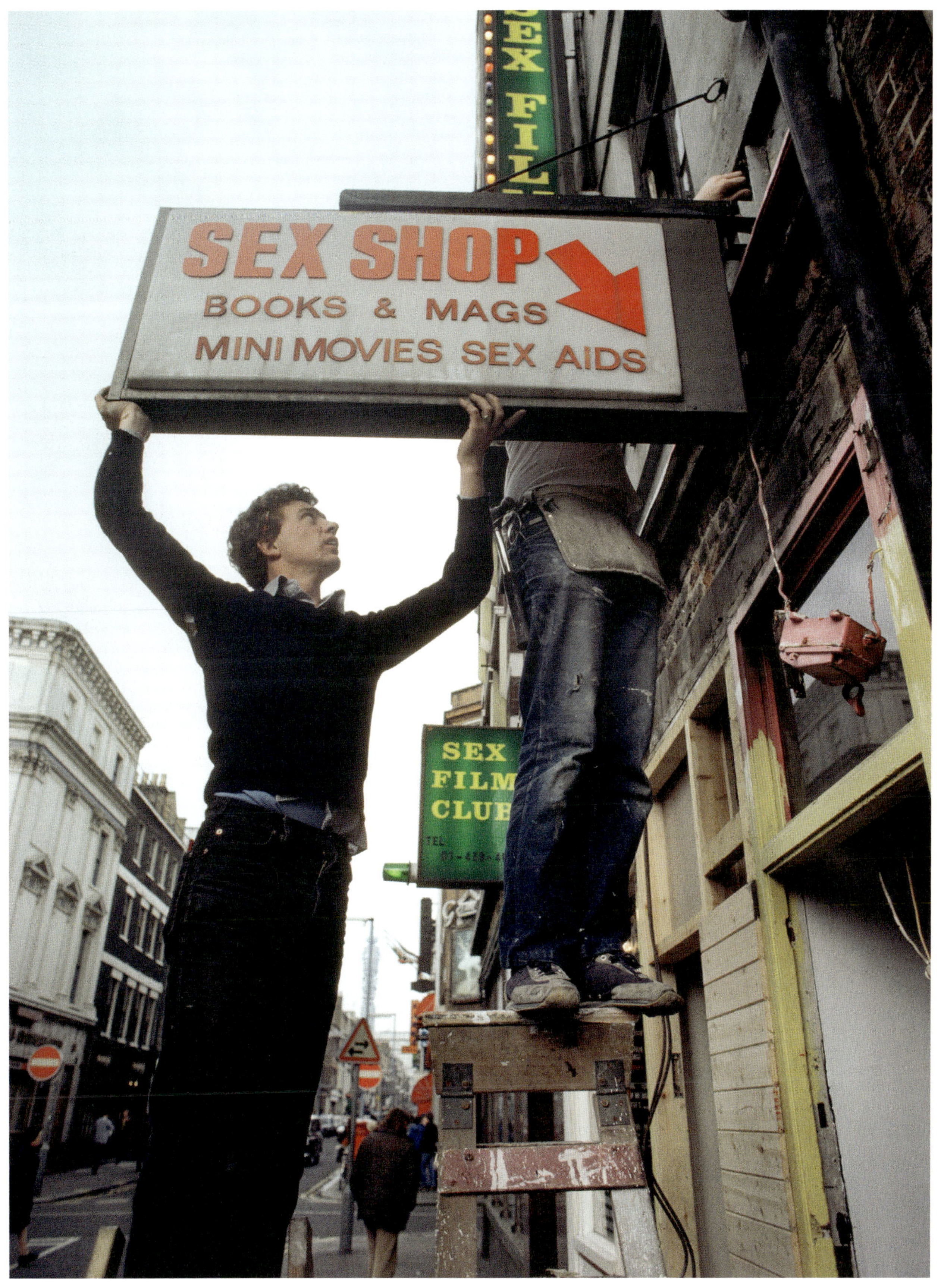

'The commerce of vice takes over another Soho shop.'

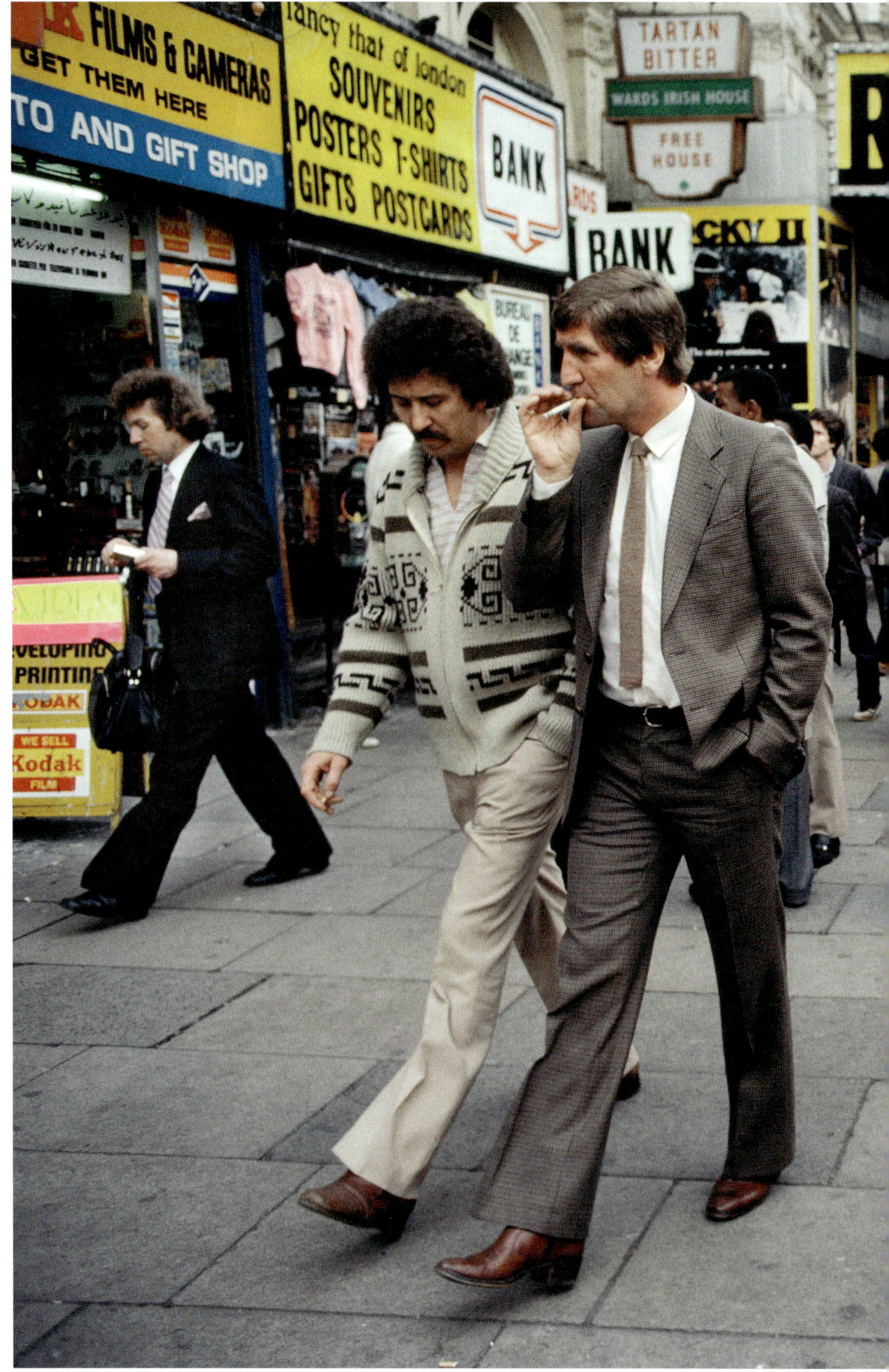

'Shoeshiner, Coventry Street, Piccadilly.'

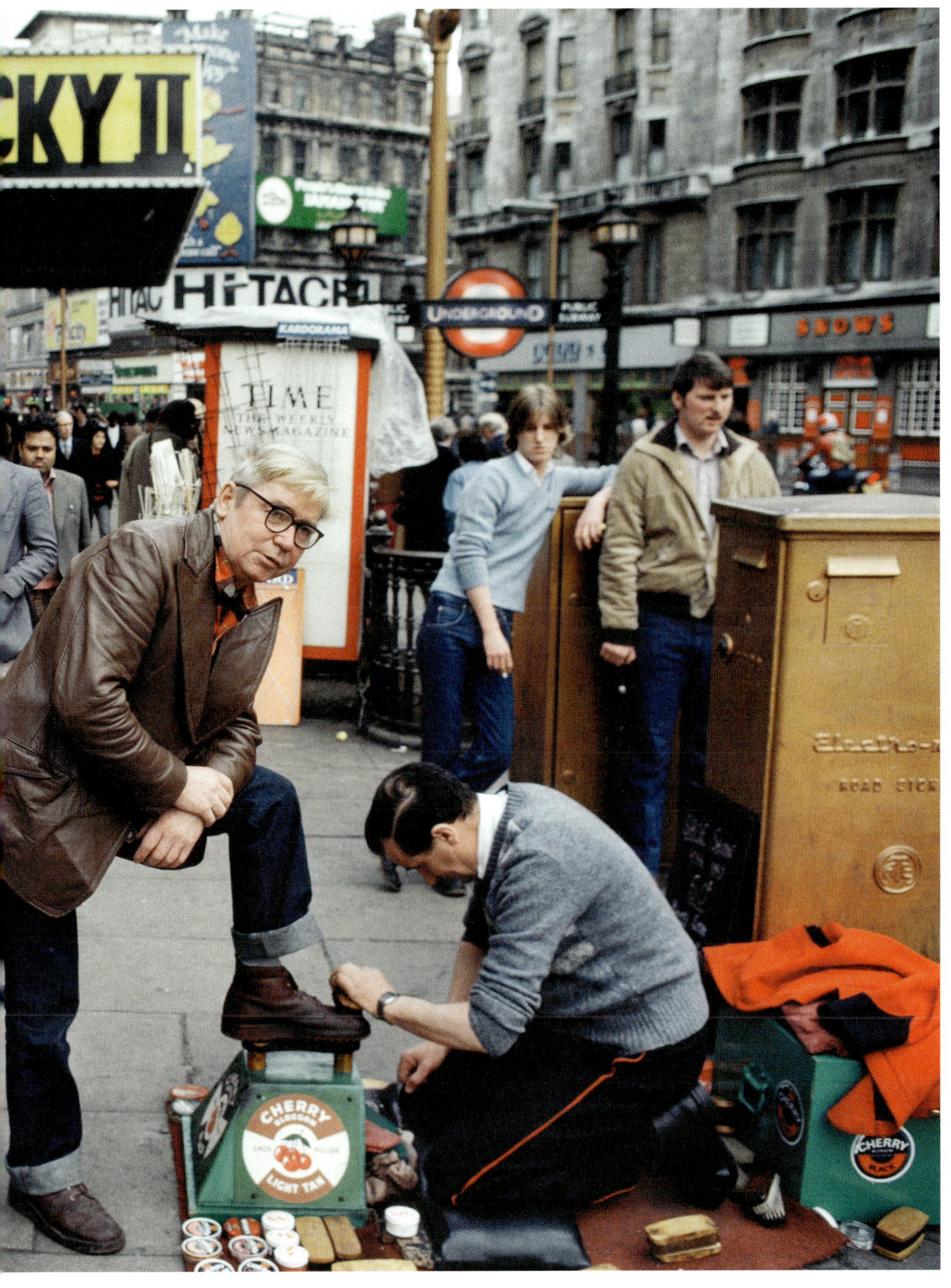
CKY II
HITACHI
UNDERGROUND
KARDORAMA
TIME
THE WEEKLY
NEWSMAGAZINE
CHERRY
BLOSSOM
LIGHT TAN
CHERRY
BLACK

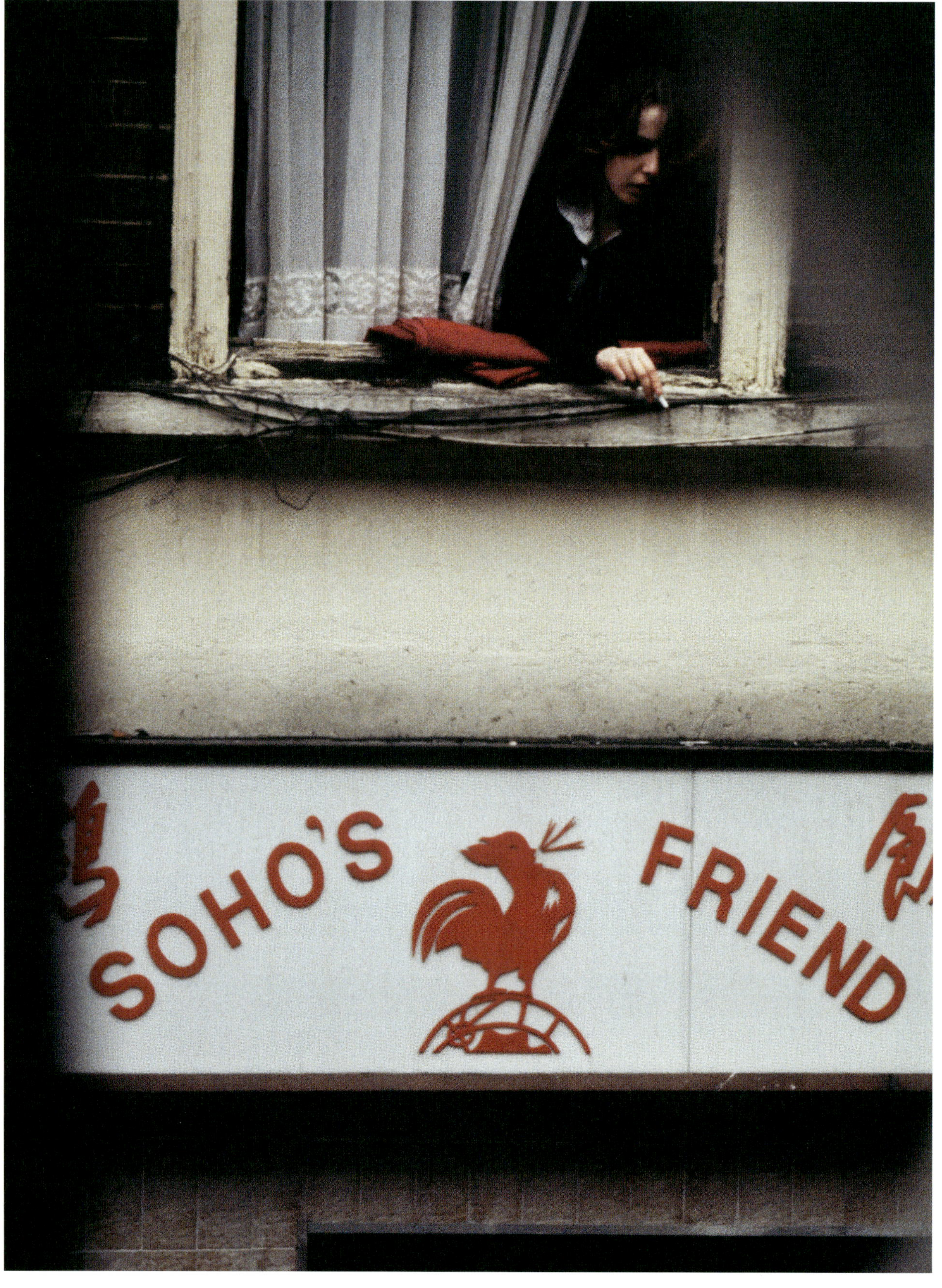

'Soho's Friend Chinese restaurant, with model's room above and Chinese Sunday school next door, Meard Street.'

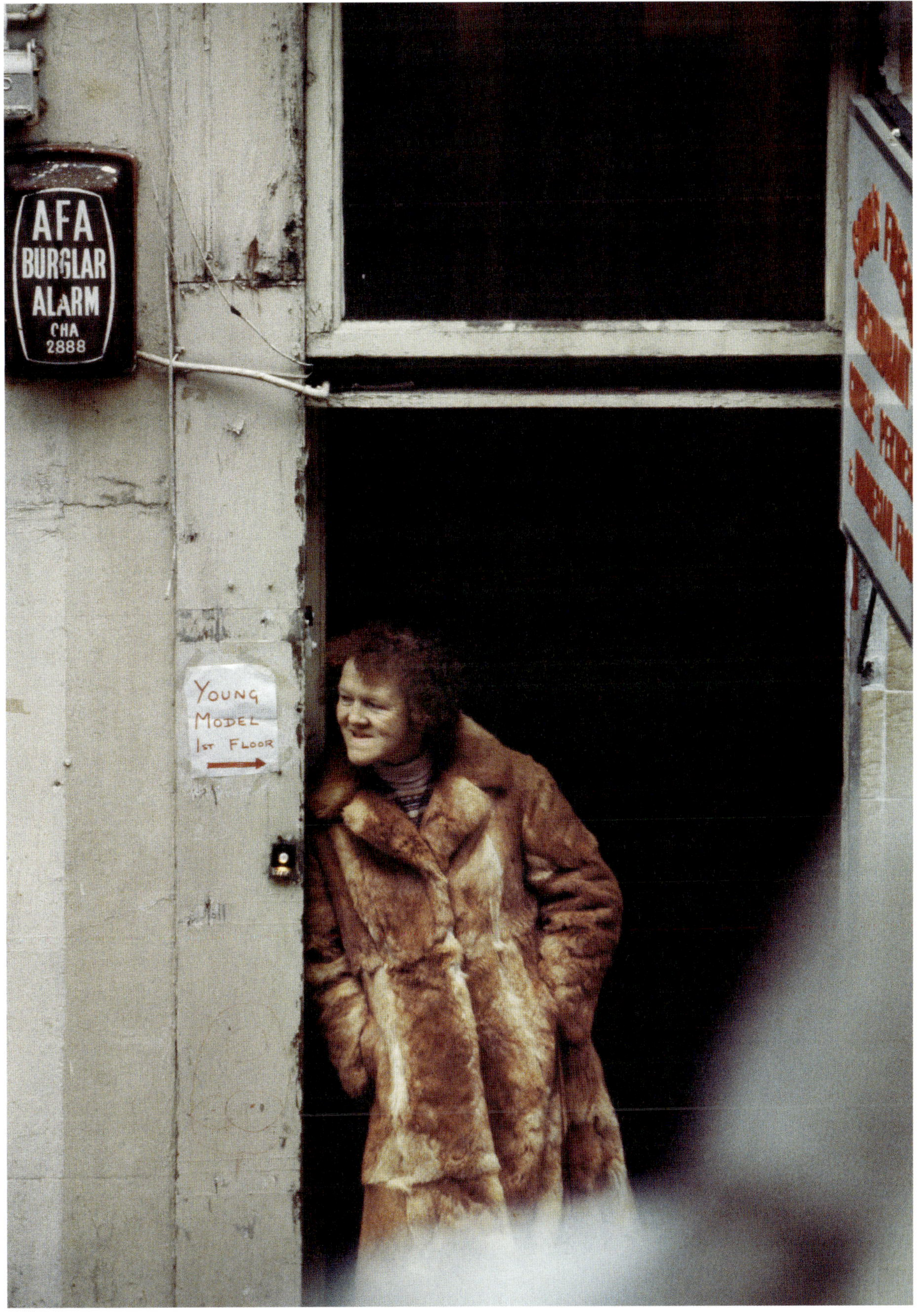

‘Model lady and a traditional business plaque.’

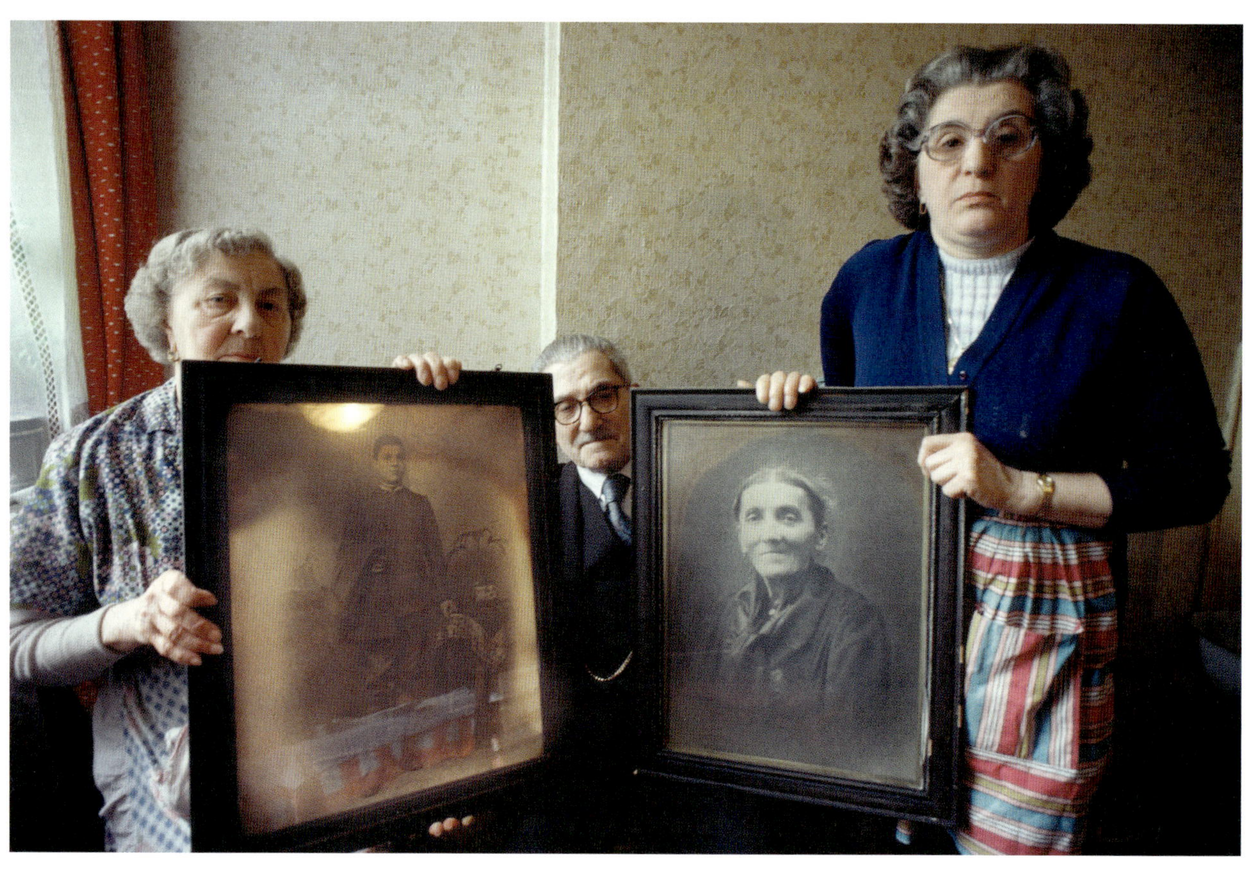

 ‘The Rotondos family and antecedents in Soho’s Little Italy.’

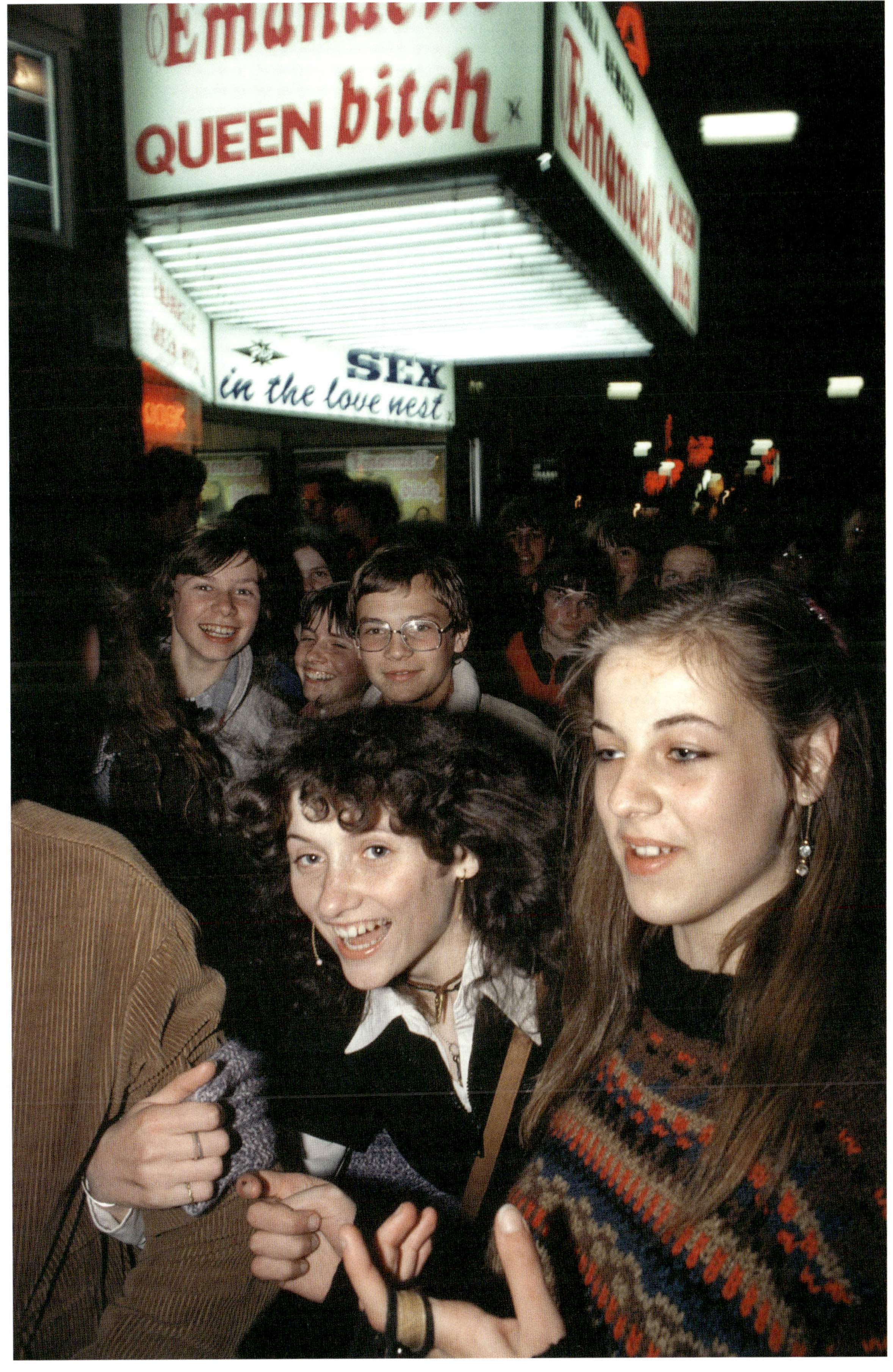

'Crowds outside a cinema showing *Emanuelle: Queen Bitch.*'

ANDERS PETERSEN

Swedish photographer Anders Petersen (b. 1944) is best known for the visceral intimacy of his black-and-white documentary photography. His first project, *Café Lehmitz* (1978), was made in a Hamburg dive bar and was an intimate portrait of its regulars. They were a wild bunch of outsiders and Petersen connected deeply with them; at the Café Lehmitz he drank, forged friendships, fell in love – and took photographs. The publication is now recognised as a key photo-book in post-war European photography.

Over the past twenty years Petersen has accepted numerous invitations for residencies in cities across the world, ranging from Okinawa and Paris to Utrecht and Valparaiso. In each place he spends several weeks or months observing the street life, getting to know people and photographing. He calls these projects 'City Diaries' – visual records of cities filtered through his uncompromising lens.

In 2011 The Photographers' Gallery invited Petersen to make such a project in its own neighbourhood, Soho. Petersen immersed himself in the life of this unique area. He had first wandered Soho's streets back in the 1970s; he found much had changed since, though some things had not. The resulting body of work contains street scenes, fleeting snapshots of tender embraces and boisterous performances to camera by some of Soho's exuberant characters. It also includes portraits of some of those he befriended on the streets, in pubs, cafés and clubs, often inviting those he found interesting to pose for him. Some were captured there and then; others were arranged for later, taken in private homes, models' working rooms or Petersen's hotel. All of Petersen's work has an element of poetic sadness that is heightened by his characteristic use of high-contrast and grain, and these qualities are abundantly present in the Soho photographs, perhaps most palpably in those generated during his night-time wanderings.

A book of the work, titled simply *Soho*, was co-published by MACK and The Photographers' Gallery in 2012, but this is the first time the work has been exhibited. Petersen's *Soho* is a testament to the dynamism and diversity of the area and the people who frequent and live in it. Always curious about his fellow humans, and unafraid to take risks, Petersen believes that taking a photograph is first and foremost a personal engagement with the world. As he said of his Soho work in 2012: 'My longings and desires are in there, too, and I felt at home in the places I visited. In the heart of many big cities, there are now only young people. I think this is sad. It is like the old have been banished. I did not feel that so much in Soho. It has changed, for sure, but there is still a big mix of people and many special characters, old and young. For me, Soho is something special.'[22]

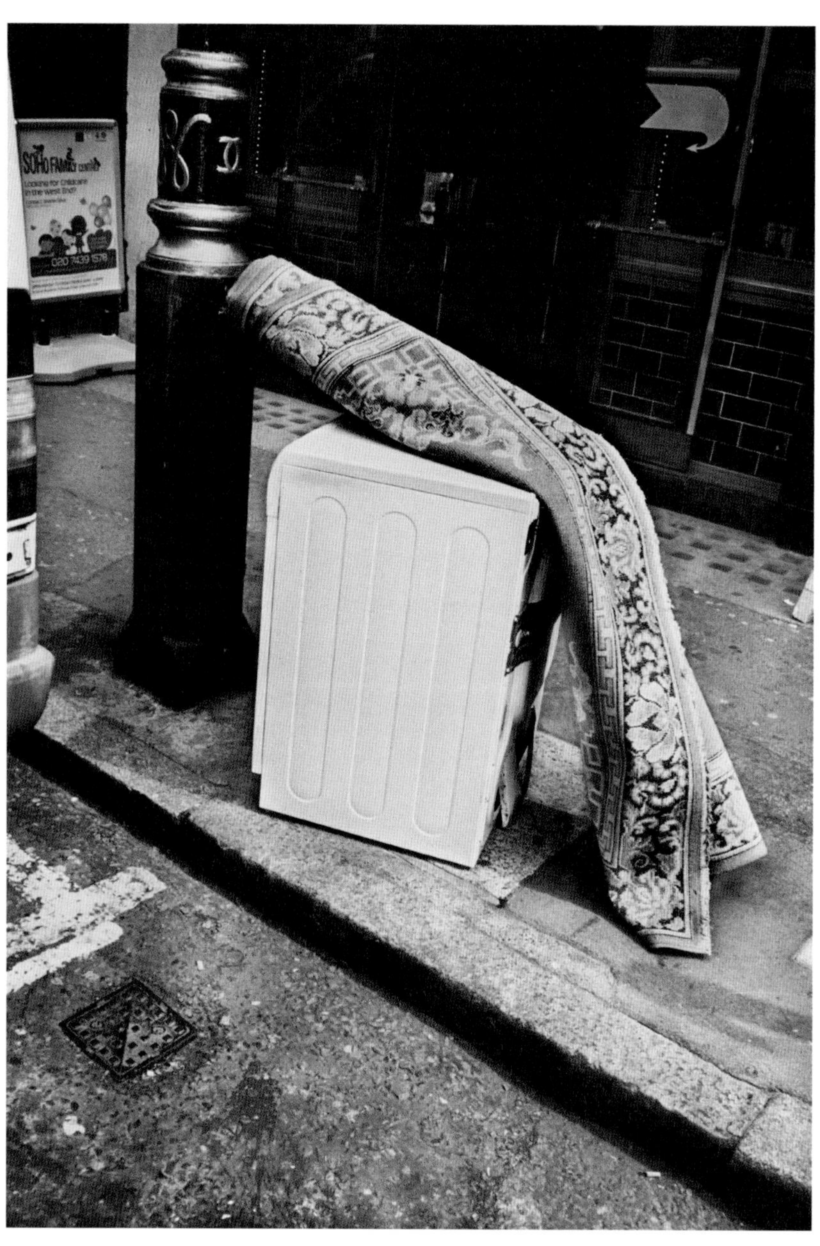

 All images are from the series *Soho*, first published by The Photographers' Gallery and MACK, 2012.

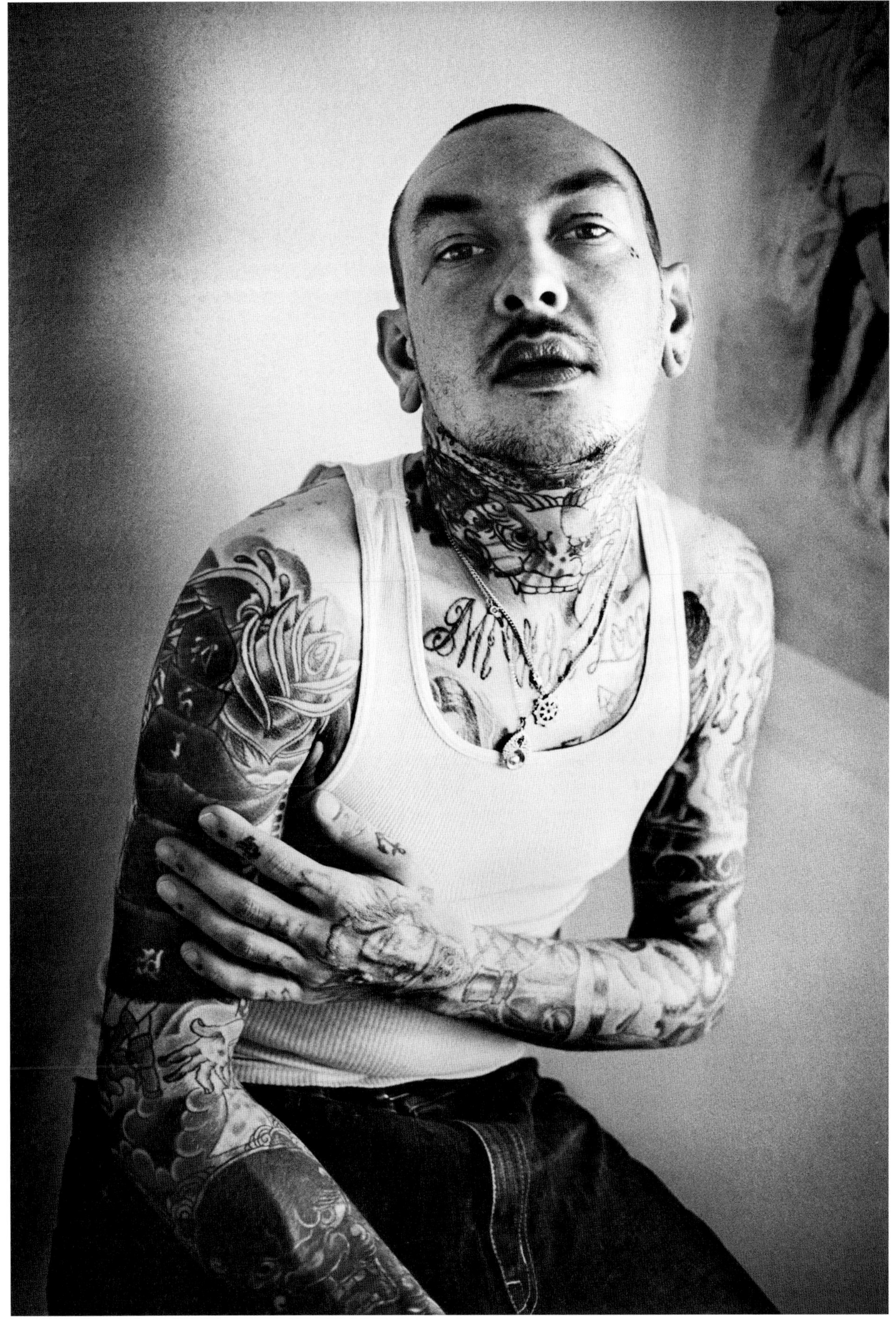

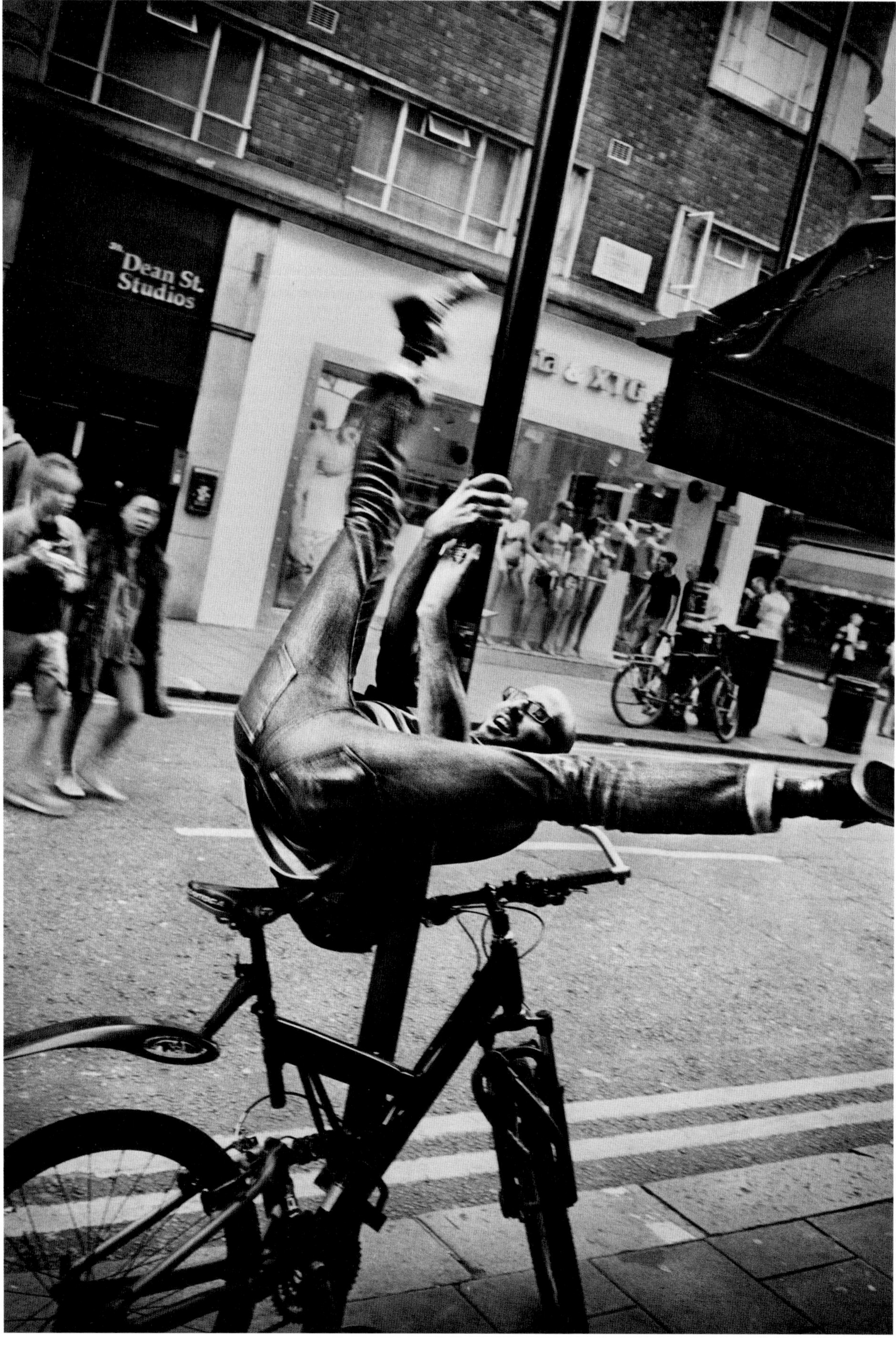
Dean St.
Studios

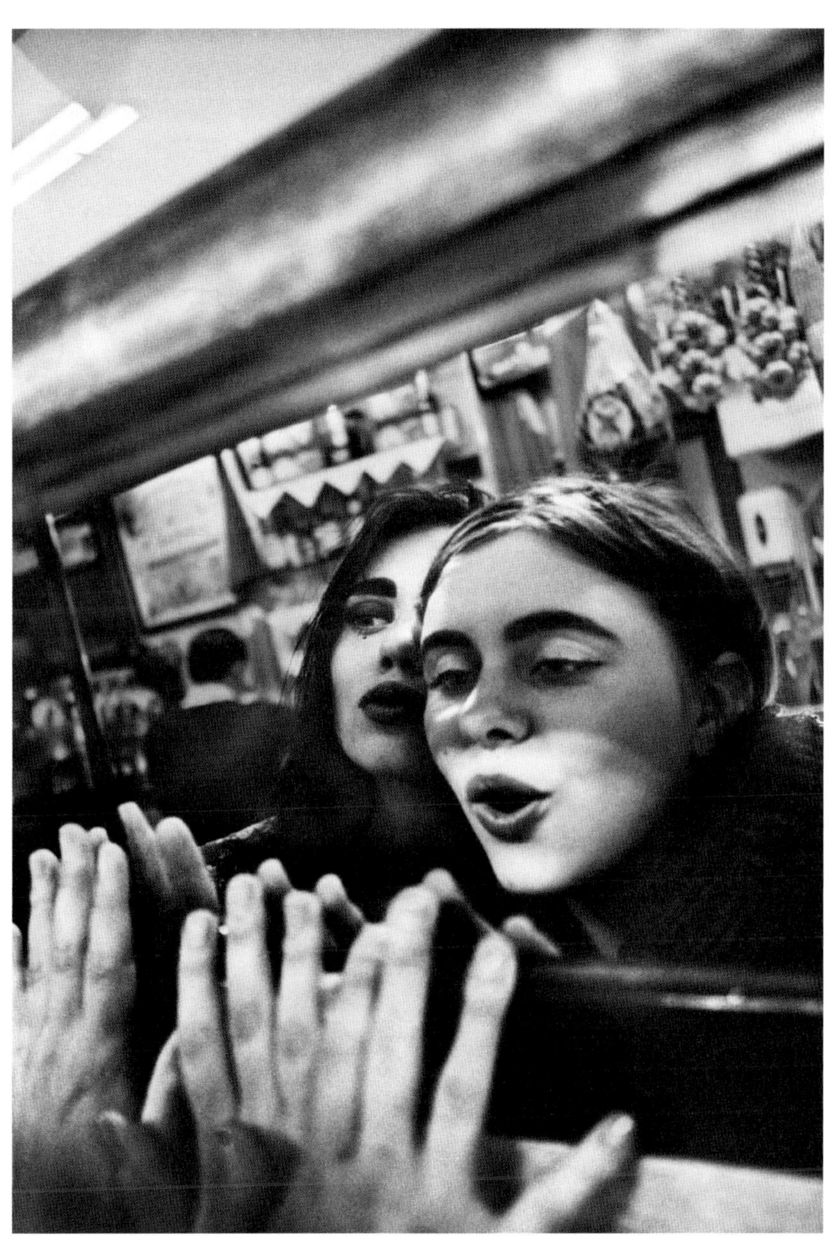

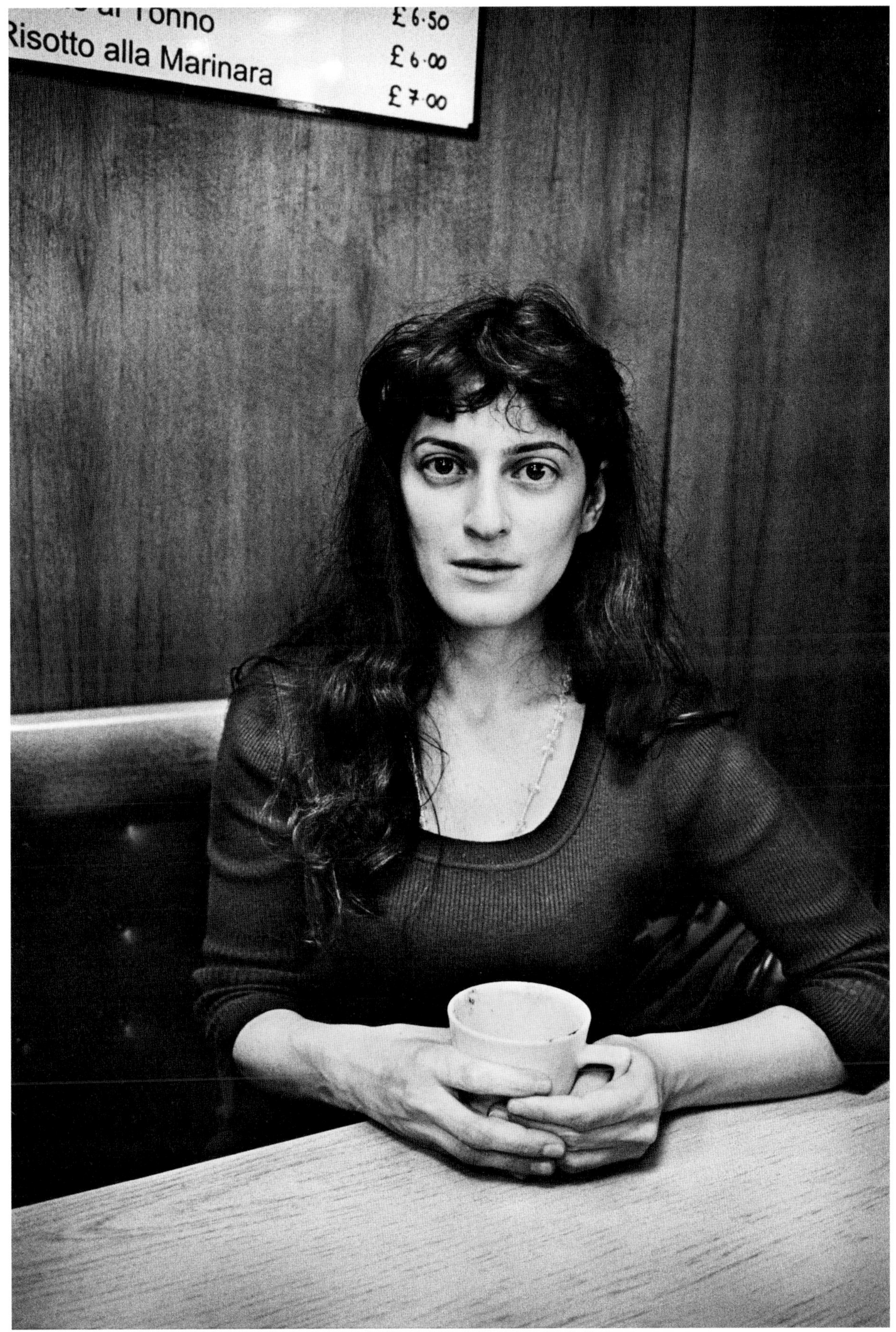
£6.50
Risotto alla Marinara
£6.00
£7.00

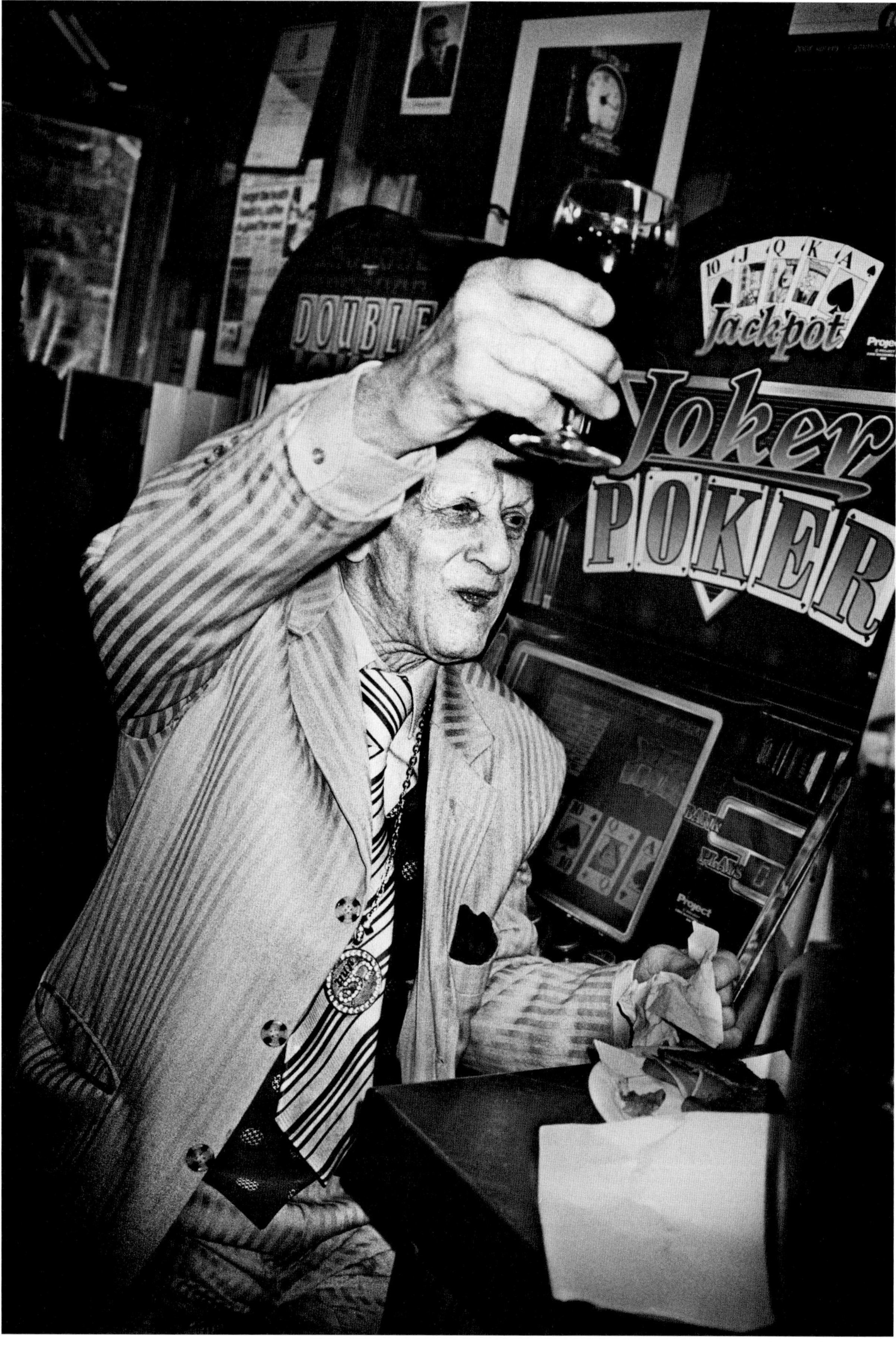
DOUBLE
10 J Q K A
Jackpot
Joker
POKER
Project

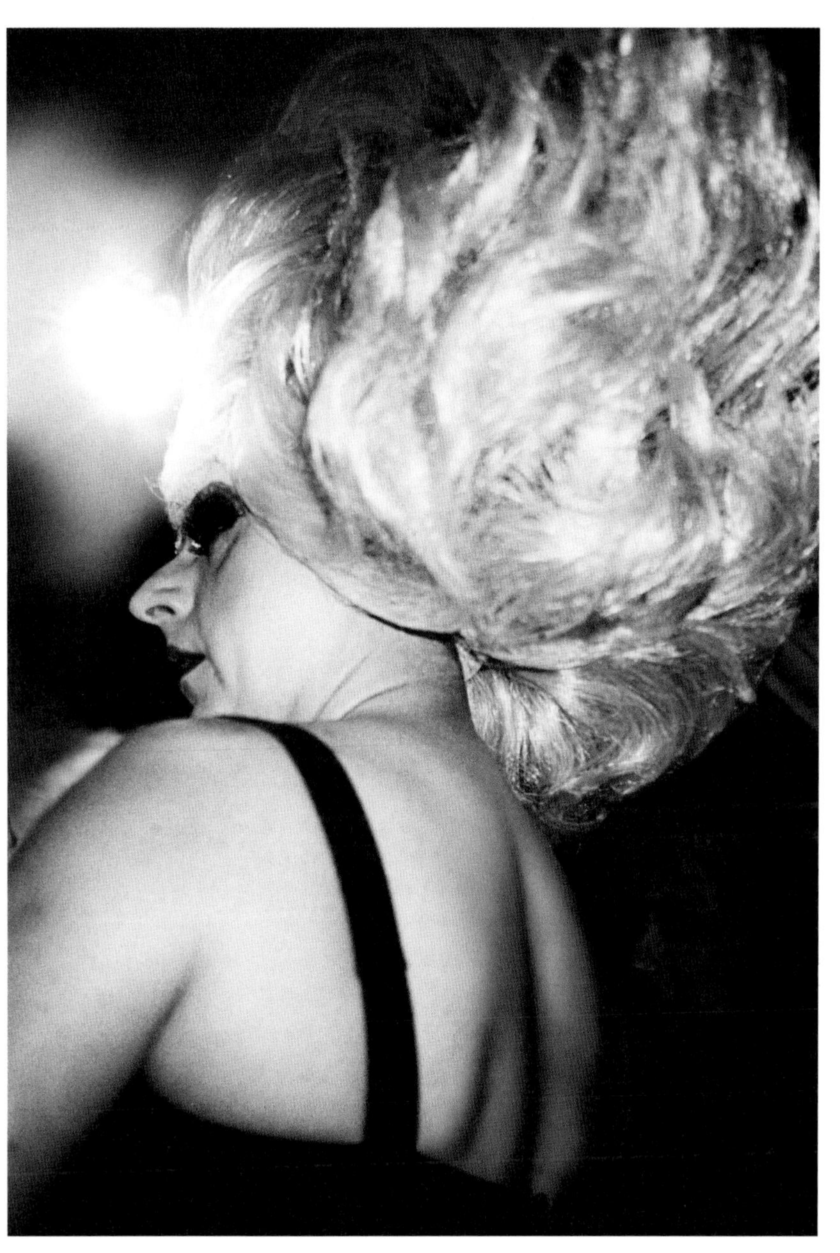

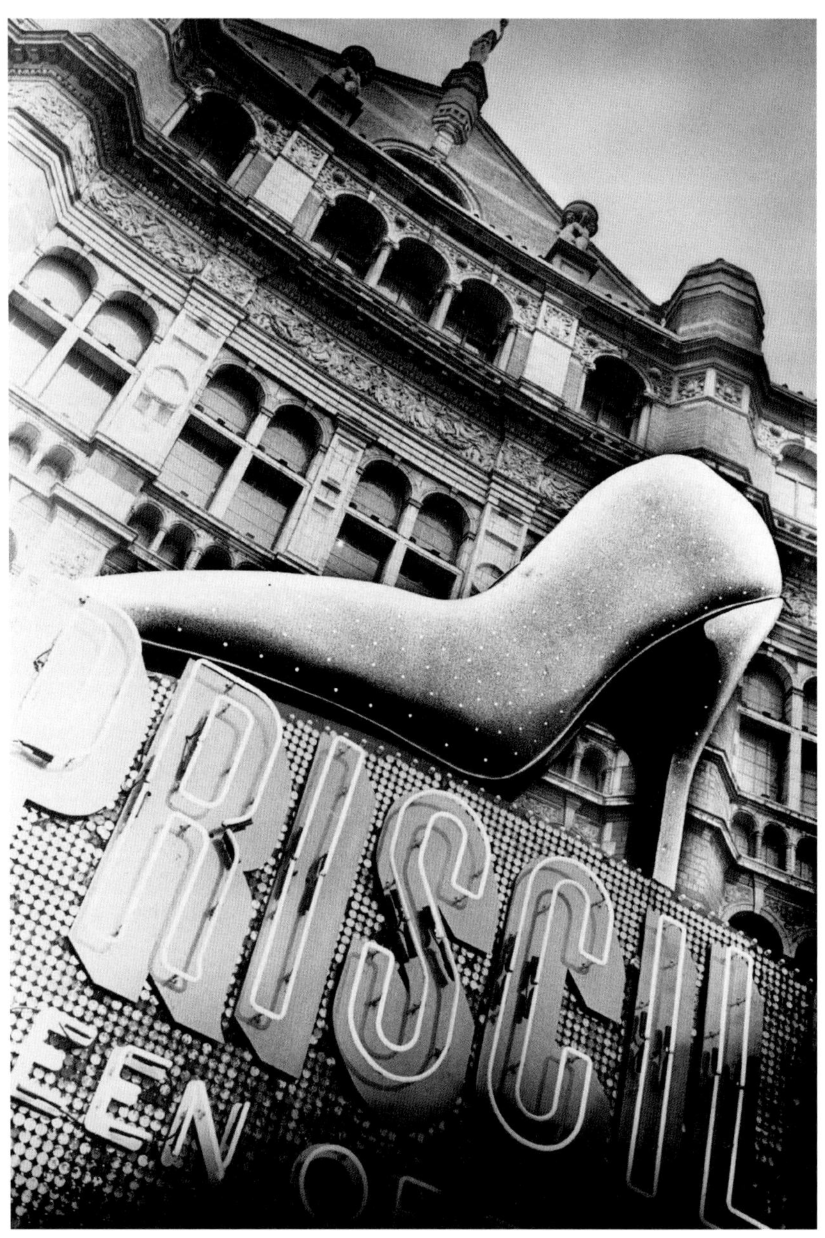
RISCIL
EN

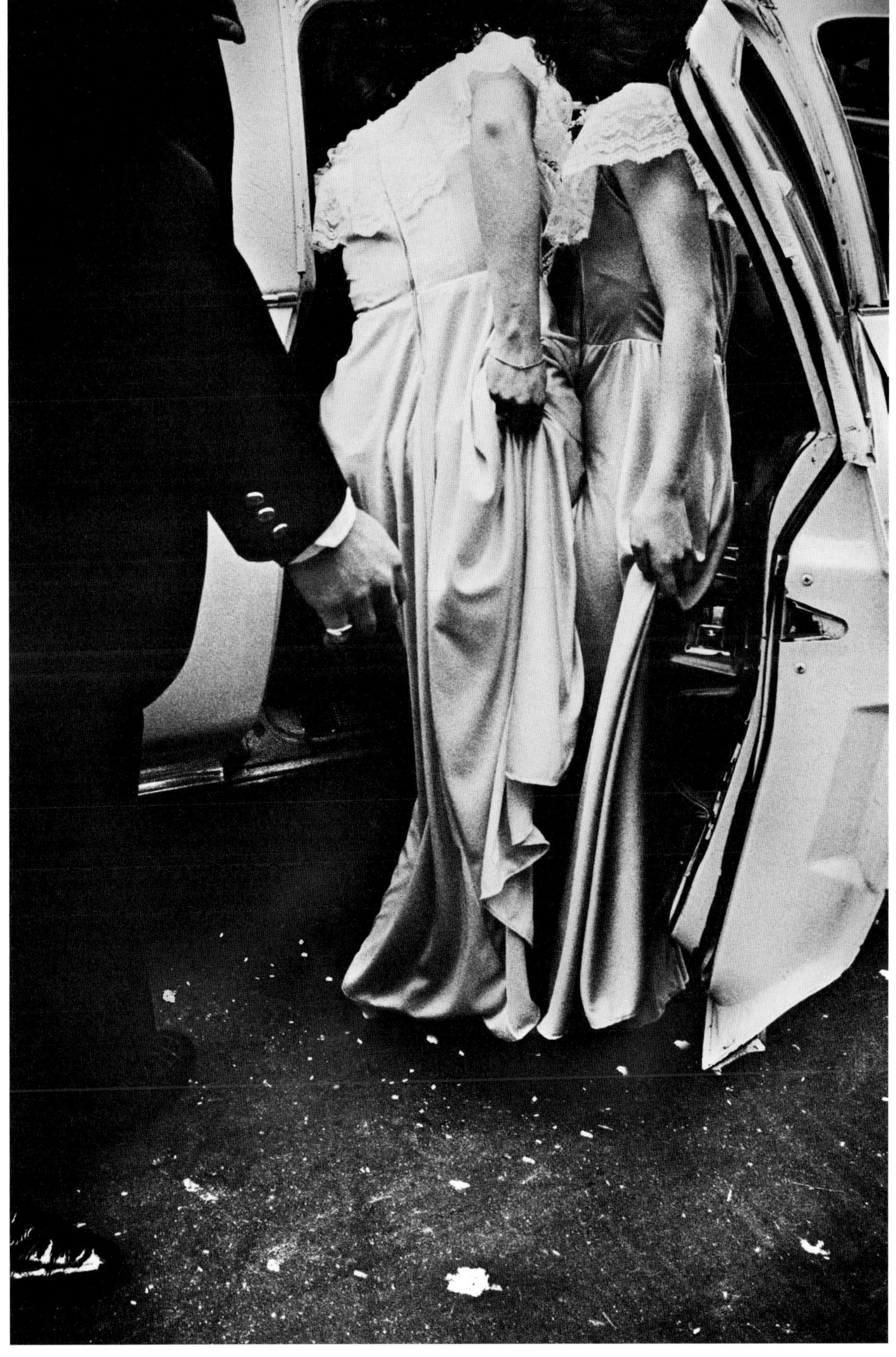

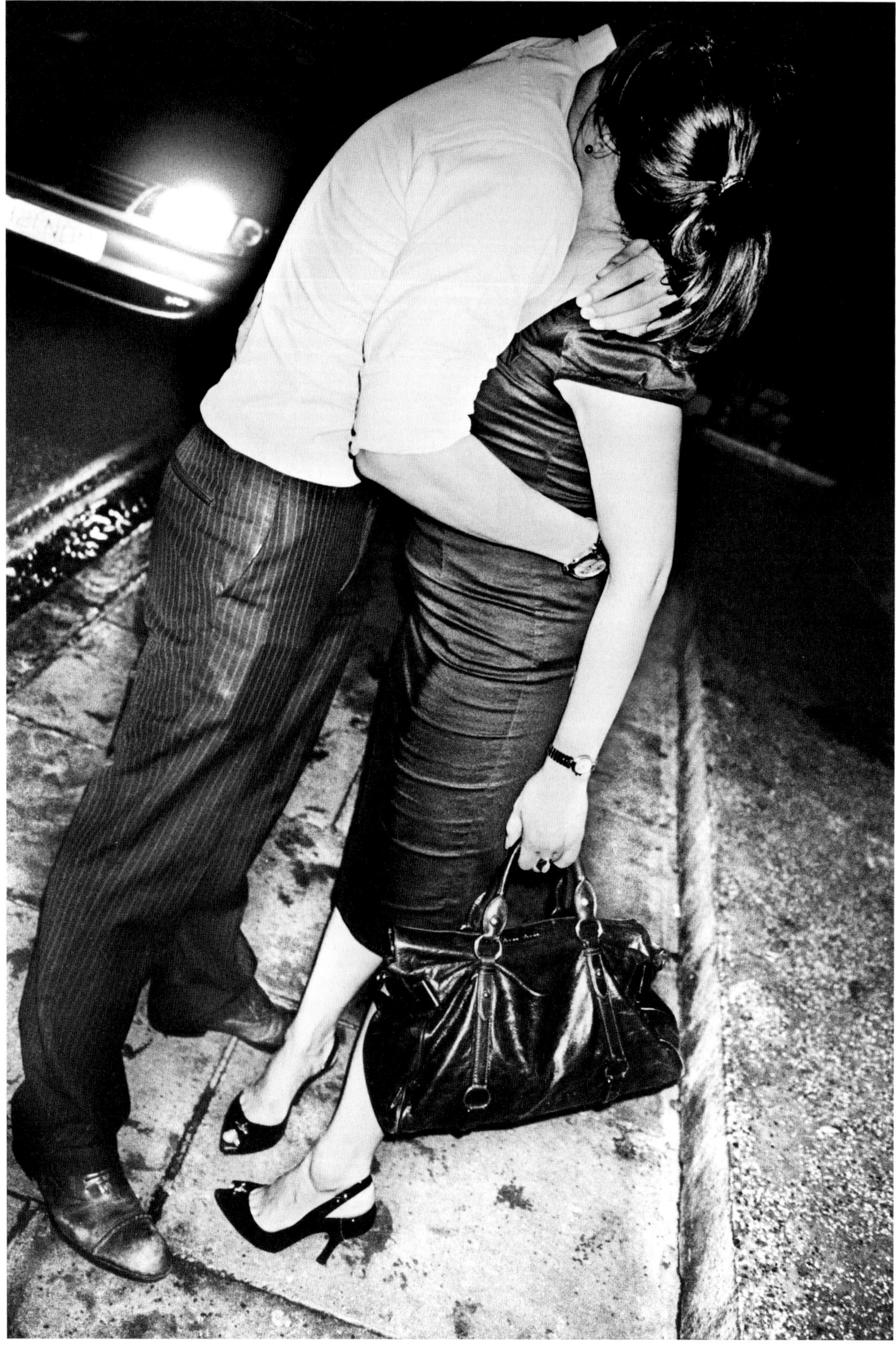

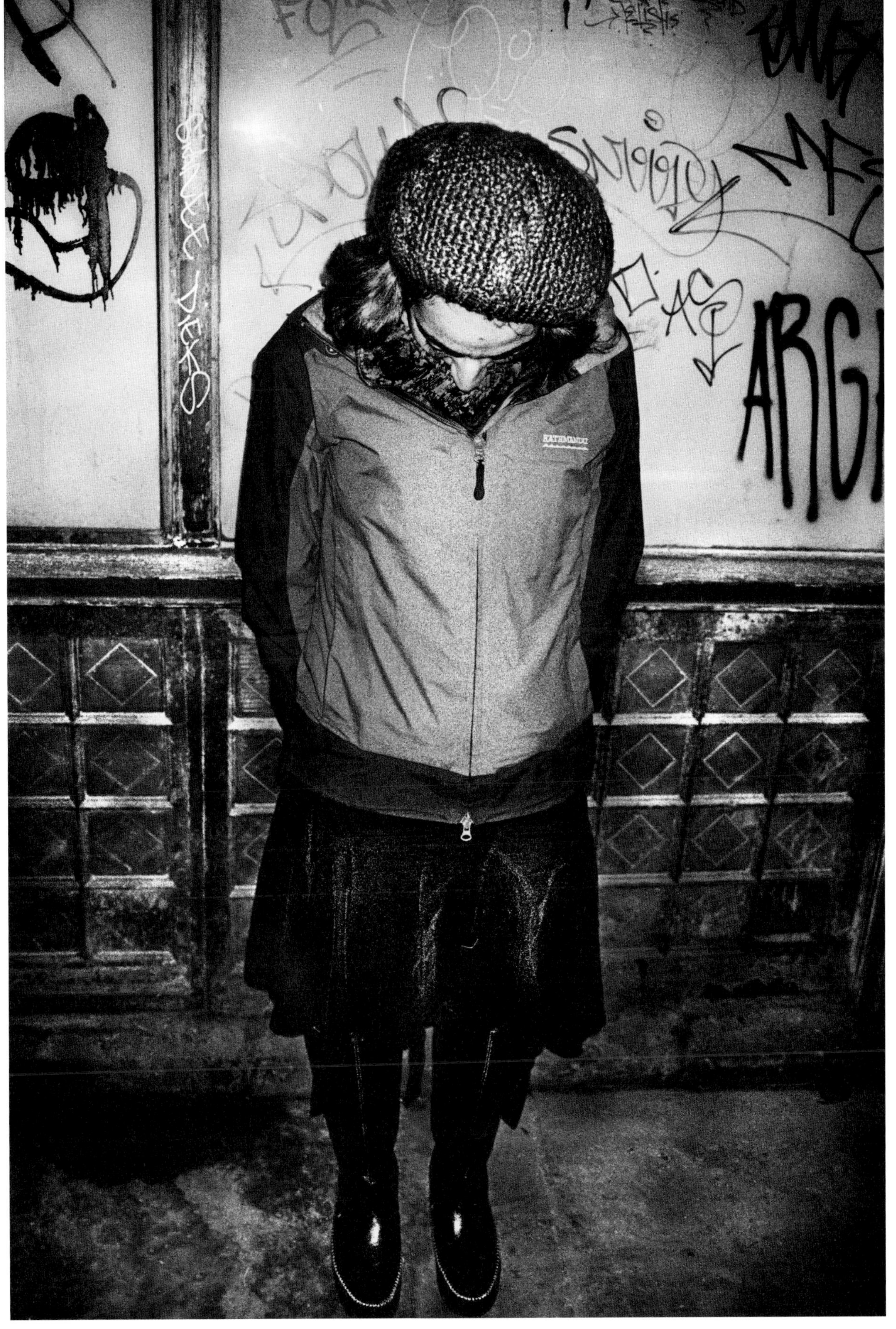
KATHMANDU
ARG

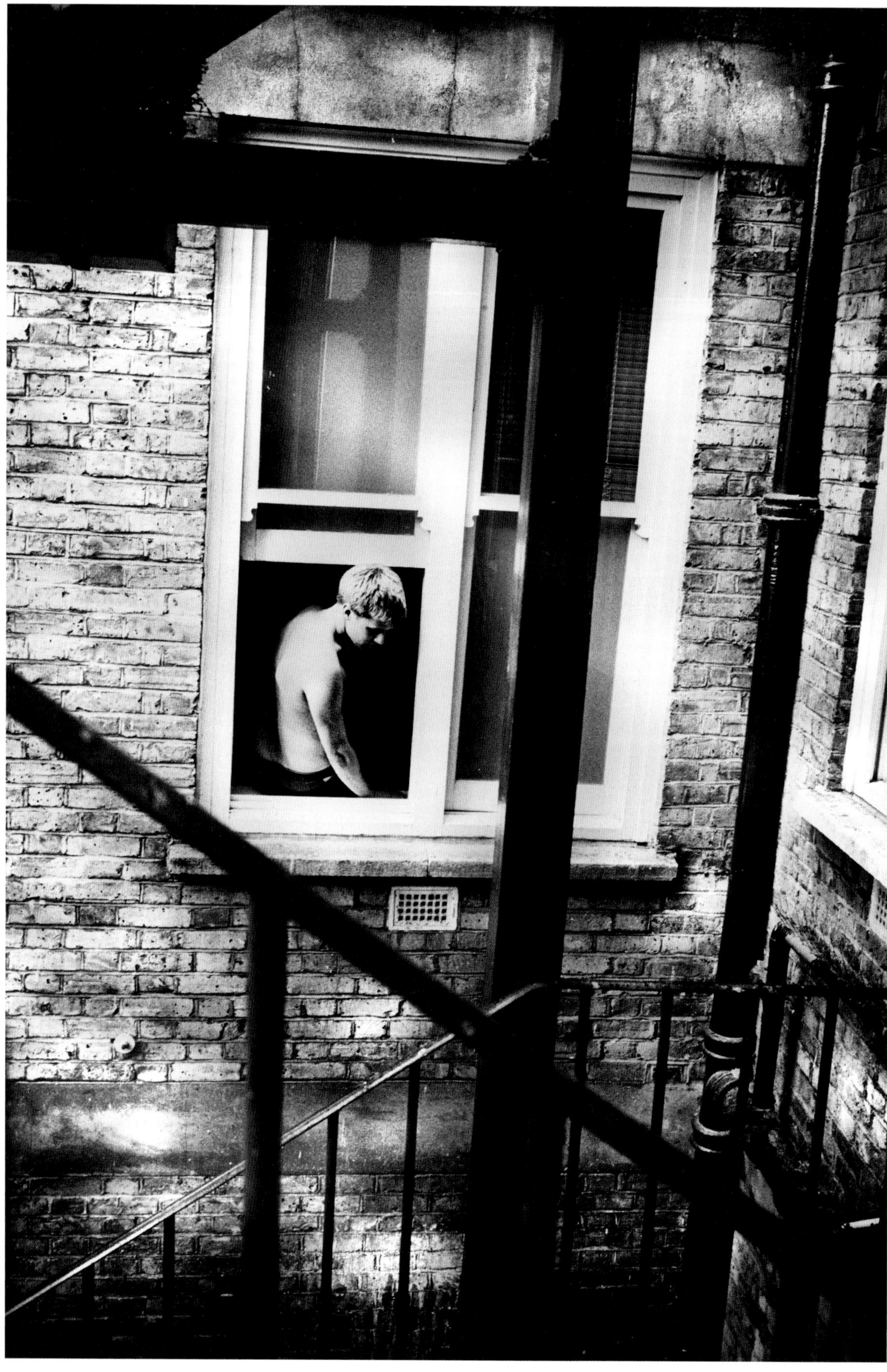

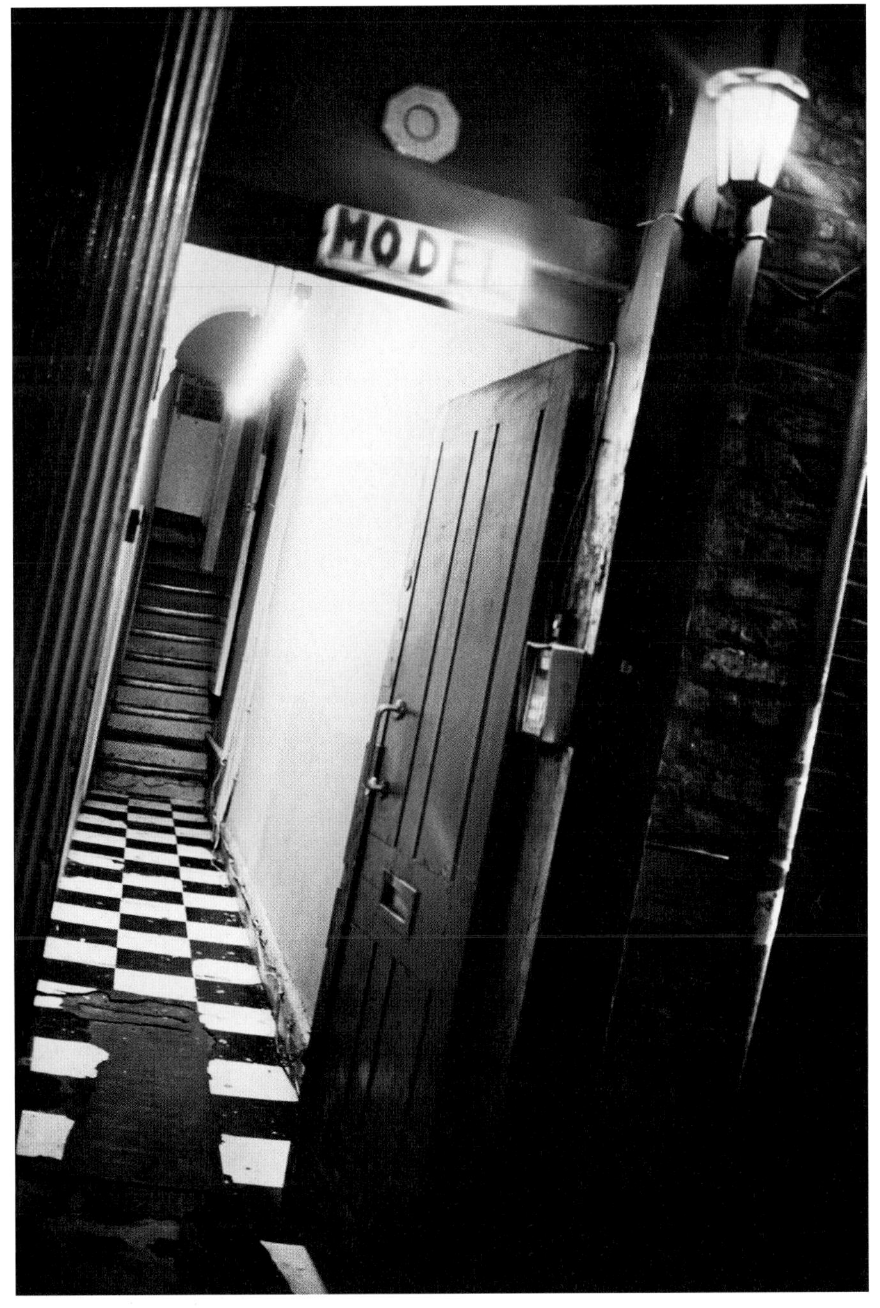
MODE

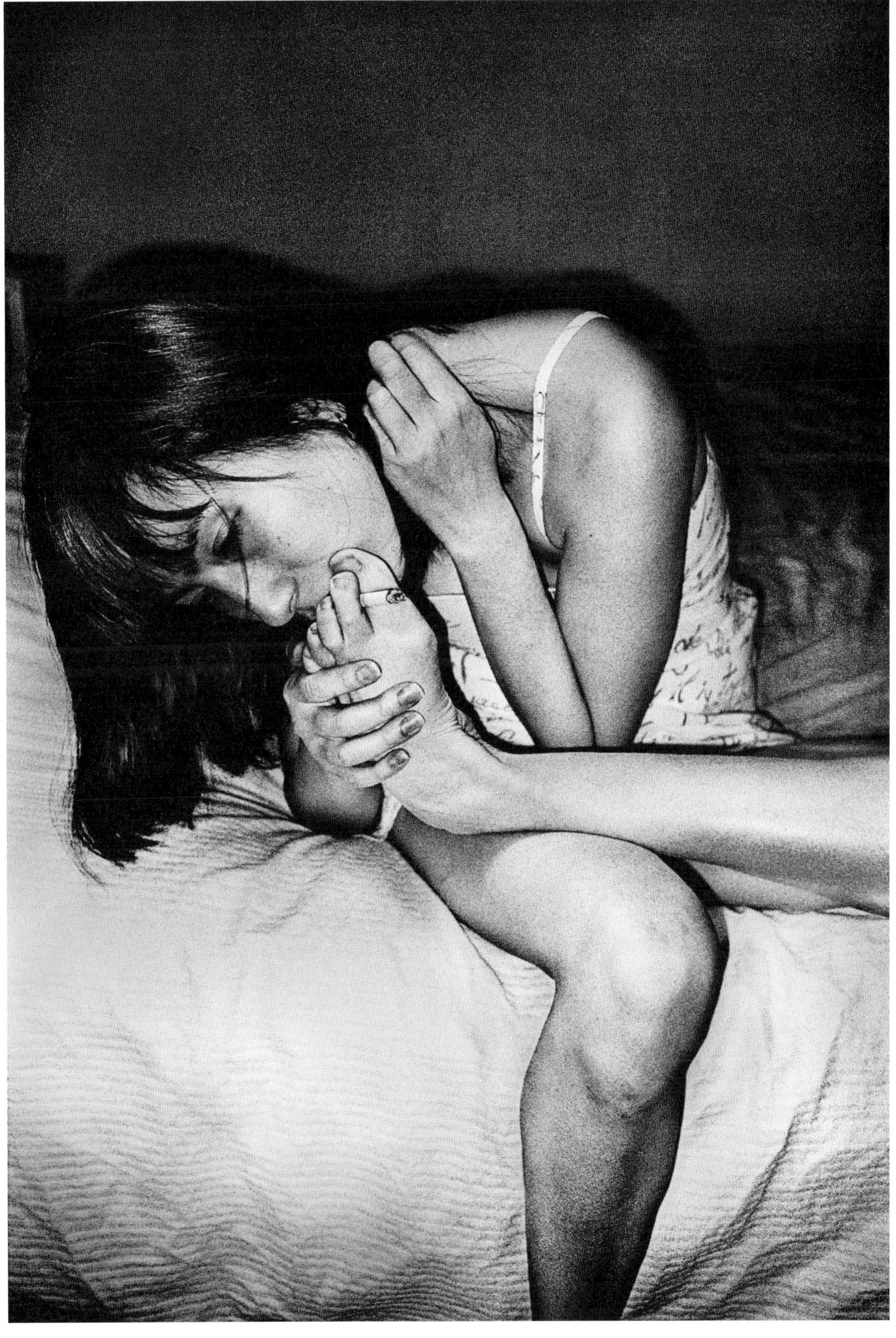

DARAGH SODEN

Daragh Soden (b. 1989) is an emerging photographer based in London. His breakthrough project, *Young Dubliners*, was made as part of his degree in documentary photography at the University of South Wales, Newport. The project captures young people in his home town at a time of national economic upheaval and won him the prestigious Photography Jury Grand Prix at the Hyères Festival of Fashion and Photography in 2017. In recent and ongoing work Soden has looked at the performance of identity, for example in *Queens and Me*, a series of portraits of drag queens in which he also appears, some of them shot in the club Heaven in London's Charing Cross.

Soden was invited by The Photographers' Gallery and the curators of *Shot in Soho* to create a contemporary portrait of Soho. *Looking for Love* is the result. In approaching the project, Soden familiarised himself with the area, initially with little agenda beyond using the camera to see what stood out to him. An interest in a particular aspect of Soho activity soon came to the fore: Soden came to see the area as a web of streets in which couples have exchanged numbers, met for first dates, kissed, argued, made up, hooked up and hailed cabs home. He set out to document this particular Soho – this constellation of corners where key moments in an endless number of relationships are mapped.

Soden often uses prose, poetry, video and installation in his practice. For *Looking for Love* he has made a short 8mm film of street, bar and club scenes, accompanied by an audio recording of an interview he conducted with an older man in which the man talks about love and relationships. Soden met the interviewee and his partner at Bearaoke, a Sunday-evening karaoke session aimed at bears at the Kings Arms on Poland Street, where they are regulars. For the piece he has also included screenshots from the apps Tinder and Grindr, captured while wandering Soho, the images chosen because their subjects maintain a degree of anonymity. They feature people in costume or are pictures of bodies that prioritise showing a torso over a face – modern love in all its complex guises. Soden has teamed these images with more traditional documentary shots of Soho people and scenes.

Looking for Love examines how we search, perform and relate in the pursuit of love, sex, romance and myriad other forms of interaction. The series spans dusk, the night hours and into daybreak; several of the quieter pictures were made at the end of the night, when, as Soden says, 'the drink is wearing off – you're thinking clearly but your guard is still down, there's no barrier to emotion. It might be the same after sex, as you lie there vulnerable, thinking about the true nature of love and loneliness.'[23] Beyond its human subjects, in *Looking for Love* Soho itself becomes a living space; a place charged with countless personal stories of discovery and connection, disappointments and thrills.

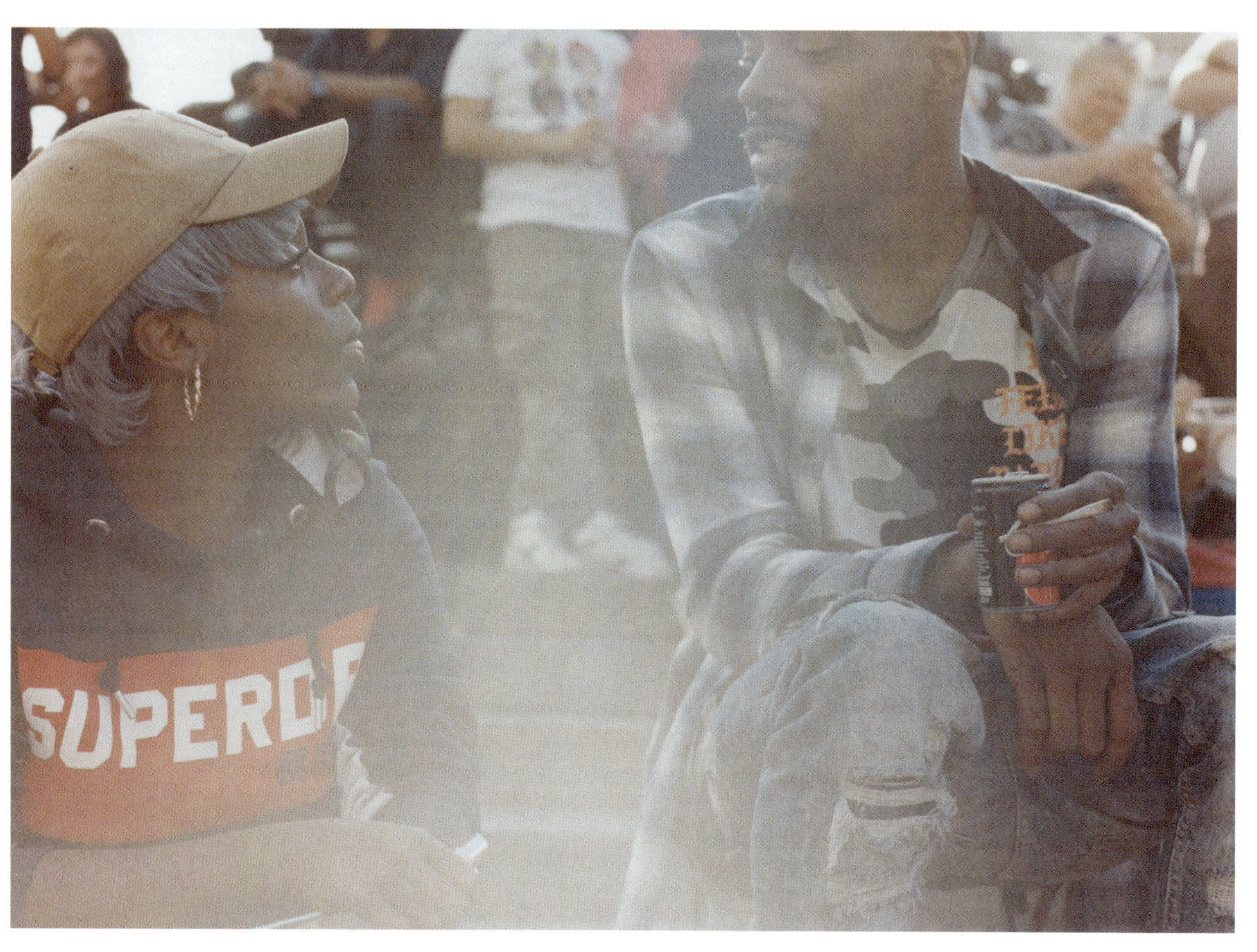

 All images are from the series *Looking for Love*, 2019, commissioned by The Photographers' Gallery.

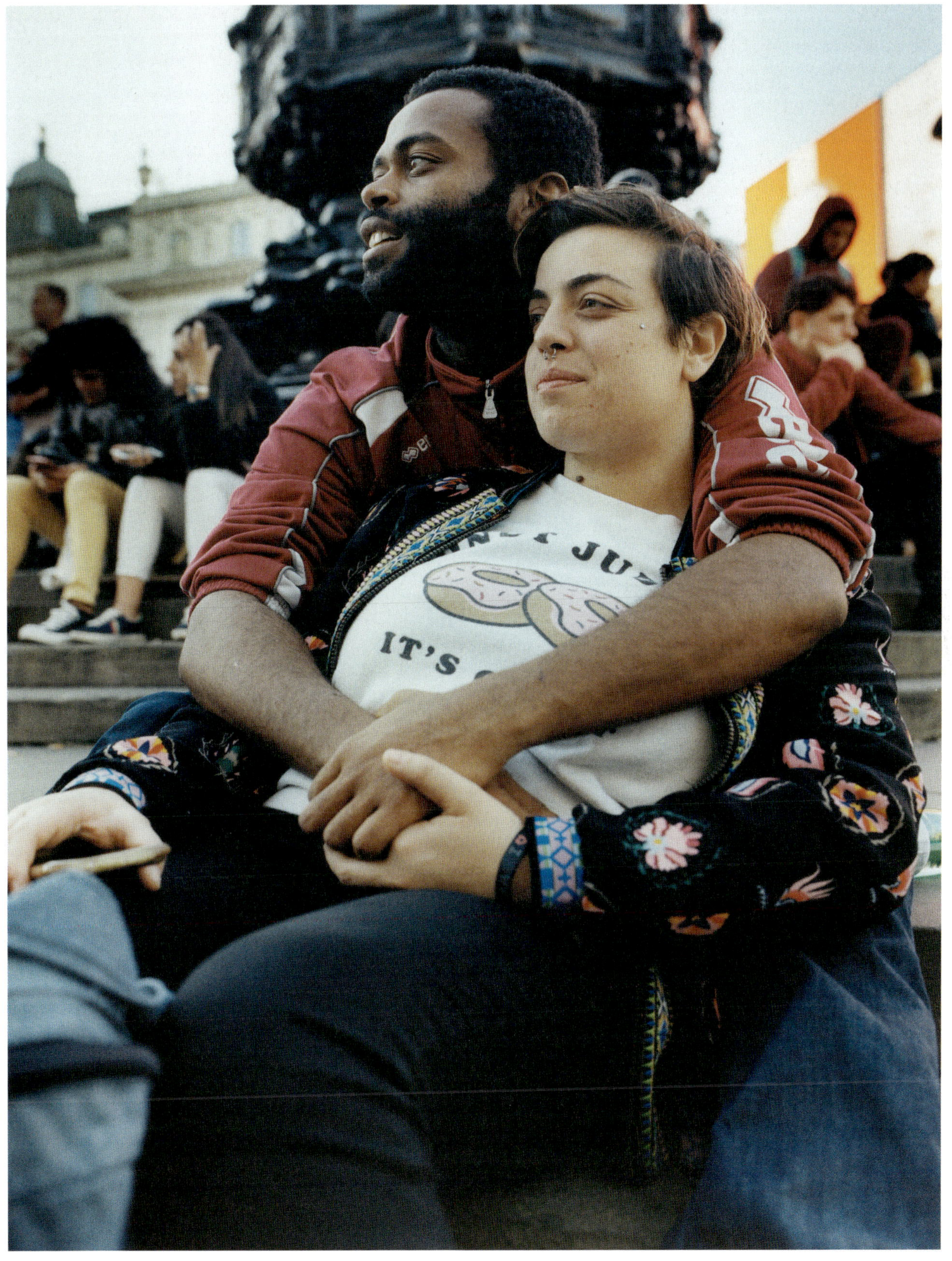
IT'S

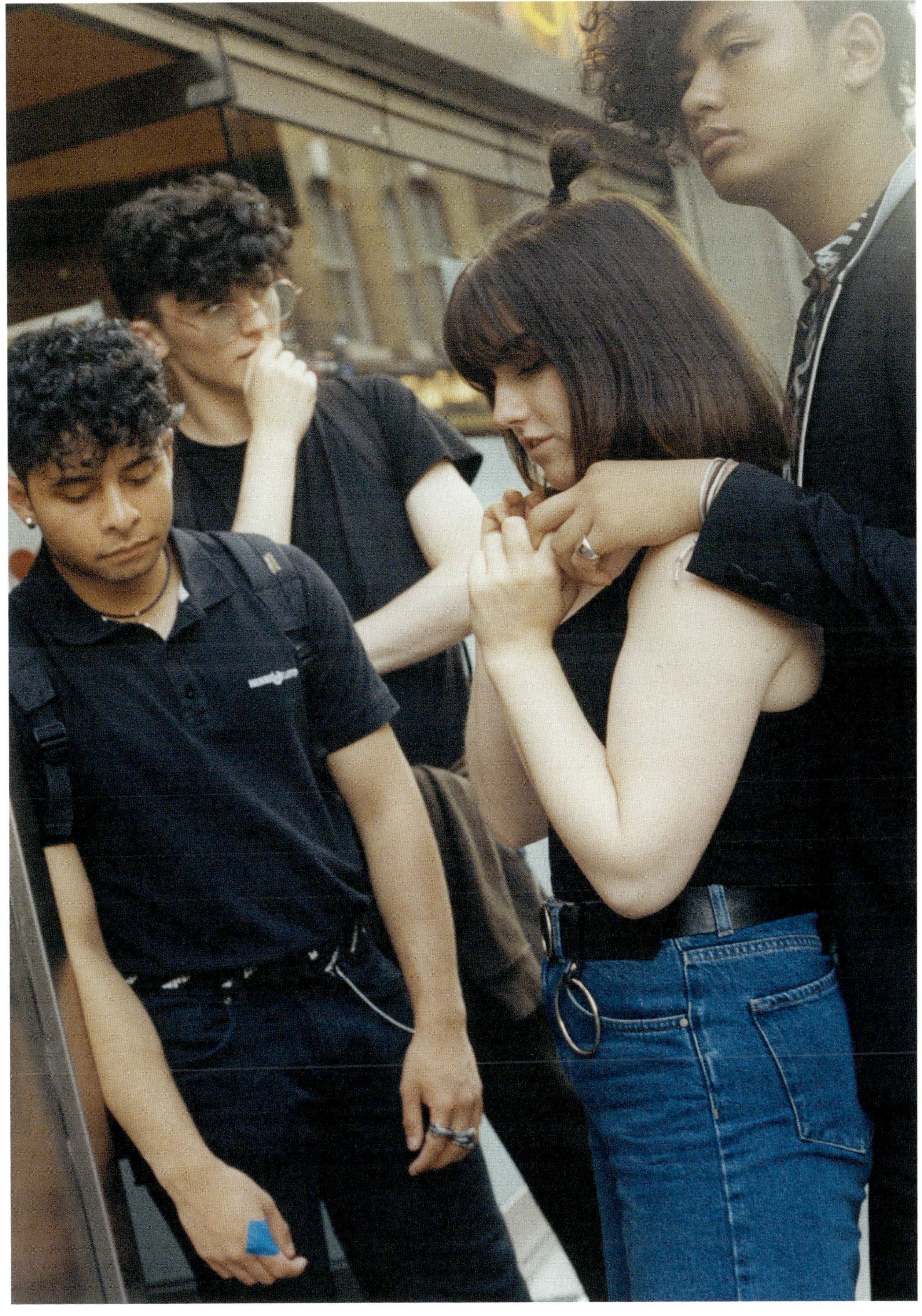

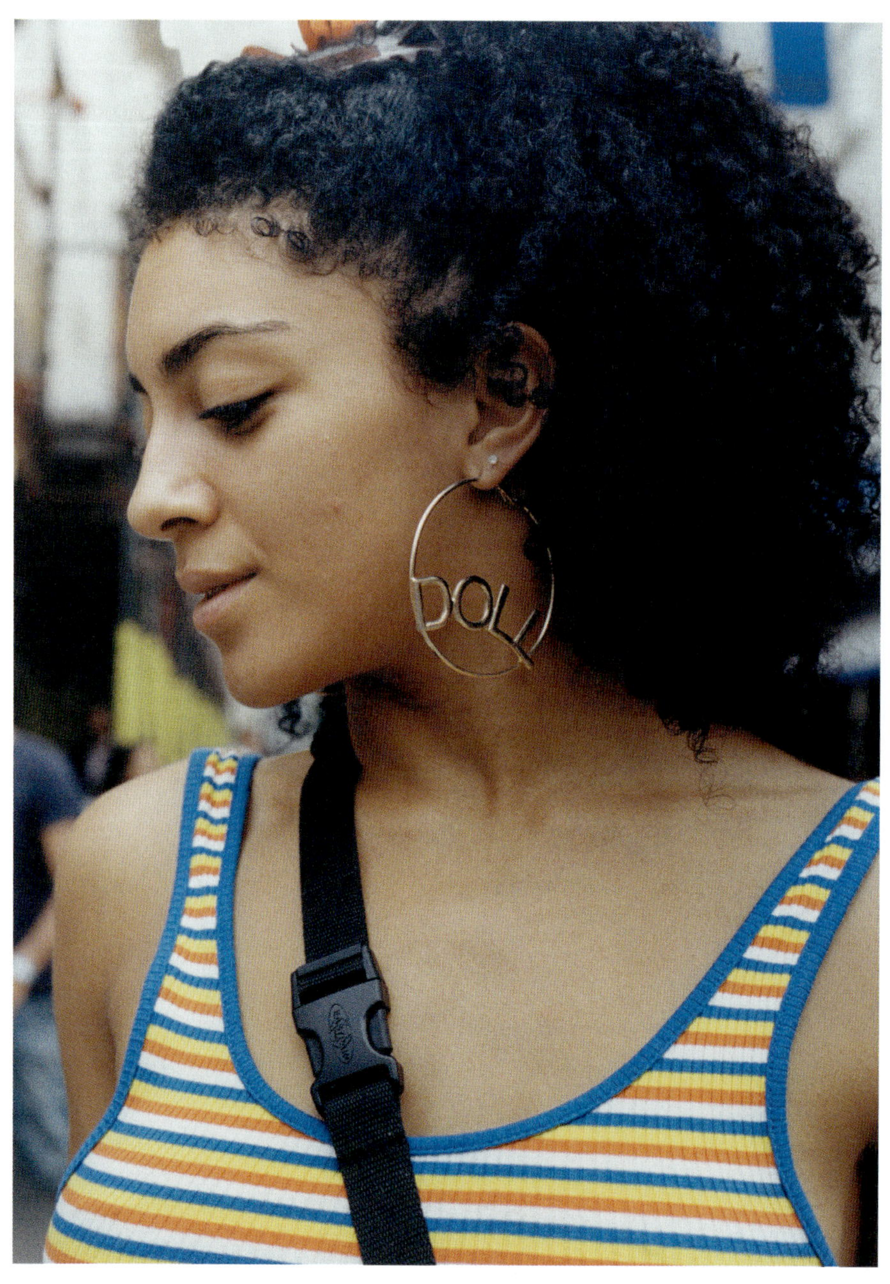
DOLL

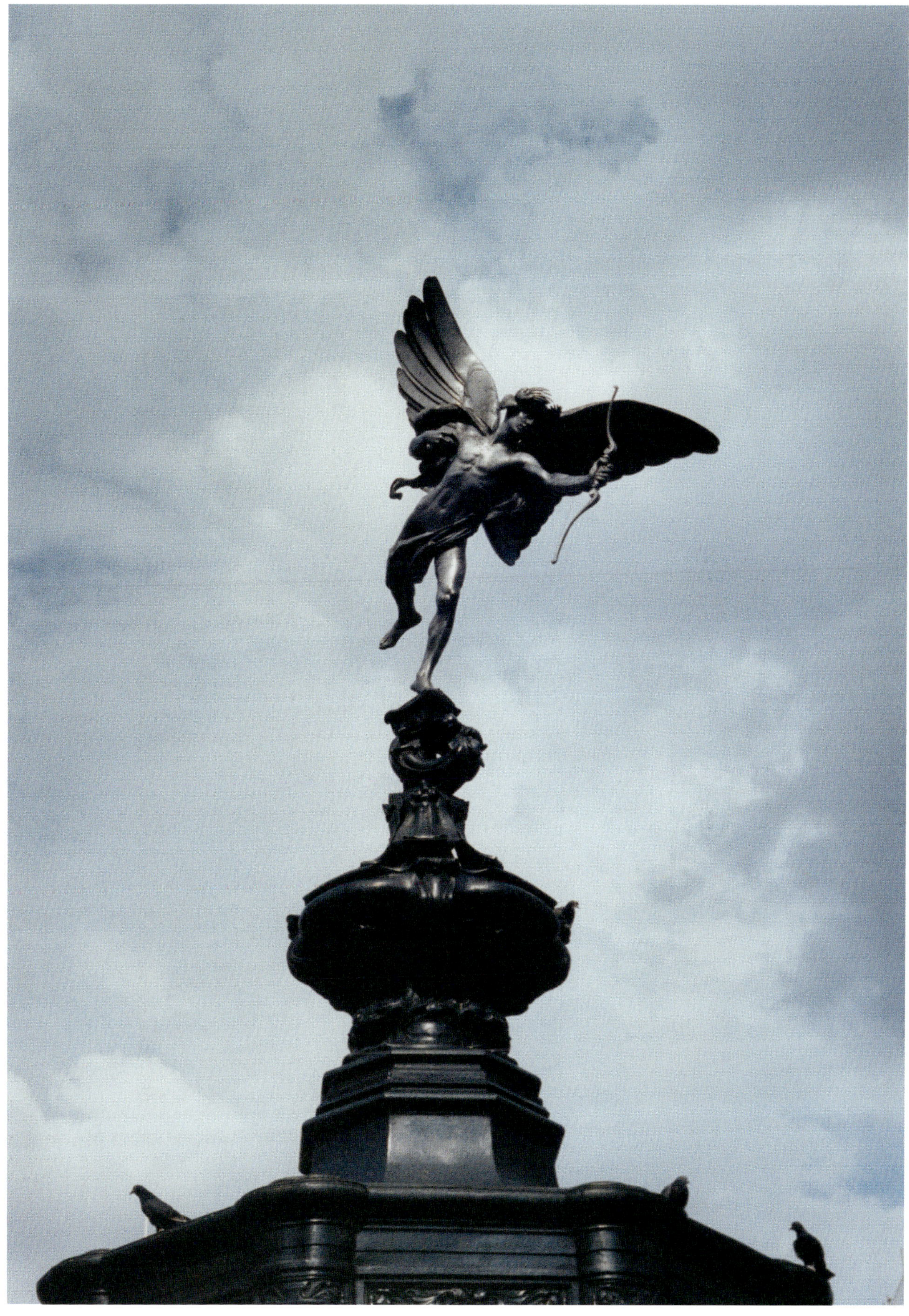

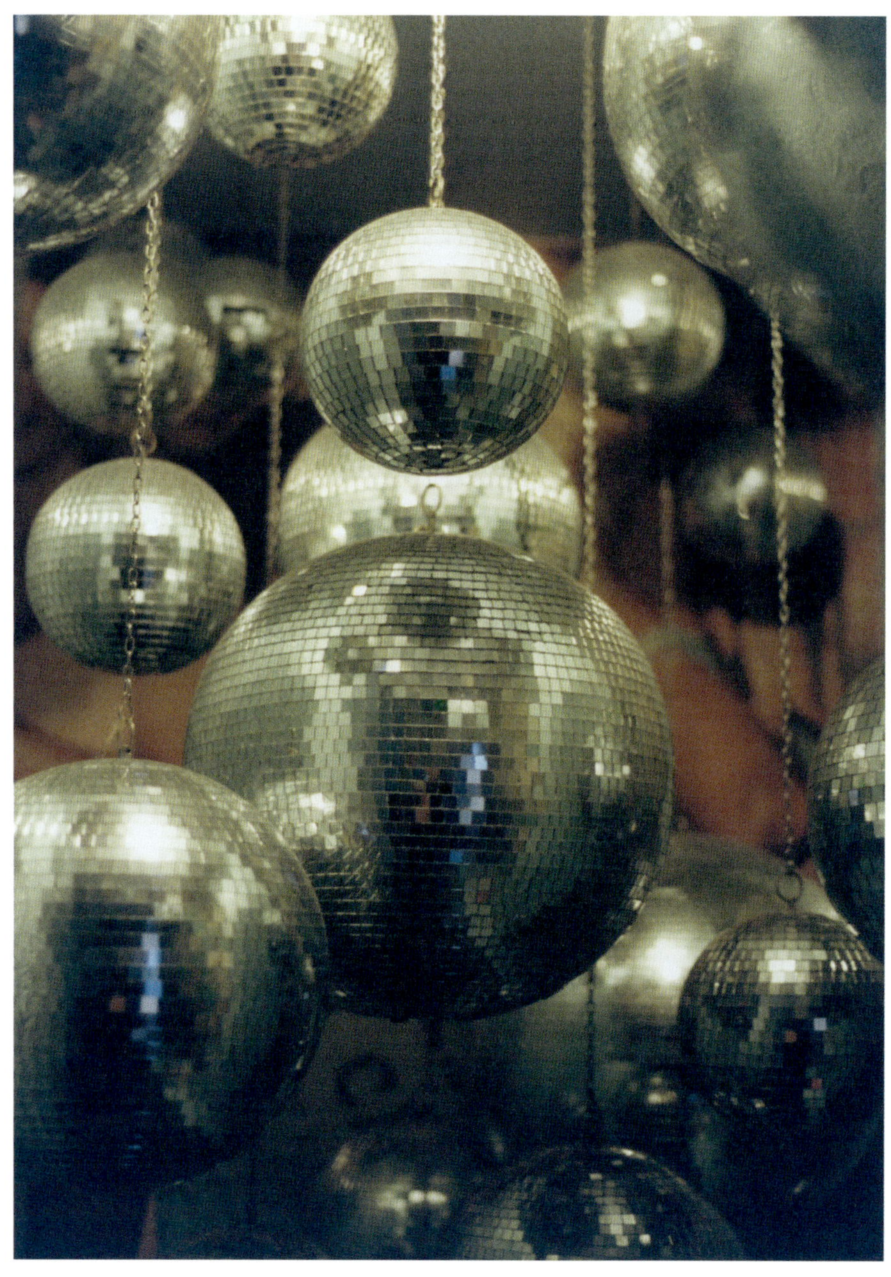

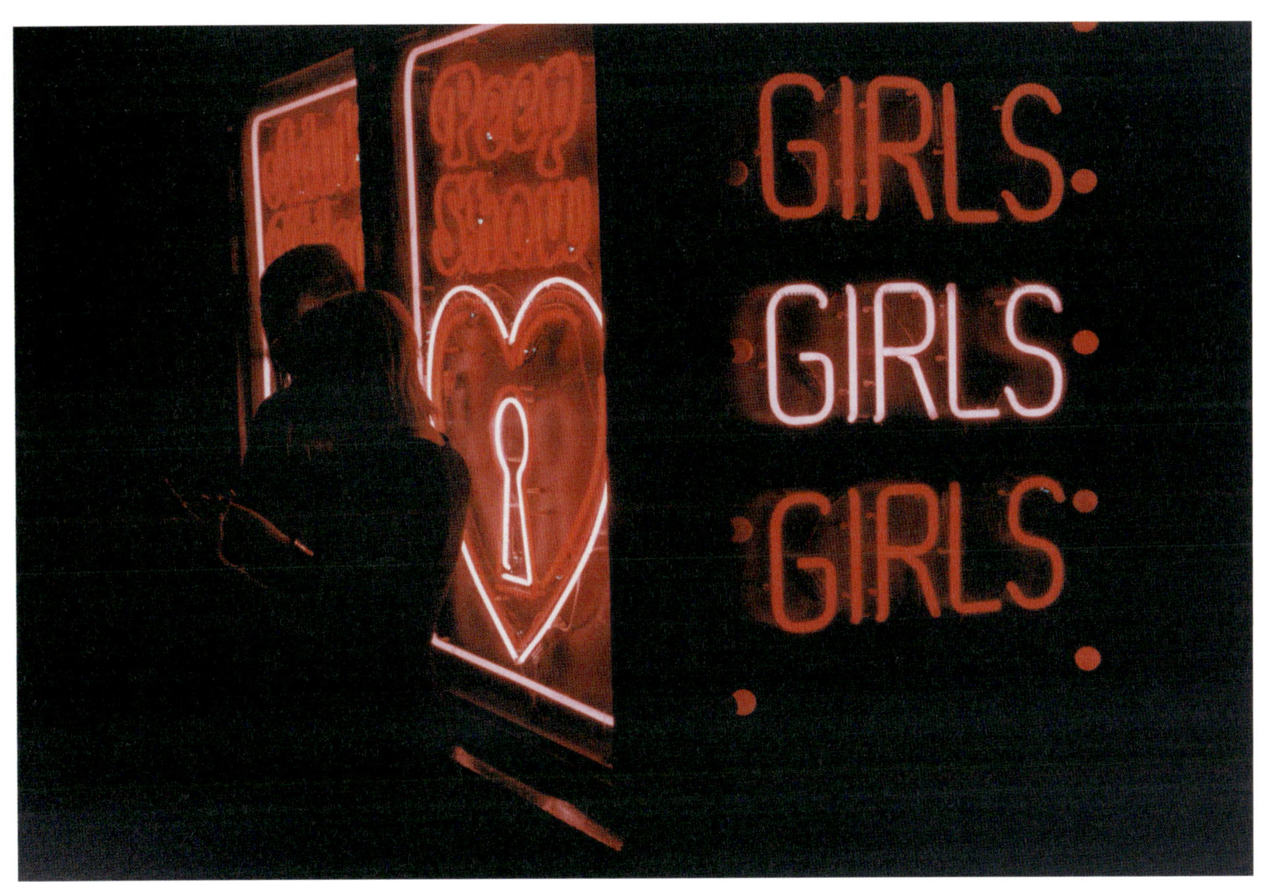
Peep
Show
GIRLS
GIRLS
GIRLS

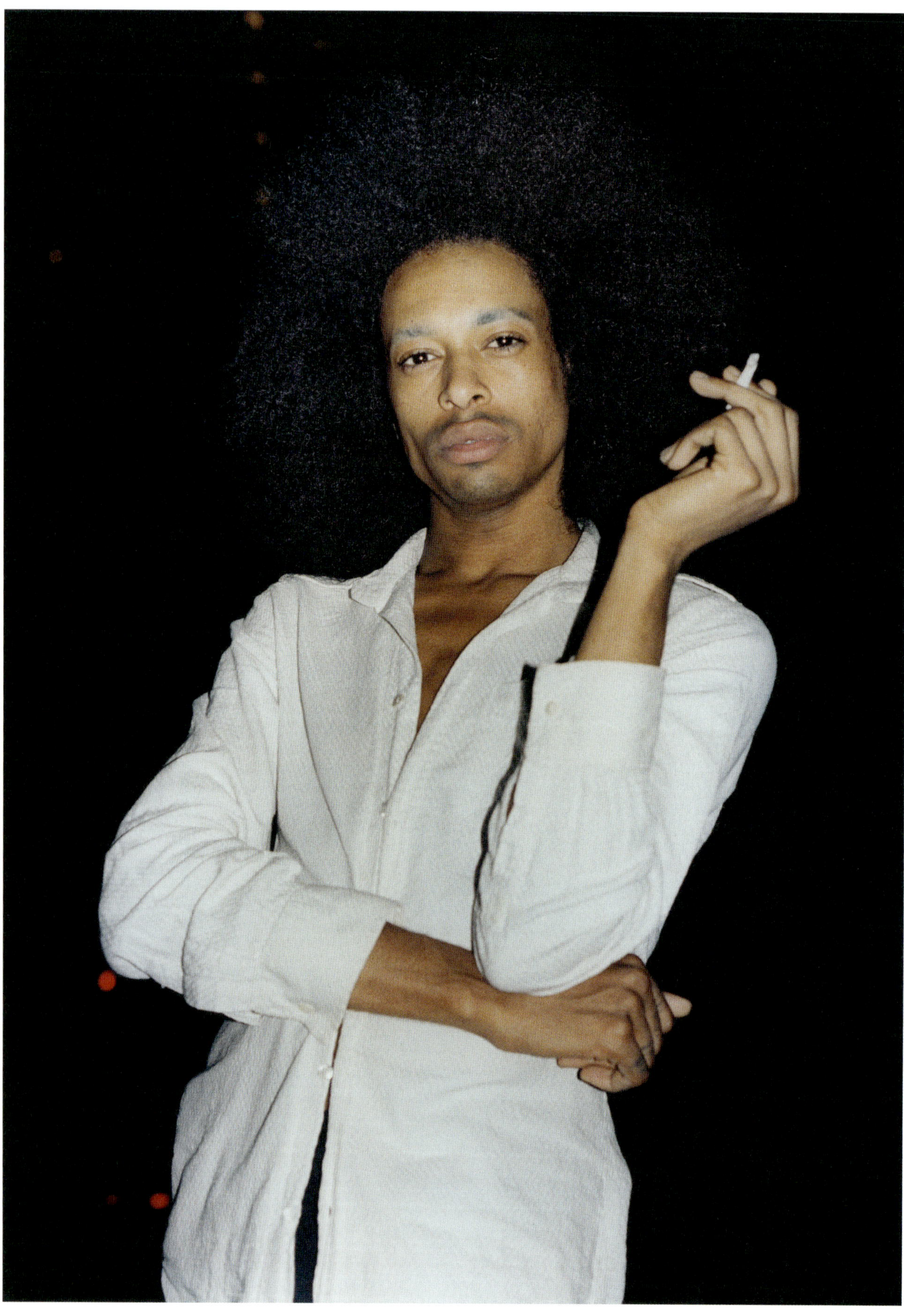

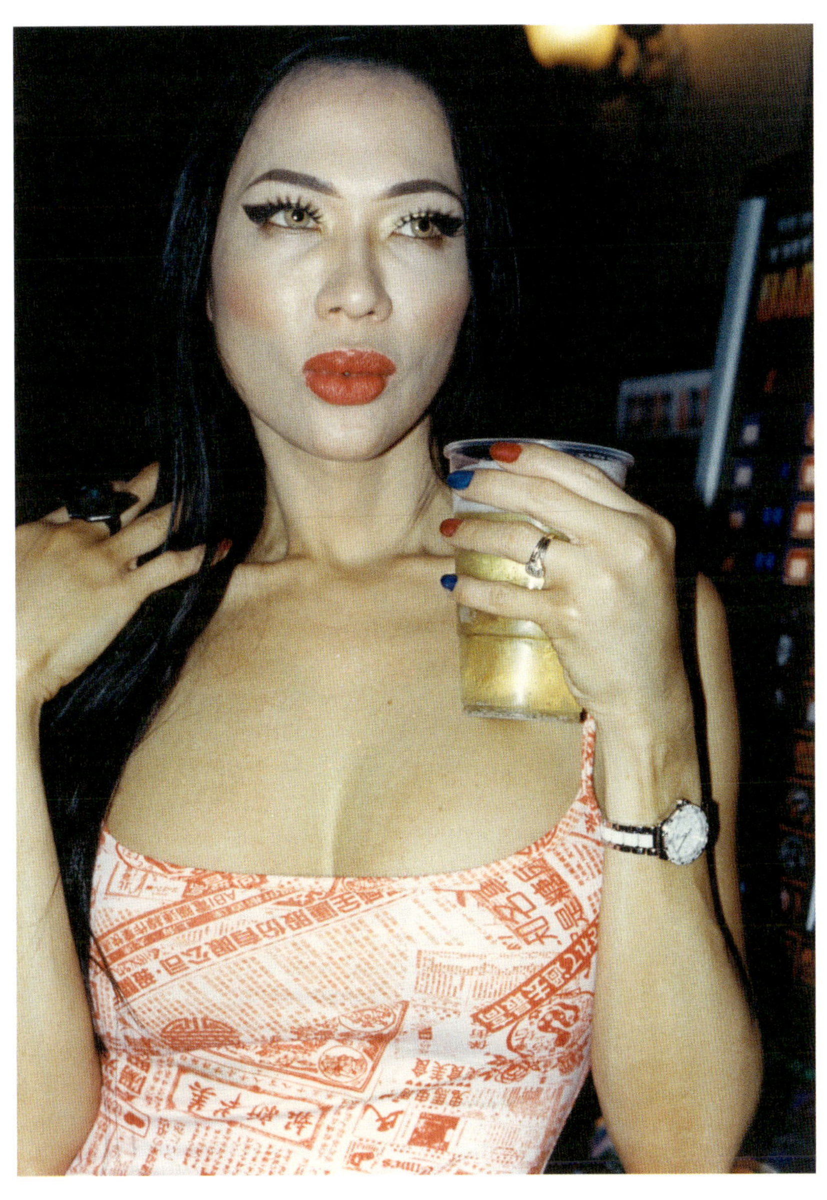

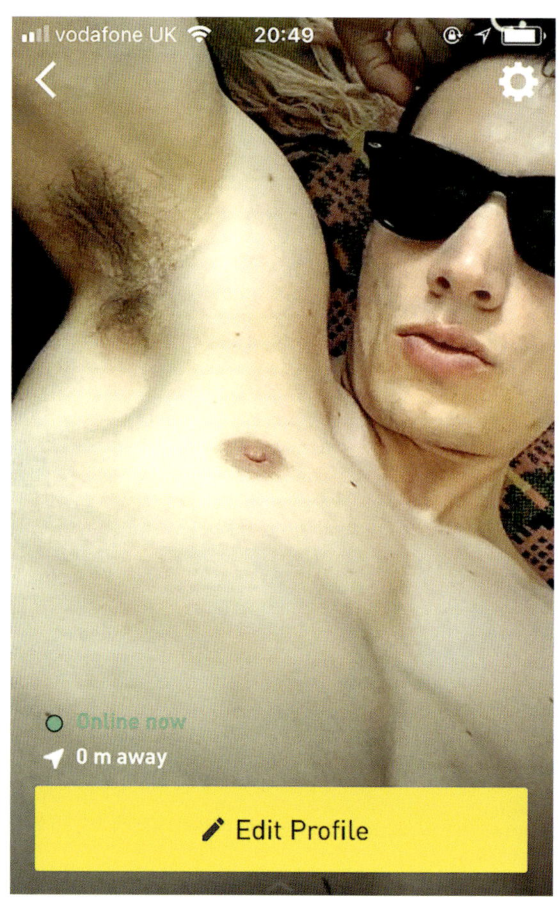
vodafone UK
20:49
Online now
0 m away
Edit Profile

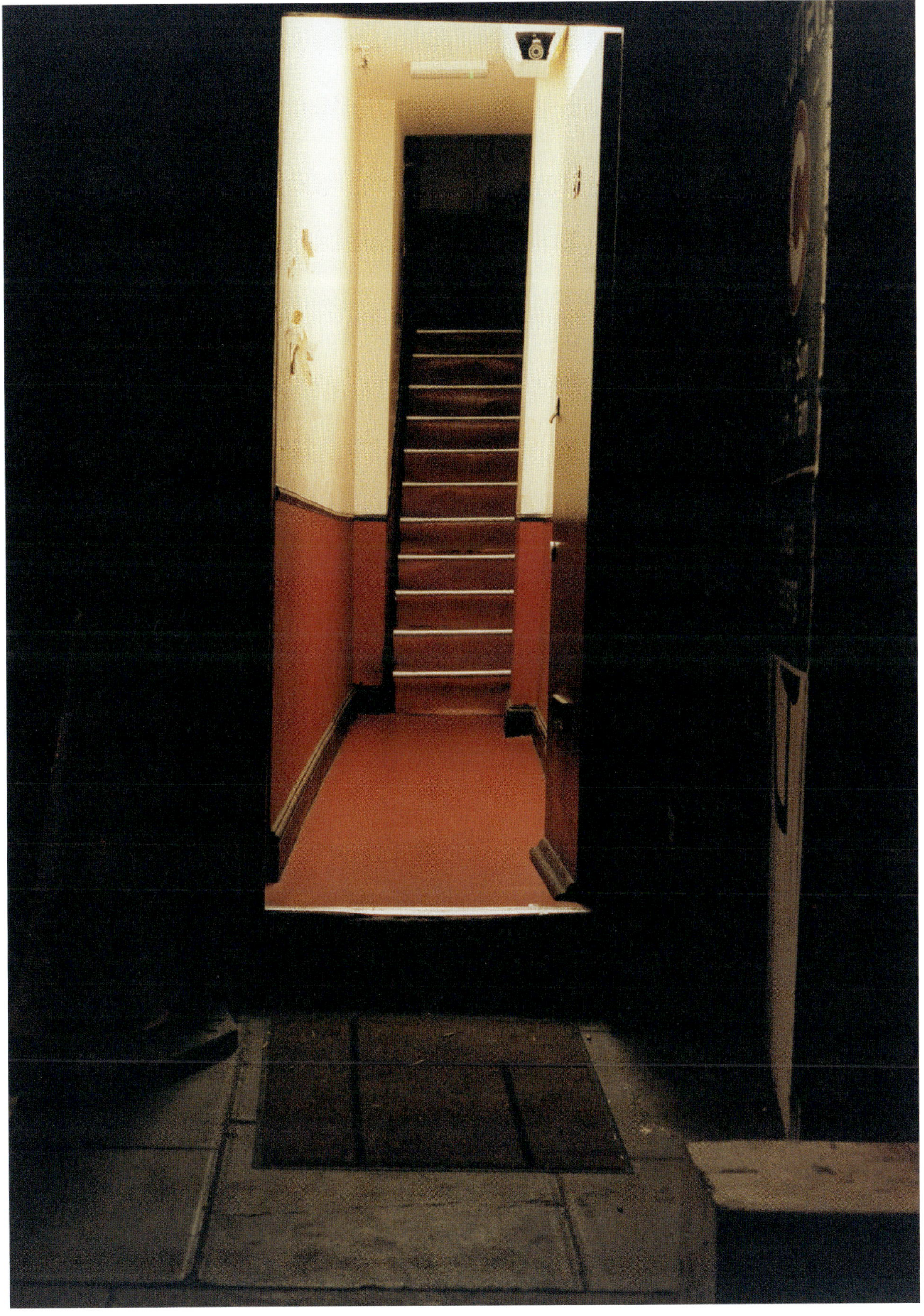

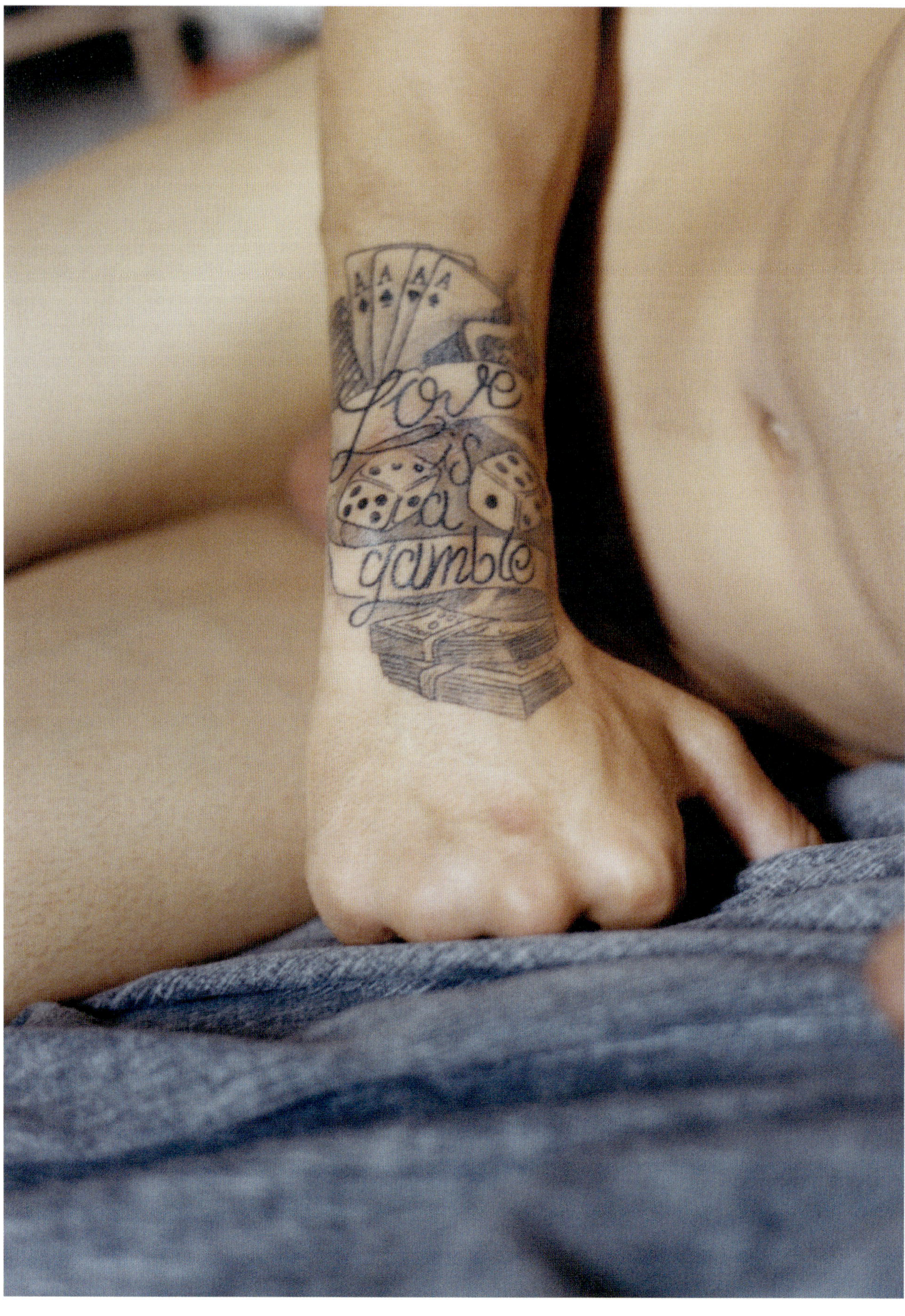
Love is a gamble

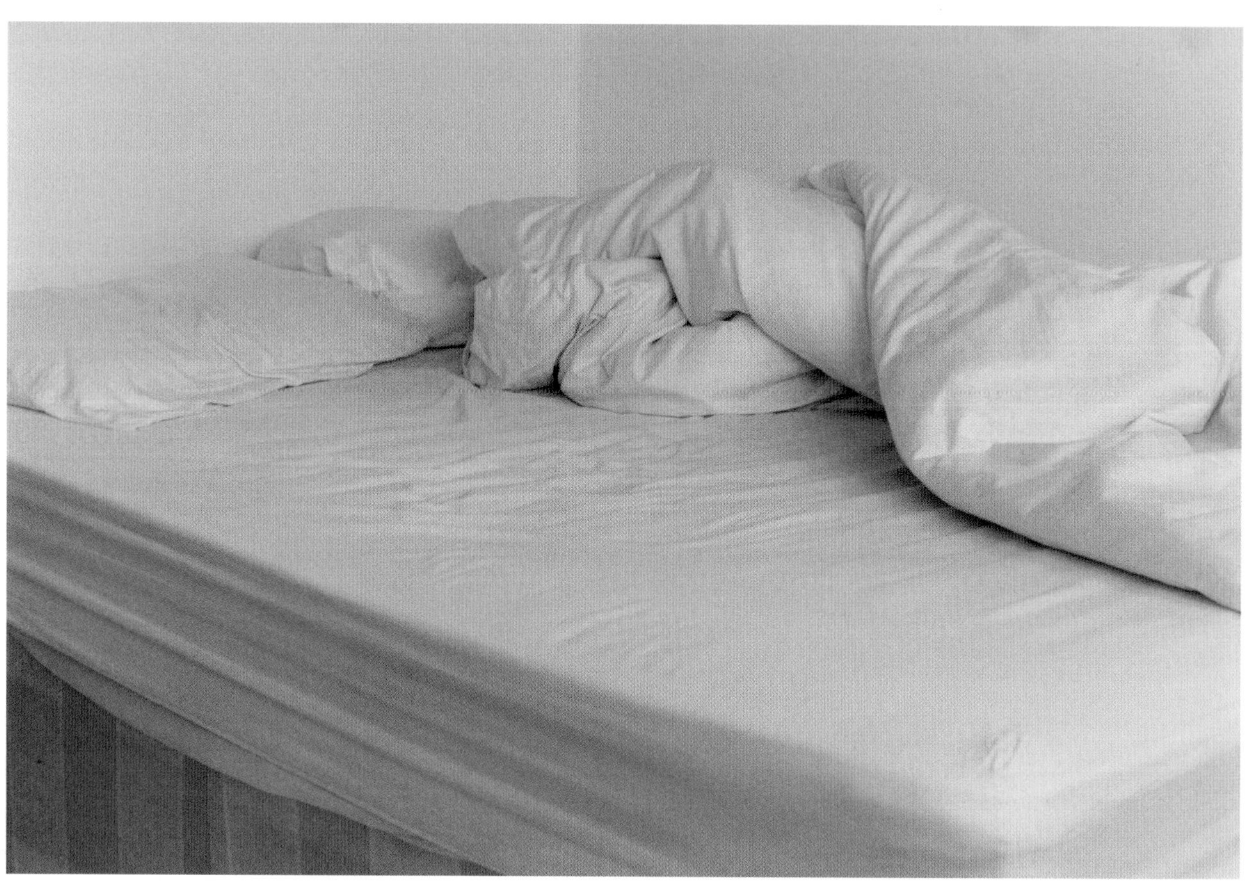

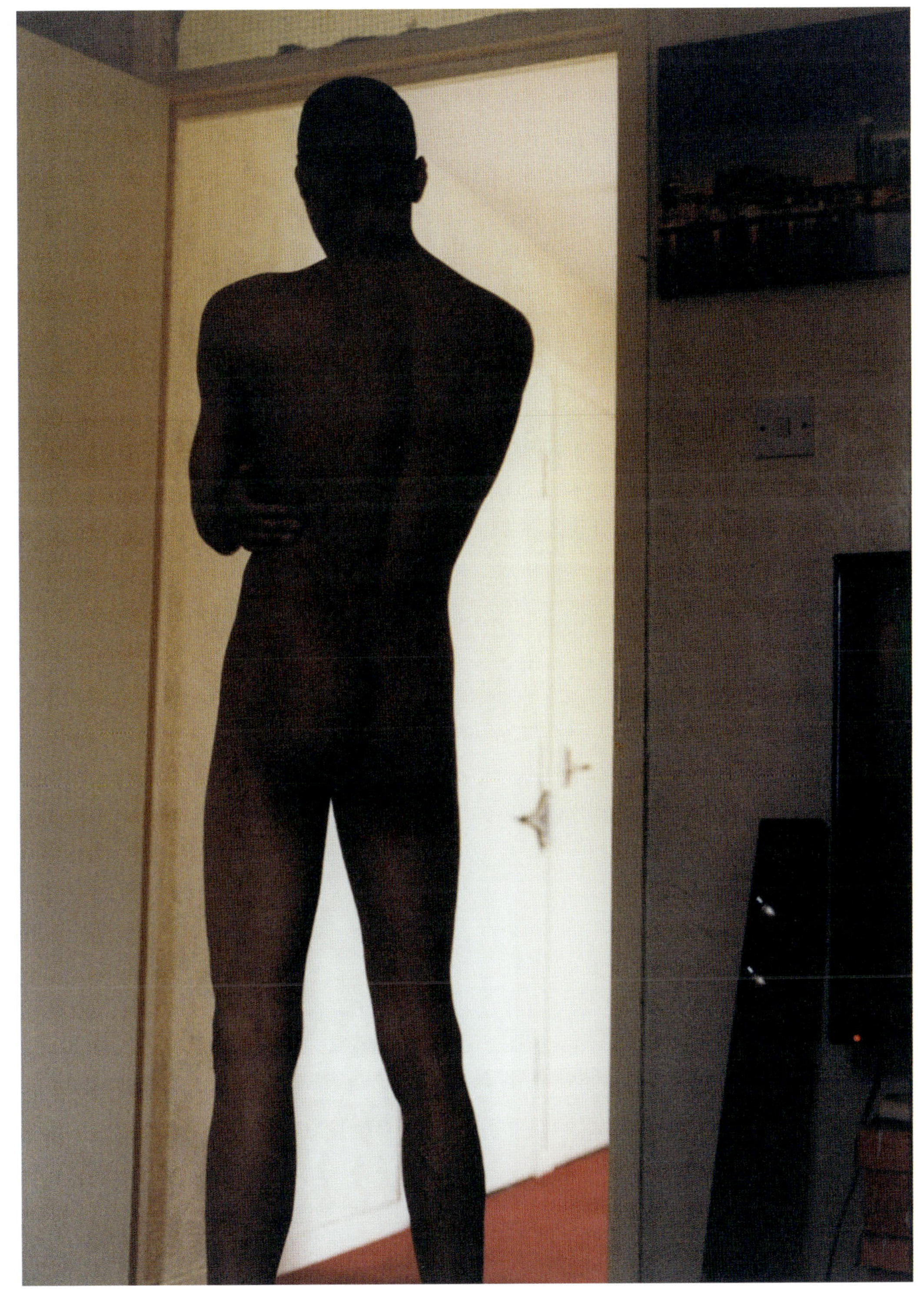

Endnotes

1 P. D. James, *Unnatural Causes*, Adam Dalgliesh Mystery #3 (New York: Simon & Schuster, 2001), p. 173.
2 'World's Wickedest Mile', *VUE: America's Photo Digest* 10:1 (January 1957), n.p.
3 Dick Hebdige, *Style of the Mods* (Birmingham: Centre for Contemporary Cultural Studies, 1974), p. 6.
4 Roy Castle, 'A Slice of Soho', *Sunday Times Magazine*, 21 January 1968, pp. 24–25.
5 'Stephen Fry Stands up for Soho', ITV News, www.itv.com/news/london, 13 January 2015.
6 Tony Wolf, *Edith Garrud: The Suffragette Who Knew Jujutsu*, ed. Kathrynne Wolf (Lulu.com, 2009), p. 67.
7 Bill Brandt, 'Back Stage at the Windmill: Ten Minutes to the Show', *Lilliput* 11:4 (October 1942), p. 329.
8 Jackson was writing in the 1950s and his choice of words is reflective of the era. Frank Jackson, 'Shopping in Soho', *What's On in London*, Soho Fair supplement, 11 July 1958, pp. xiv–xv.
9 Harold Evans in conversation with the author (Julian Rodriguez), 8 January 2019.
10 Denis Hamilton, *Editor in Chief: Fleet Street Memoirs* (London: Hamish Hamilton, 1989), p. 104.
11 Harold Evans, *My Paper Chase: True Stories of Vanished Times* (London: Little, Brown, 2009), p. 344.
12 John Withington, *London's Disasters* (Stroud: The History Press, 2010), p. 96.
13 Ibid., p. 98.
14 James Morton, *Fighters: The Lives and Sad Deaths of Freddie Mills and Randolph Turpin* (London: Time Warner, 2005), pp. 298–304.
15 Harold Evans in conversation with the author (Julian Rodriguez), 8 January 2019.
16 David Leitch, 2002, at www.bryanwharton.com/review.htm, accessed 12 July 2019.
17 Corinne Day in Diane Smyth, 'Day Light', *PDN* 48–49 (February 2008), p. 44.
18 Clancy Gebler Davies in conversation with the author (Karen McQuaid), 27 June 2019.
19 John Goldblatt, 'The Undressing Room', *Creative Camera* 52 (October 1968), p. 347.
20 William Klein in conversation with the author (Julian Rodriguez), 'Against the Grain', *British Journal of Photography* 144:7114 (February 1997), pp. 25–27.
21 Ibid.
22 Anders Petersen interviewed by Sean O'Hagan, 'Anders Petersen: "For Me, Soho is Something Special"', www.theguardian.com, 13 May 2012.
23 Daragh Soden, correspondence with the author (Karen McQuaid), 26 June 2019.

Image Credits

7 Photograph by Eleni Parousi. Courtesy The Photographers' Gallery.
8 Photograph by Dorothy Bohm. Courtesy The Photographers' Gallery.
11 Courtesy *Daily Herald* © Mirrorpix.
12 Photograph by Arthur Tanner © Arthur Tanner/Fox Photos/Getty Images.
13 Photograph by Valentine Blanchard © Historic England Archive. Howarth-Loomes Collection.
15 © Historia/Shutterstock.
16 Photograph by Felix H. Man © Picture Post/Hulton Archive/Getty Images.
17 Photograph: Hulton Deutsche stringer © Hulton Archive/Getty Images.
18 Photograph by Charlie Ley for the *Daily Mirror* © Mirrorpix.
19, 26 Photographs by Sergio Larraín © Sergio Larraín/Magnum Photos.
20 Photograph by Neil Libbert. Courtesy Francis Bacon MB Art Foundation, MB Art Collection © Neil Libbert.
21, 24 Photographs by Ray Stevenson © Ray Stevenson/Shutterstock.
22 Photograph by Lewis Morley © Lewis Morley Archive/Seymour Platt.
25 Photograph taken for the *Daily Mirror* in 1965 © Mirrorpix.
36–49 All images © Kelvin Brodie. Courtesy the *Sunday Times Magazine*/News Licensing.
52, 54–67 All images courtesy and © The Corinne Day Estate.
53 Image by Corinne Day/Mark Szaszy. Courtesy and © The Corinne Day Estate.
70–85 All images courtesy and © Clancy Gebler Davies.
88–103 All images courtesy and © The John Goldblatt Estate.
107–21 All images courtesy and © William Klein.
124–39 All images courtesy and © Anders Petersen.
142–57 All images courtesy and © Daragh Soden.

Acknowledgements

We would like to thank the participating photographers for their invaluable contributions to this book: Clancy Gebler Davies, William Klein, Anders Petersen and Daragh Soden. We are also indebted to Michael-John Jennings and Marcelle Price for enabling us to bring to light under-sung bodies of work by Kelvin Brodie and John Goldblatt respectively, and to Mark Szaszy for joining in our enthusiasm for looking again at Corinne Day's Brewer Street work in the context of the energy and creativity of Soho.

We are grateful to our wider colleagues at The Photographers' Gallery and Kingston University for their support and advice. In developing this book we have relied extensively on the expertise of Prestel editors Anna Godfrey and Lincoln Dexter, and the design talents of Sarah Boris. We are indebted to the following people, all of whom played an important role in the research, development and execution of this book: Dr Sarah Bennett, Stefanie Braun, Oliver Craske, Marc Cutler, Sir Harold Evans, Simon Flavin, Rosa Maria Falvo, Julie Grahame, Michael Hoppen, Michael Mack, Jenny McKinley, Russ O'Connell, Marc Russell, Tony Shrimplin, James Smith and Bryan Wharton.

The curators and the William Klein Studio would like to thank Pierre-Louis Denis and Tiffanie Pascal for research and direction, and Bruno Ryterband for his generous advice. Thanks also to Sidonie Gaychet (Polka Galerie) and Boris Gayrard and François George (PICTO) for digital artworks.

We are also grateful to the following organisations and institutions for access to their collections: City of Westminster Archives Centre, Historic England Archive, Hulton Archive at Getty Images, Magnum Photos, Michael Hoppen Gallery, Mirrorpix, News UK Archive, the Prints and Drawings Study Room at the Victoria & Albert Museum, and Rex Features/Shutterstock.

Thanks to The Visible Institute at Kingston School of Art for additional research support.

We are grateful to Majid Boustany, founder of the Francis Bacon MB Art Foundation, and to the foundation for their support.

Finally, we would like to thank all the photographers of Soho throughout the passage of time. Their work provides a basis for understanding the community of Soho as it continues to change and thrive in the heart of London.

Karen McQuaid and Julian Rodriguez

This book is published to coincide with the exhibition *Shot in Soho* at The Photographers' Gallery (18 October 2019 – 9 February 2020). Curated by Karen McQuaid and Julian Rodriguez. www.thephotographersgallery.org.uk

Julian Rodriguez is a photography educator, writer, and Head of Film and Photography at Kingston School of Art.

Karen McQuaid is Senior Curator at The Photographers' Gallery.

Editors: Karen McQuaid and Julian Rodriguez
Editorial direction: Lincoln Dexter and Anna Godfrey
Copyediting: Aimee Selby
Design: Sarah Boris
Production: Corinna Pickart

Paper: Profibulk, Tauro

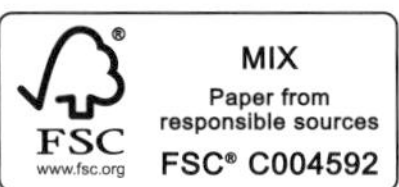

Printed in Germany

ISBN 978-3-7913-5889-5

Front Cover: Corinne Day, 'George in Stilettos', from the feature 'Goths on Acid' for *Ray Gun* magazine, June–July 1995.

Prestel Publishing Ltd.
14–17 Wells Street
London W1T 3PD

Prestel Publishing
900 Broadway, Suite 603
New York, NY 10003

Library of Congress Control Number is available; British Library Cataloguing-in-Publication Data: a catalogue record for this book is available from the British Library

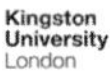

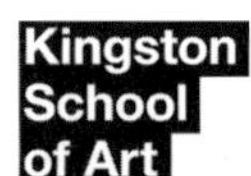

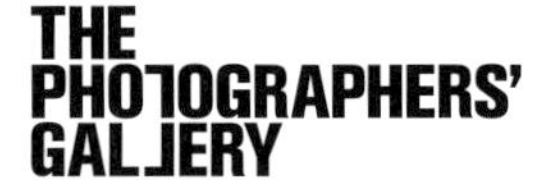